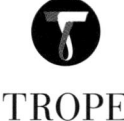

TROPE

TROPE EDITION

VOLUME III

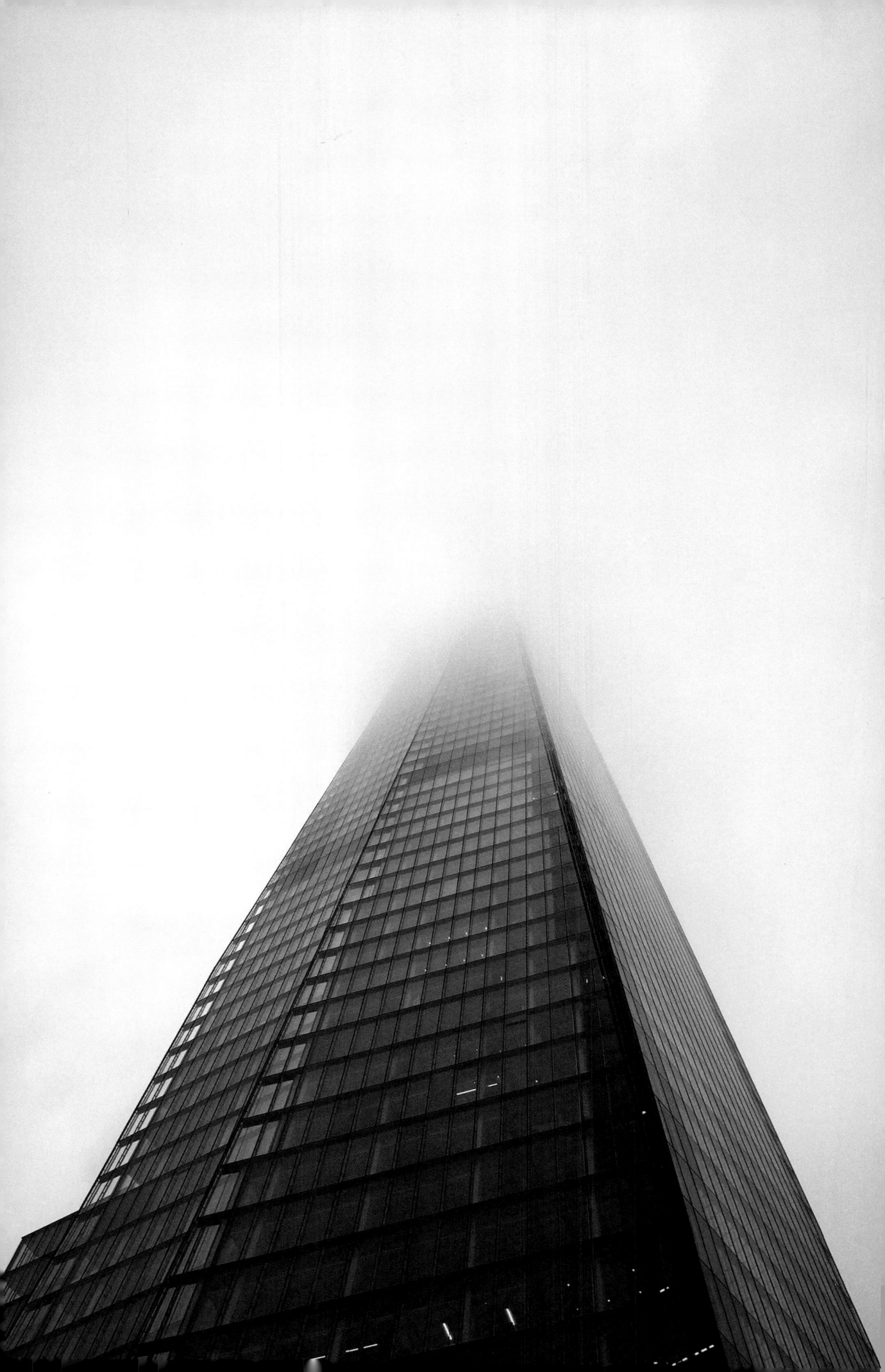

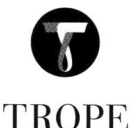

TROPE

RON TIMEHIN
London Fog

TROPE EDITION

VOLUME III

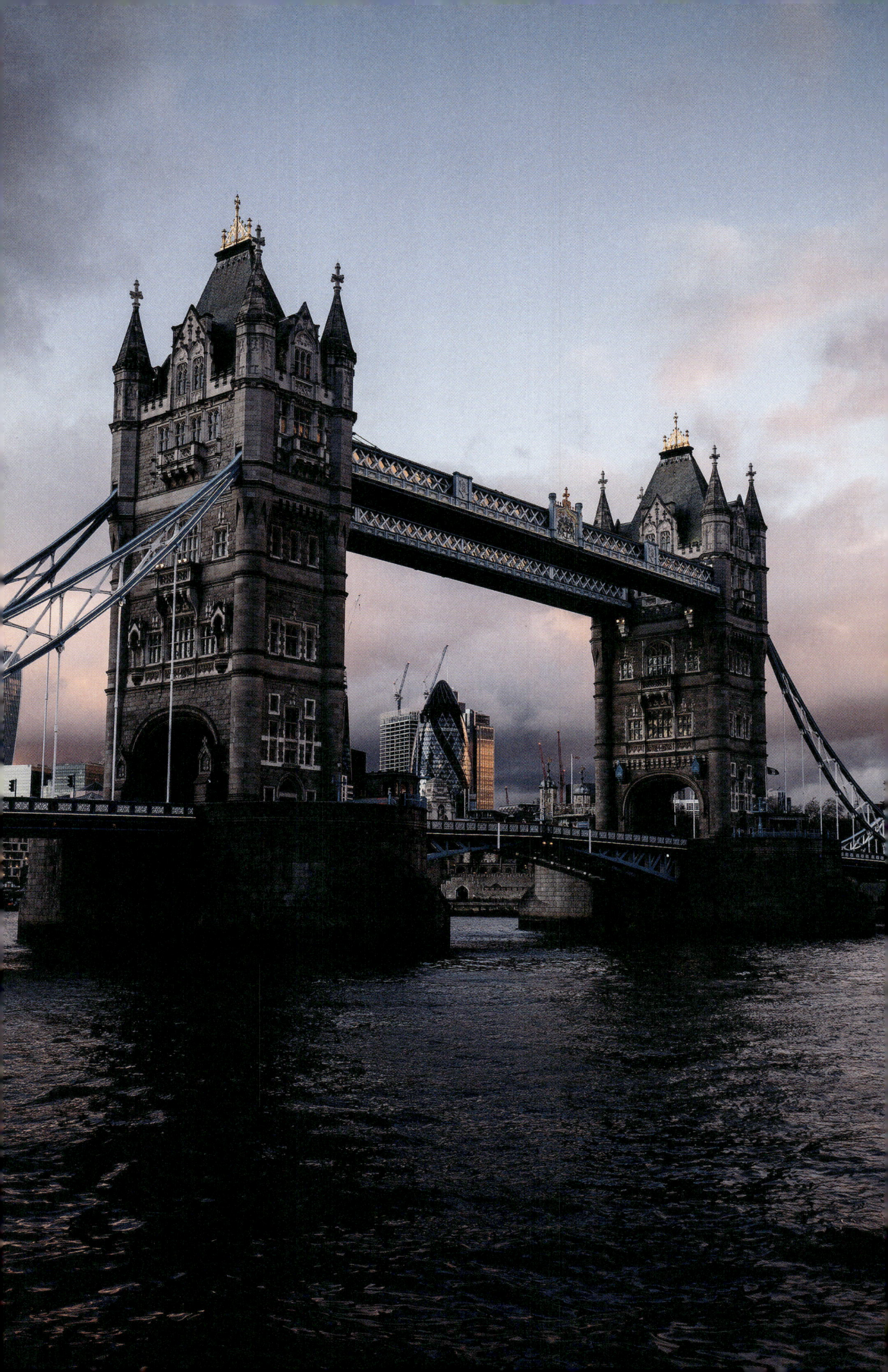

INTRODUCTION

London Fog is the third volume in the Trope Editions Emerging Photographers Series. This edition presents Ron Timehin's tireless exploration of London at its most extreme; at dawn and at dusk, in the rain, and under its most volatile weather conditions – *especially* in fog.

Ron talks about weather with regularity, the way most people might check their phones. He is always on the lookout for a particular light or moment to capture an original view of an endlessly photographed city. Often shooting before sunrise, when fog seems to appear from nowhere, Ron is 'on-call' 24/7, searching out new perspectives on the familiar. It's a 'conversation' that Ron is having with London through the language of weather, making the city feel like an old friend sharing a new story.

A serious musician until age sixteen, Ron travelled extensively around the world playing trumpet in various jazz ensembles. During those travels he discovered his true passion – photography. What began as a means of documenting the places he visited around the world quickly became a full-time endeavor.

Music continues to play a role in how he shoots today. Ron often talks about his images as being 'atmospheric', 'moody', or 'dark' – the way a jazz artist might describe their compositions.

We created this new contemporary book series to introduce young and emerging artists from around the world to a wider audience. Enjoy Ron's mercurical London, one that most of us never experience. The resulting images are hauntingly beautiful and majestic.

Sam Landers
Editor

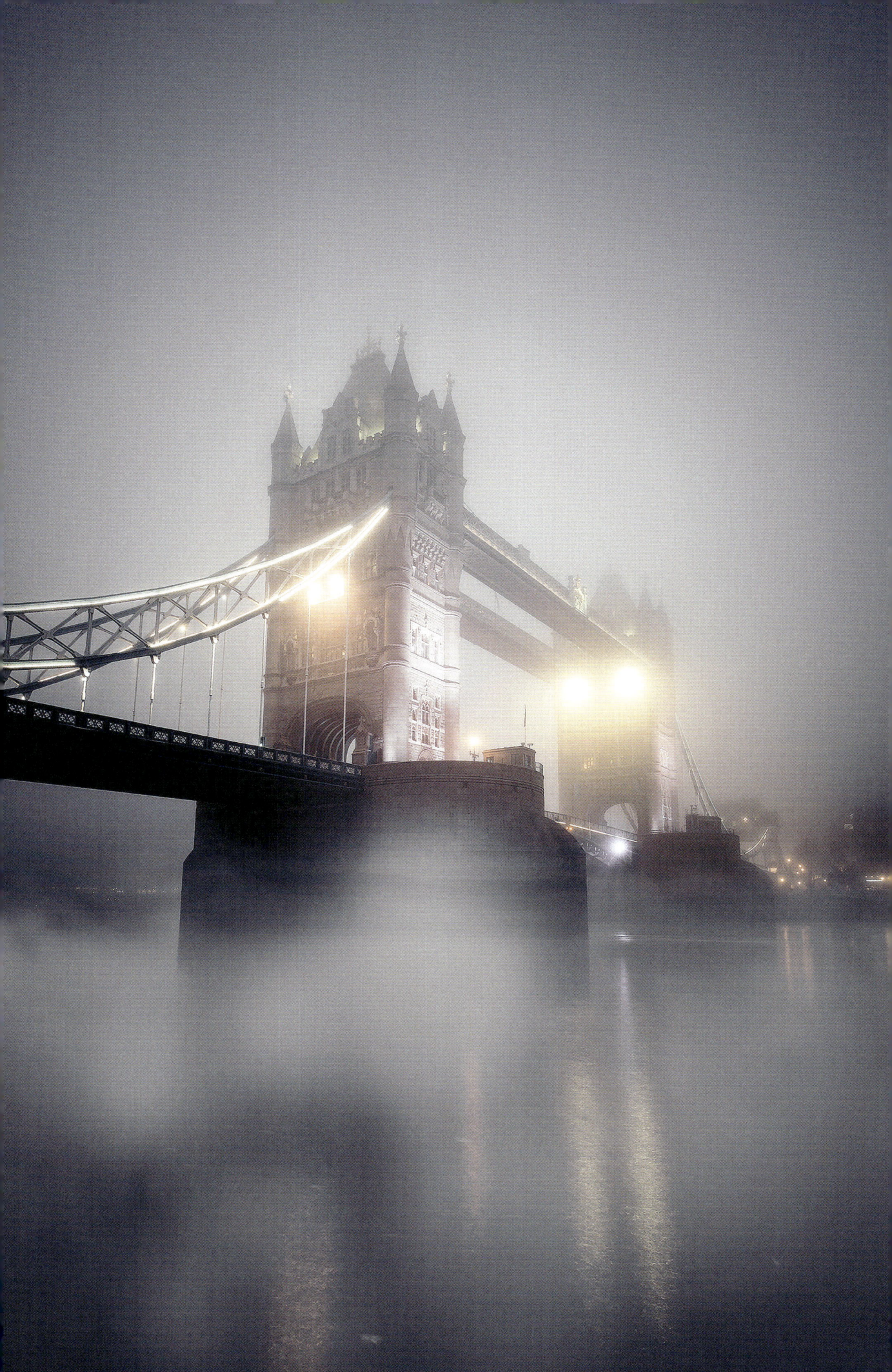

ABOUT THE WEATHER...

London Fog is a curated collection of atmospheric and evocative imagery captured over the last four years. I started the series to explore and celebrate the beauty in the often negatively perceived 'bad' weather that London is renowned for. Although London is typically grey and rainy, fog is actually a rarity, so there were many challenges whilst attempting to photograph it. I had to plan meticulously, and the number of failed shoots was high, but ultimately the end product is beautiful.

London's architectural landscape is a hybrid of old and new, which makes it fairly easy to capture different settings in a small radius. However, the average height of the buildings is relatively small compared to cities such as Chicago or New York, which makes shooting fog limited unless it is extremely low. Areas such as Bank, Canary Wharf and London Bridge contain the highest concentration of tall structures and so these areas are where London fog looks the most dramatic.

Fog can be very temperamental. Even after keeping a close eye on the weather forecast, I could turn up to my pre-planned location only to find the fog gone, or not as thick or low as I'd hoped for.

There are actually many different types of fog, which changes depending on the microclimate. London most typically sees precipitation fog, which occurs during rainfall. The most favourable for photography, however, is advection fog, commonly seen in San Francisco. Advection fog happens when moist air is carried over a cold surface by the wind and cooled, so the River Thames can sometimes harbour climates like these. The best time to see London fog is often very early morning to sunrise during autumn and winter, when humidity levels are in the 90th percentile.

The feeling of immersing myself in the London fog and generally moody scenes is unrivalled for me. The imagery captured in these environments resonates within me more than the typical happy motifs explored in popular culture.

I hope you enjoy this book as much as I have enjoyed creating it.

My photographic journey actually started with another creative art form: music.

From the age of seven I began learning to play the trumpet in both classical and jazz genres. It was my ambition to one day play music for films, so for the next 12 years I would practice three hours a day to make that dream a reality. By the age of 16 I had achieved my Grade 8 on the trumpet and began playing music internationally on tour with different bands and orchestras, in between school terms.

This is what sparked my passion for photography. Visiting incredible places like Lake Bled, Slovenia and Florence, Italy, I began taking and editing photos on my iPhone, albeit very bad ones! Around this time Instagram was born and I began sharing my images on the social media platform.

After I finished my A-levels, I attended the University of Gloucestershire to study Music & Media Management to get a wider knowledge as to how those industries operate. Upon graduation in 2015, I returned to my home of South London and to my disappointment, I realised that my real passion was in creating, and not so much the business side – reaffirming my belief that it is easier to succeed at something you love doing than something you don't.

With my interest in photography growing at a rapid pace, it eventually became my number one passion point. I had started to notice that the theme of my photography was atmospheric – dark but beautiful – whether the subject was oriented to landscape, cityscape or portraiture.

Two years after uploading my first photo to Instagram, I had posted 600 images and grown my audience to over 8000 followers. This is when everything changed for me. Instagram contacted me to say that they were going to follow me and make me a 'Suggested User' for two weeks on the app. Every new user who signed up to the app would see my profile, as an example of what a good Instagrammer is. By the end of the two-week feature, I had gained over 20,000 new followers!

Since then, I have worked tirelessly to improve my craft and create compelling content in hopes that I will continue to grow and learn as a photographer.

Ron Timehin

London Fog

I was a musician when I was younger and played the trumpet. I travelled with different bands and orchestras and as I was travelling, that is when photography kind of took my eye.

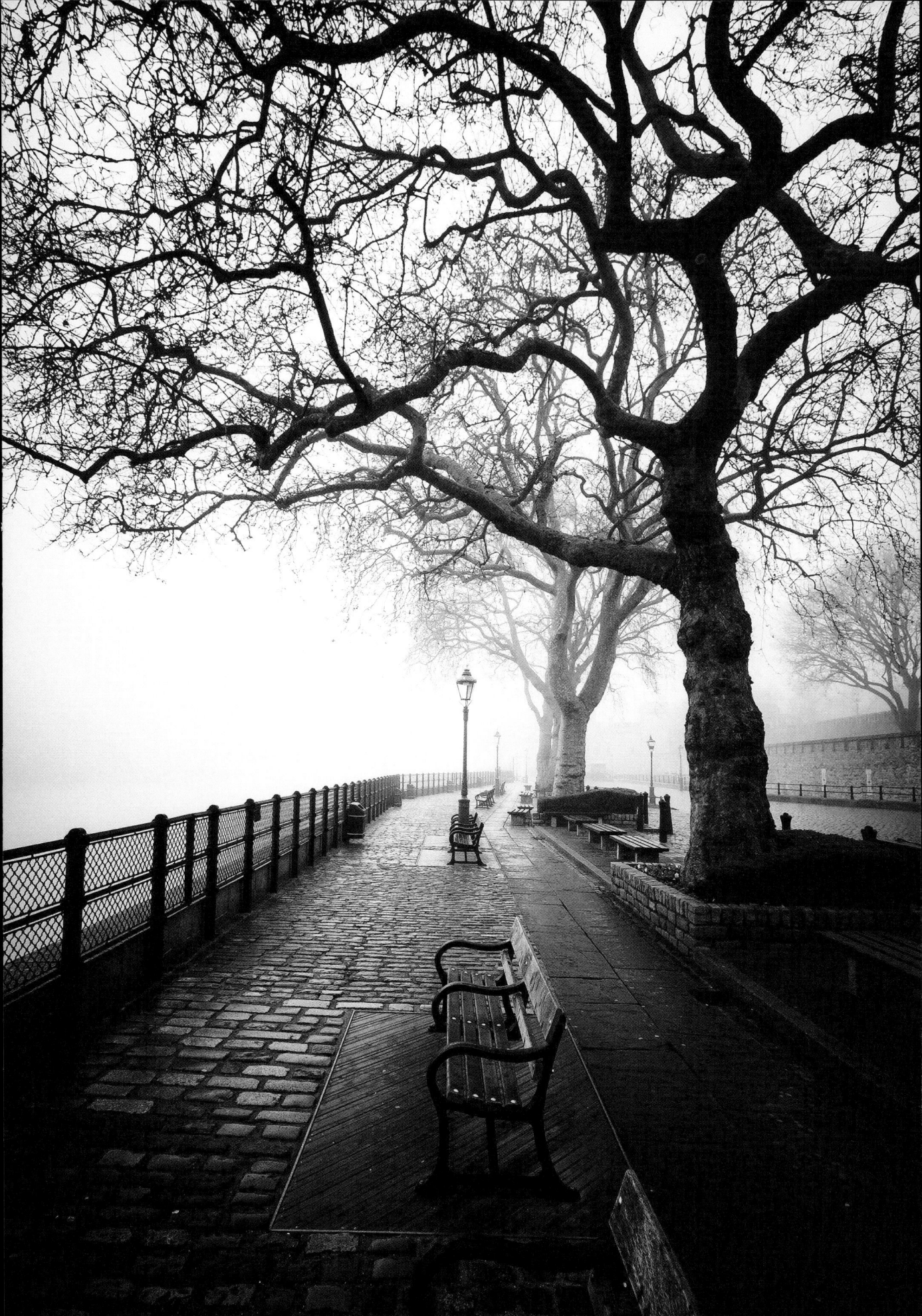

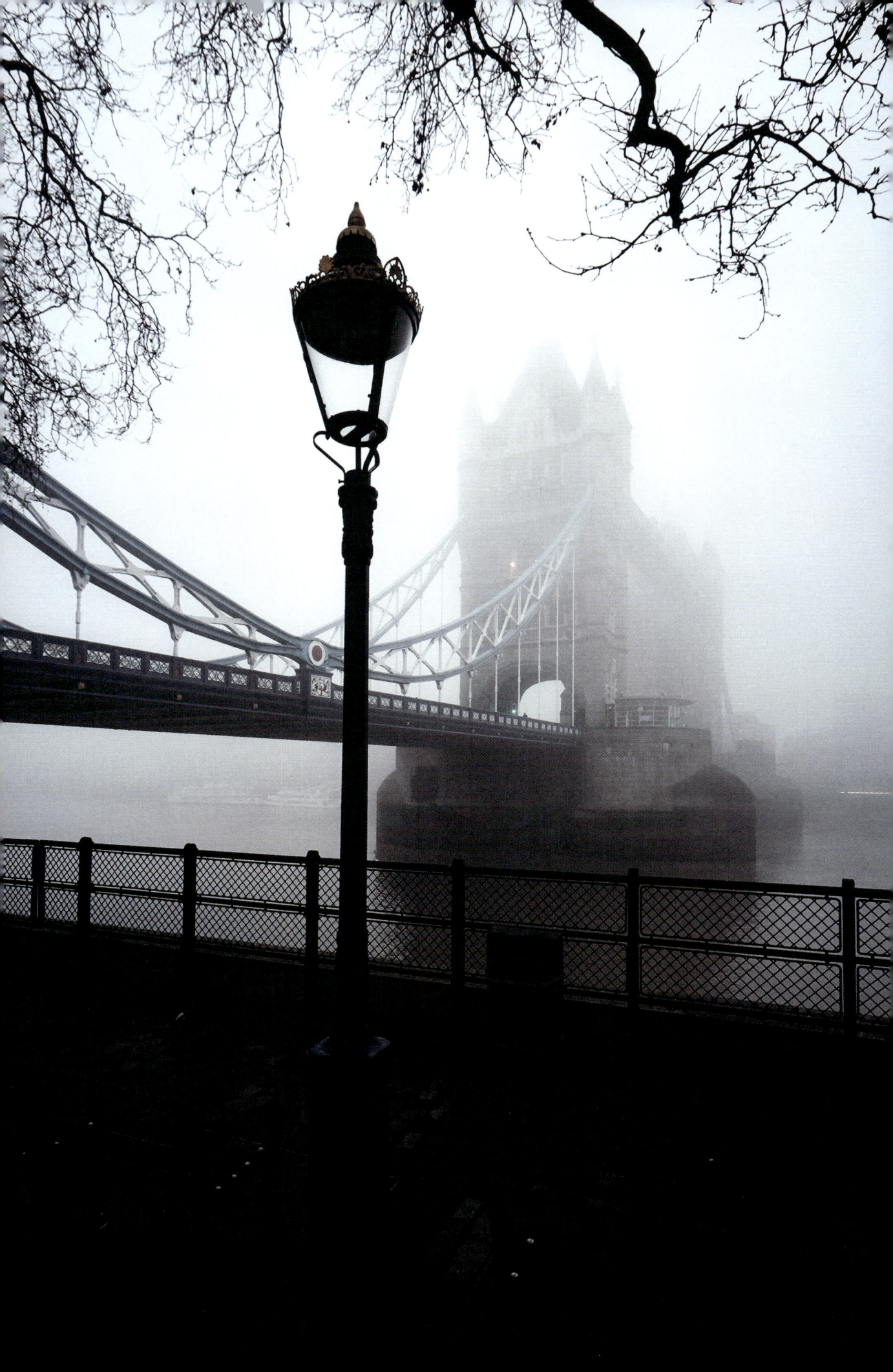

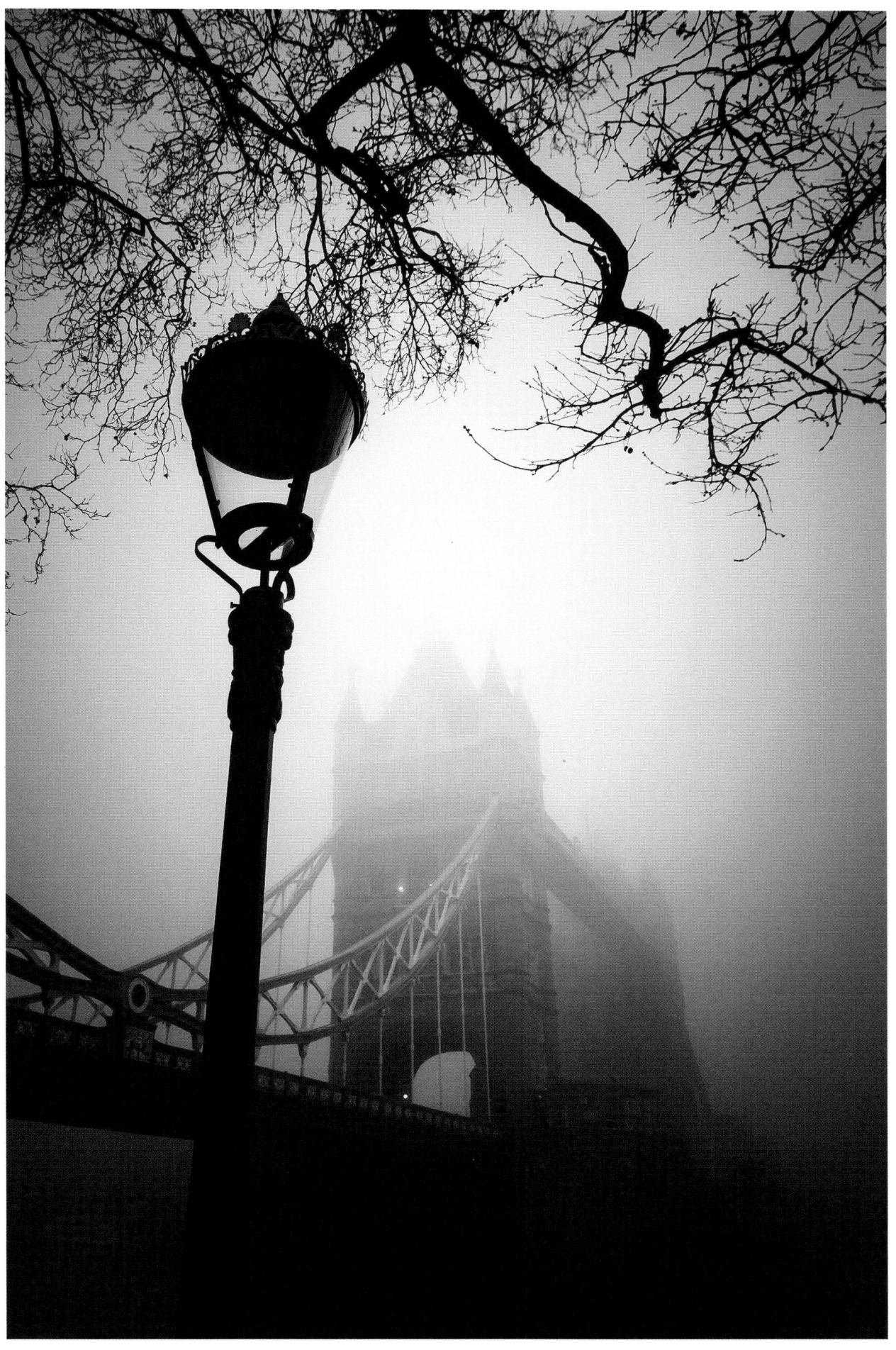

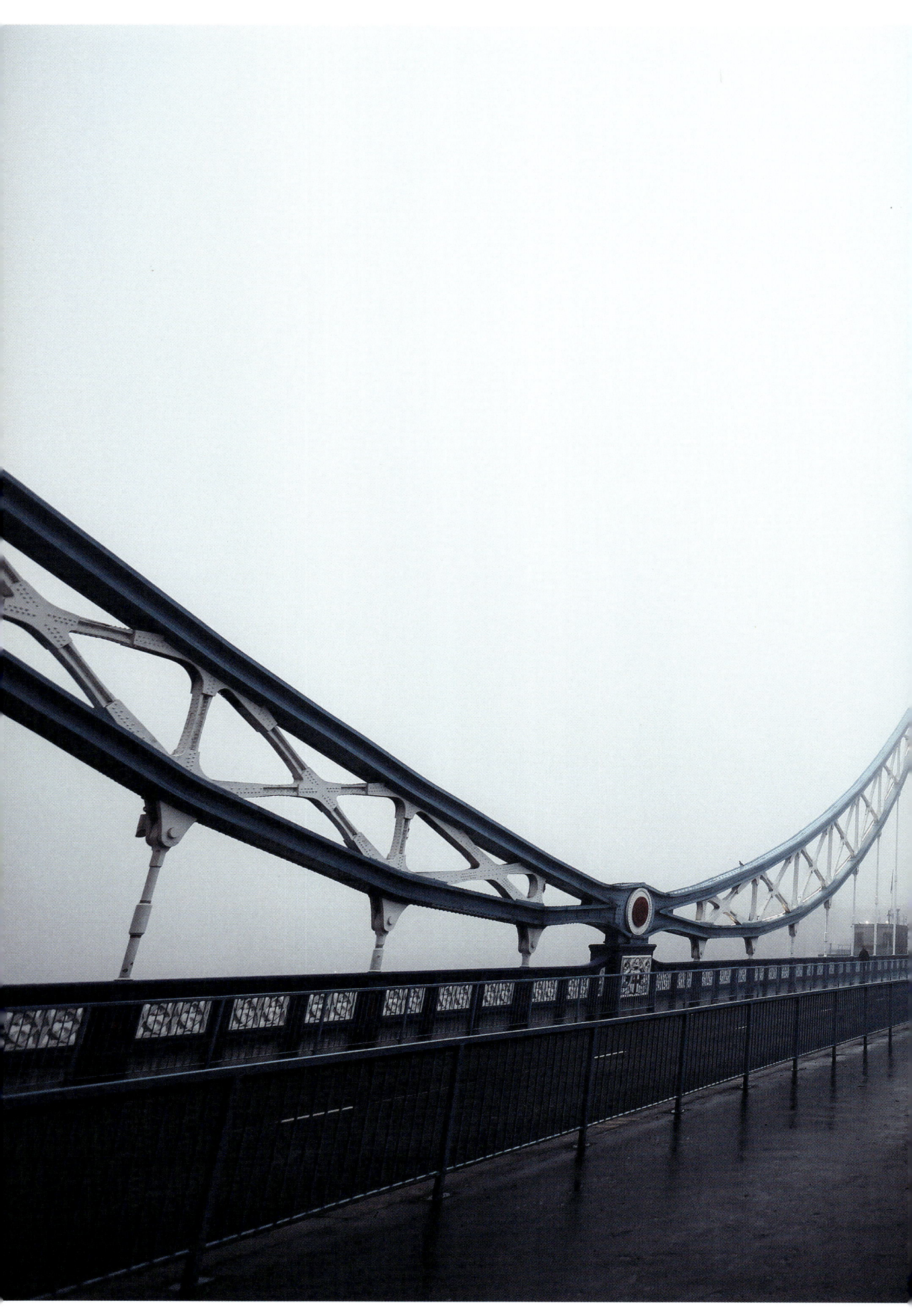

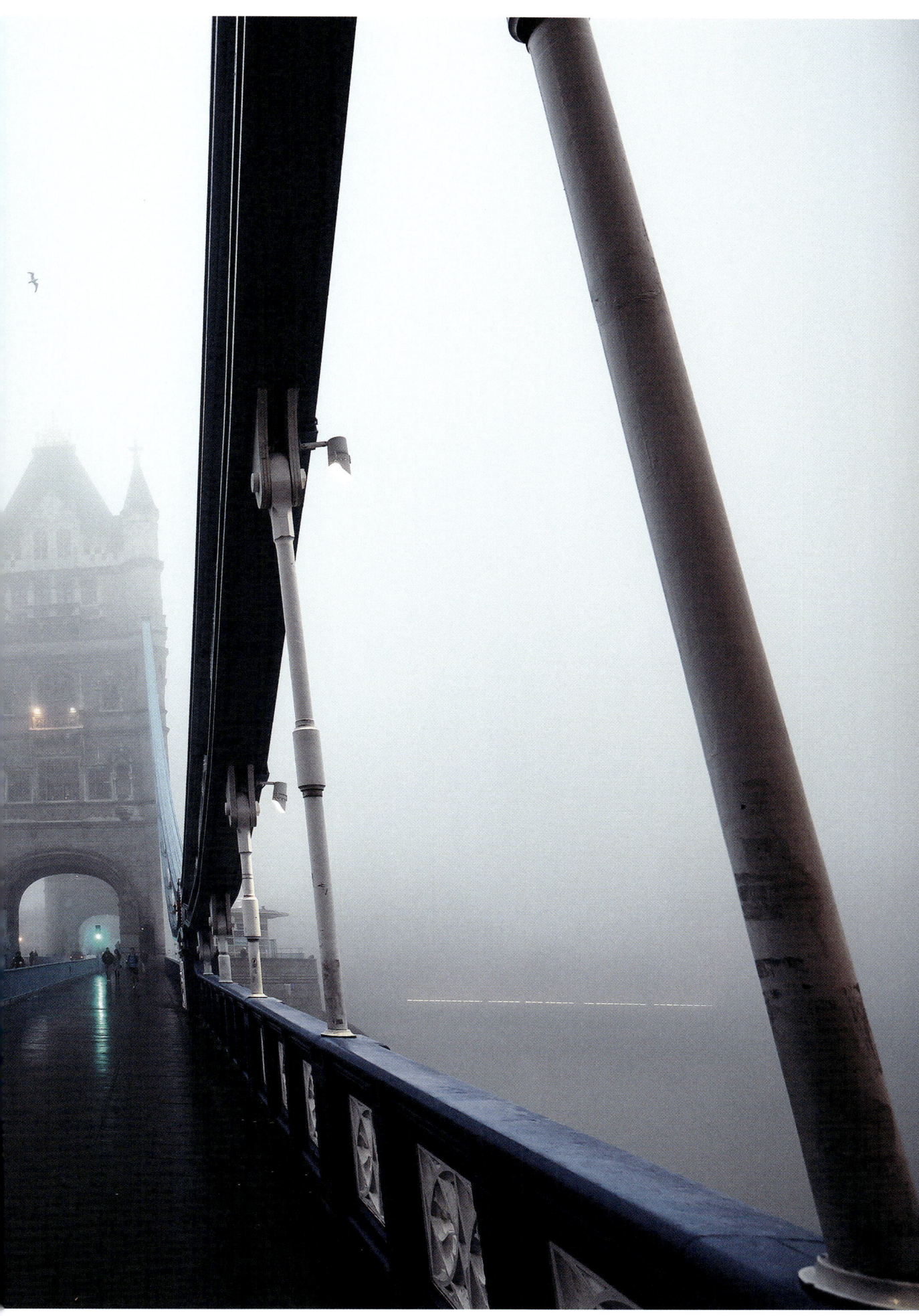

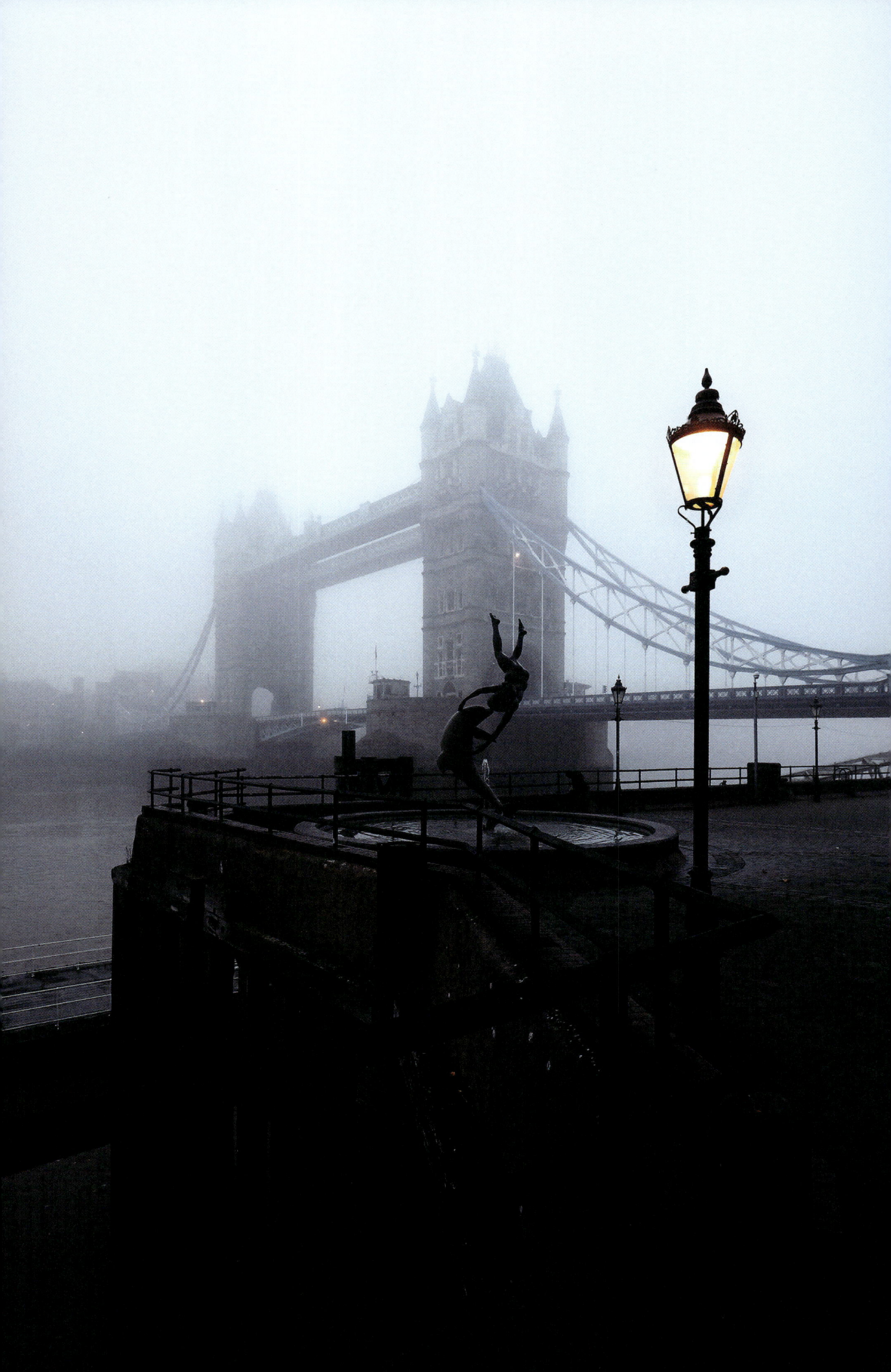

I'll go to places like Tower Bridge at 4am and catch it all foggy. It kind of became my style — very atmospheric, an empty and a moody looking London. I just like to give myself a unique perspective of the city.

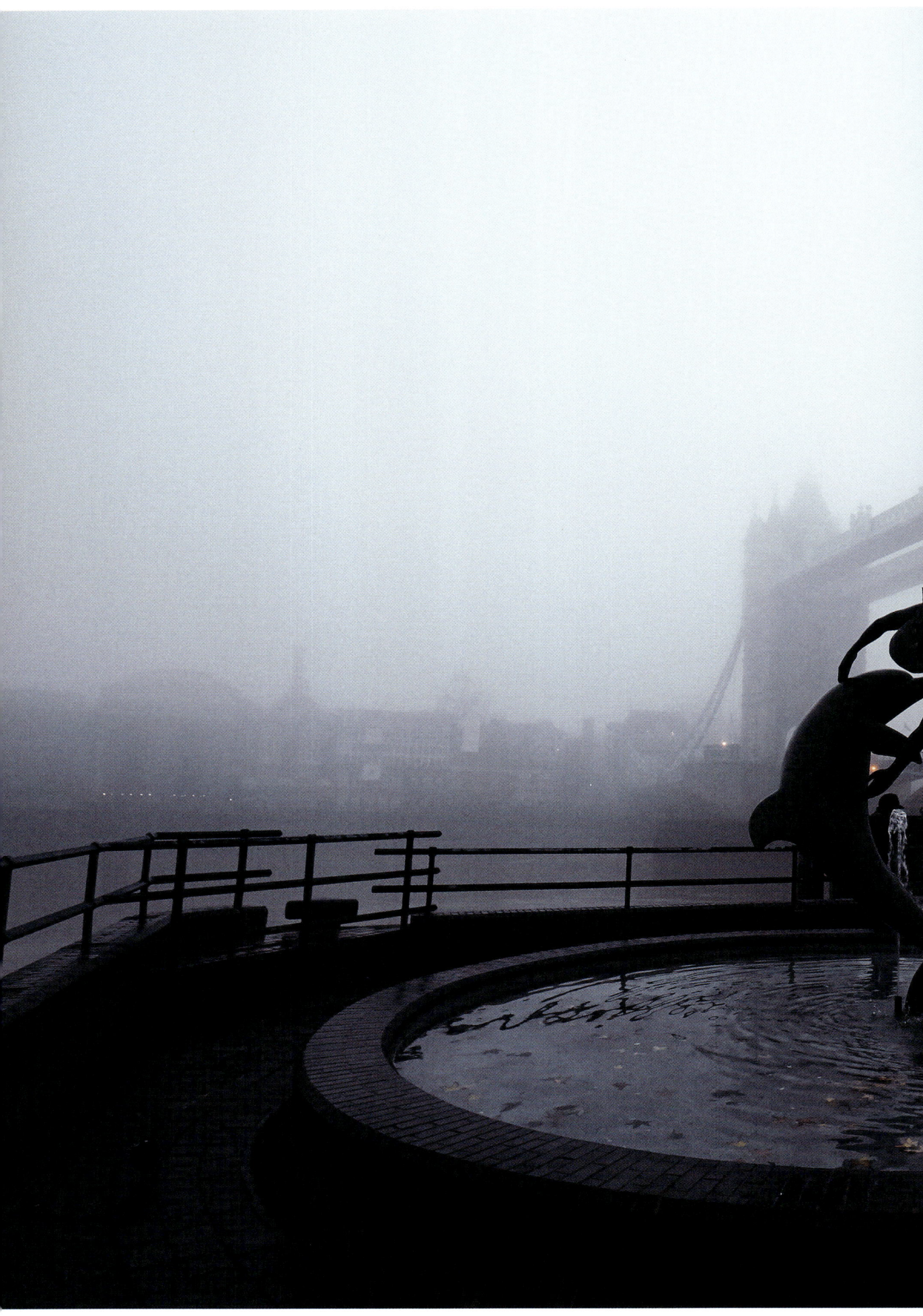

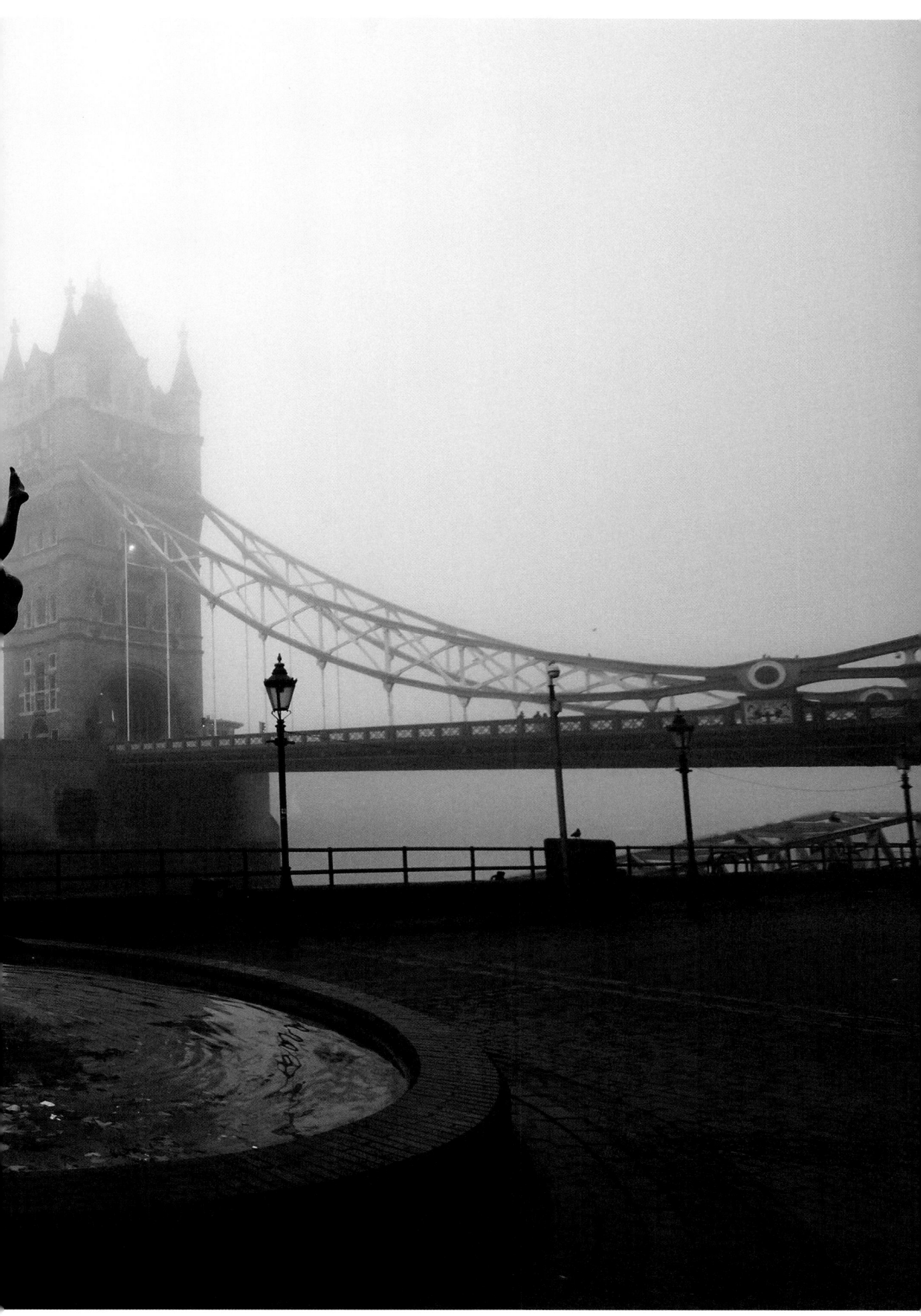

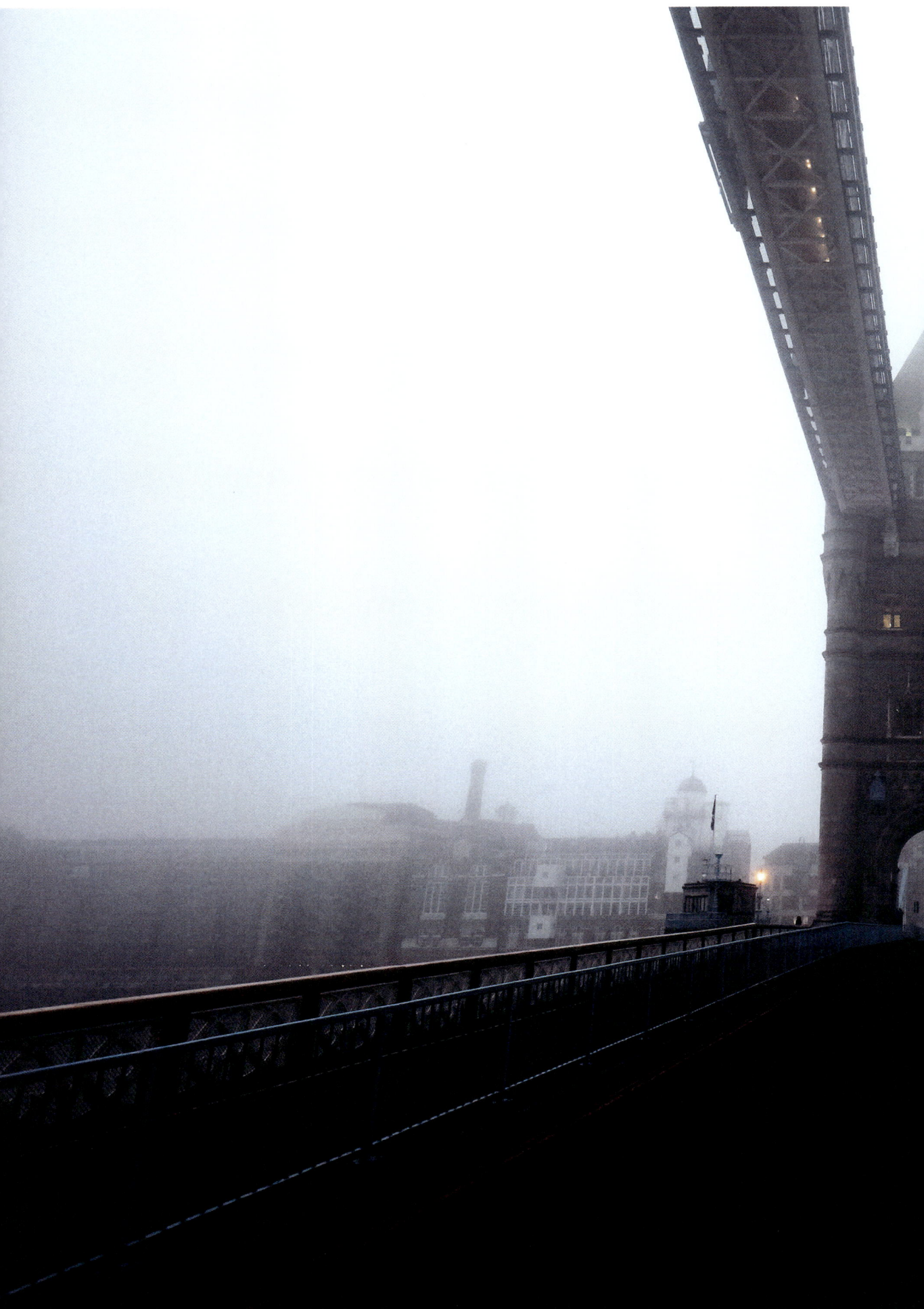

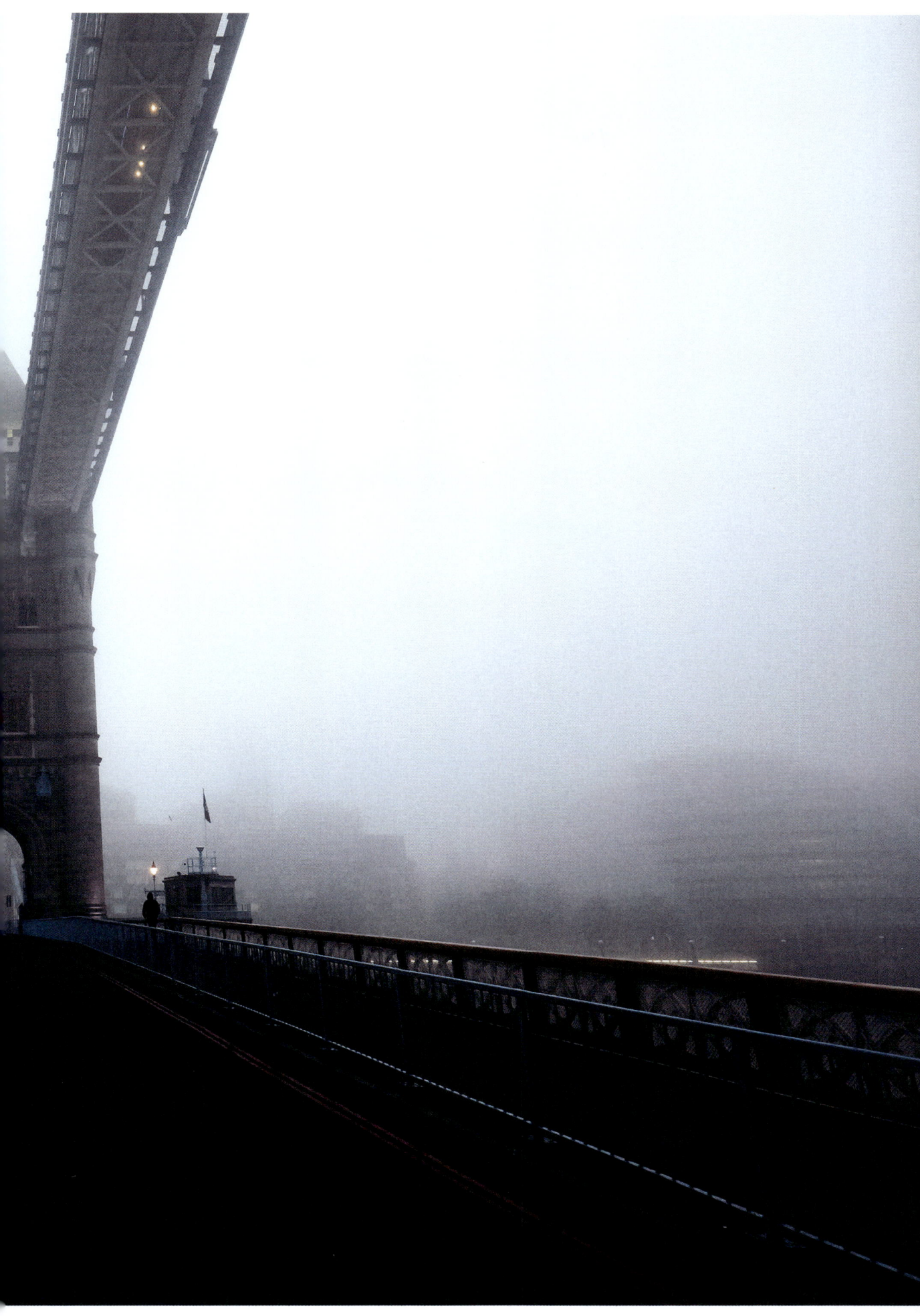

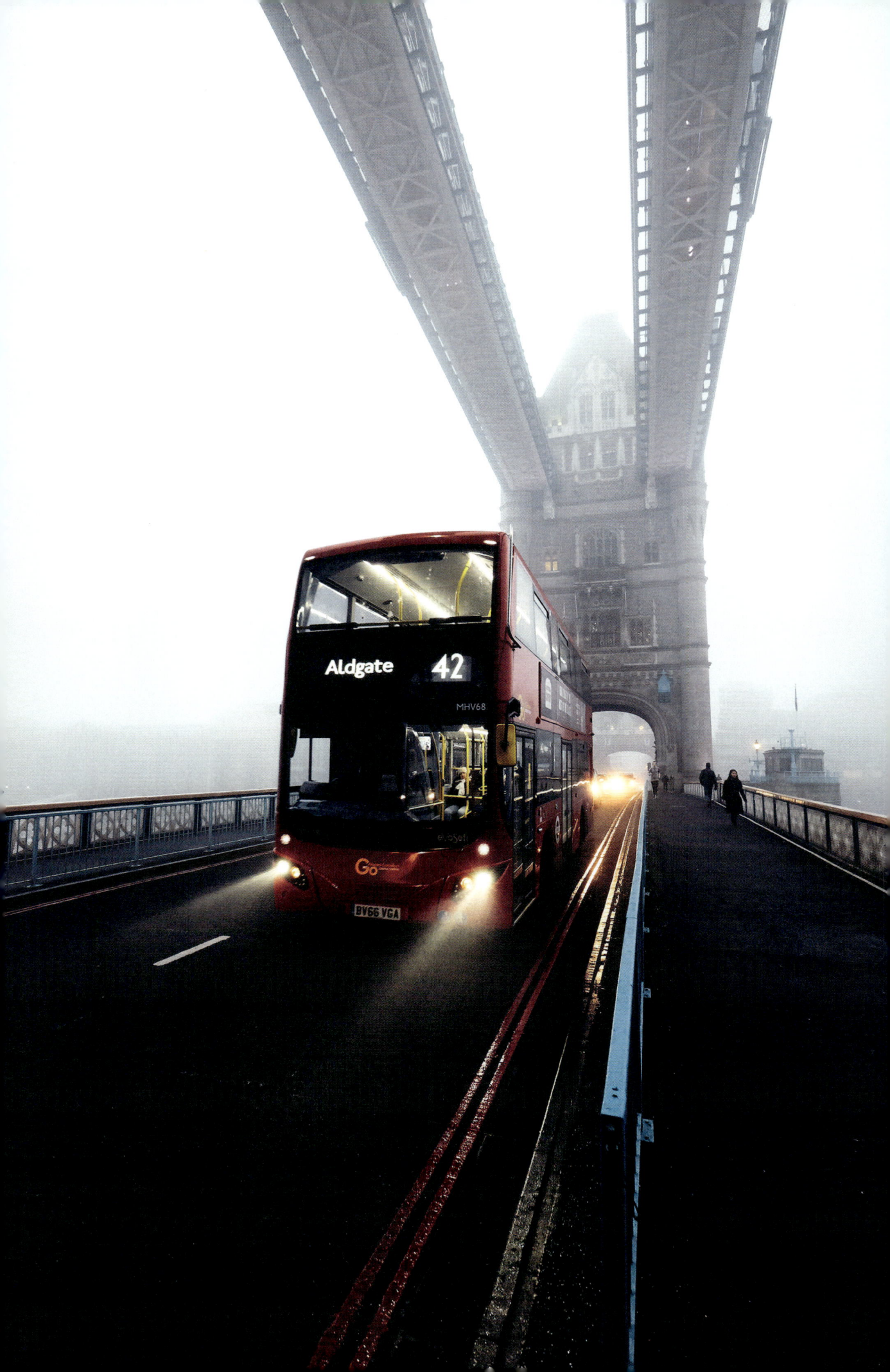

I prefer it when the skies are dramatic and mysterious. When I played the trumpet, I used to play a lot of jazz. Jazz can be sad yet beautiful at the same time, and that feeling likes to come through when I shoot with the camera.

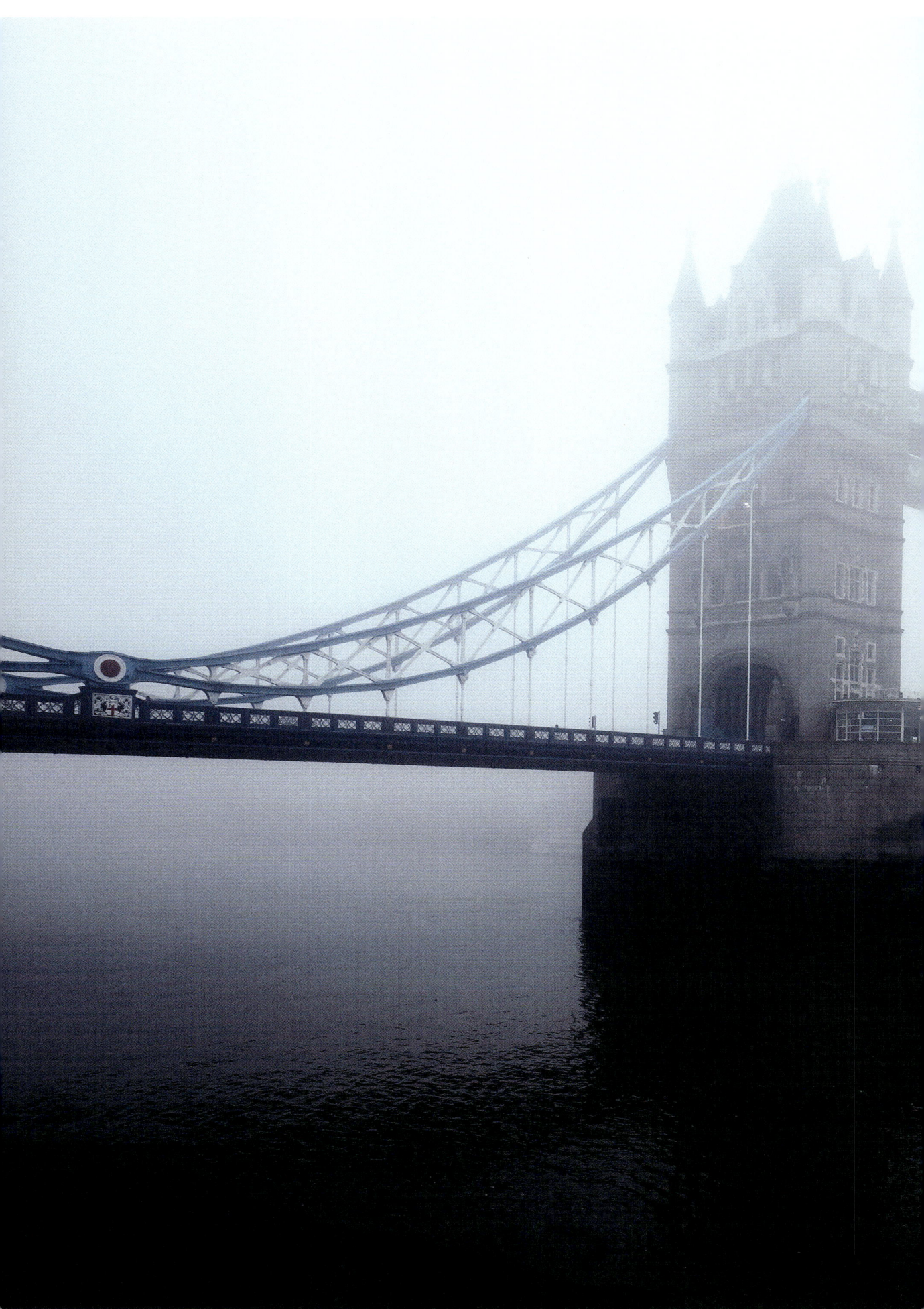

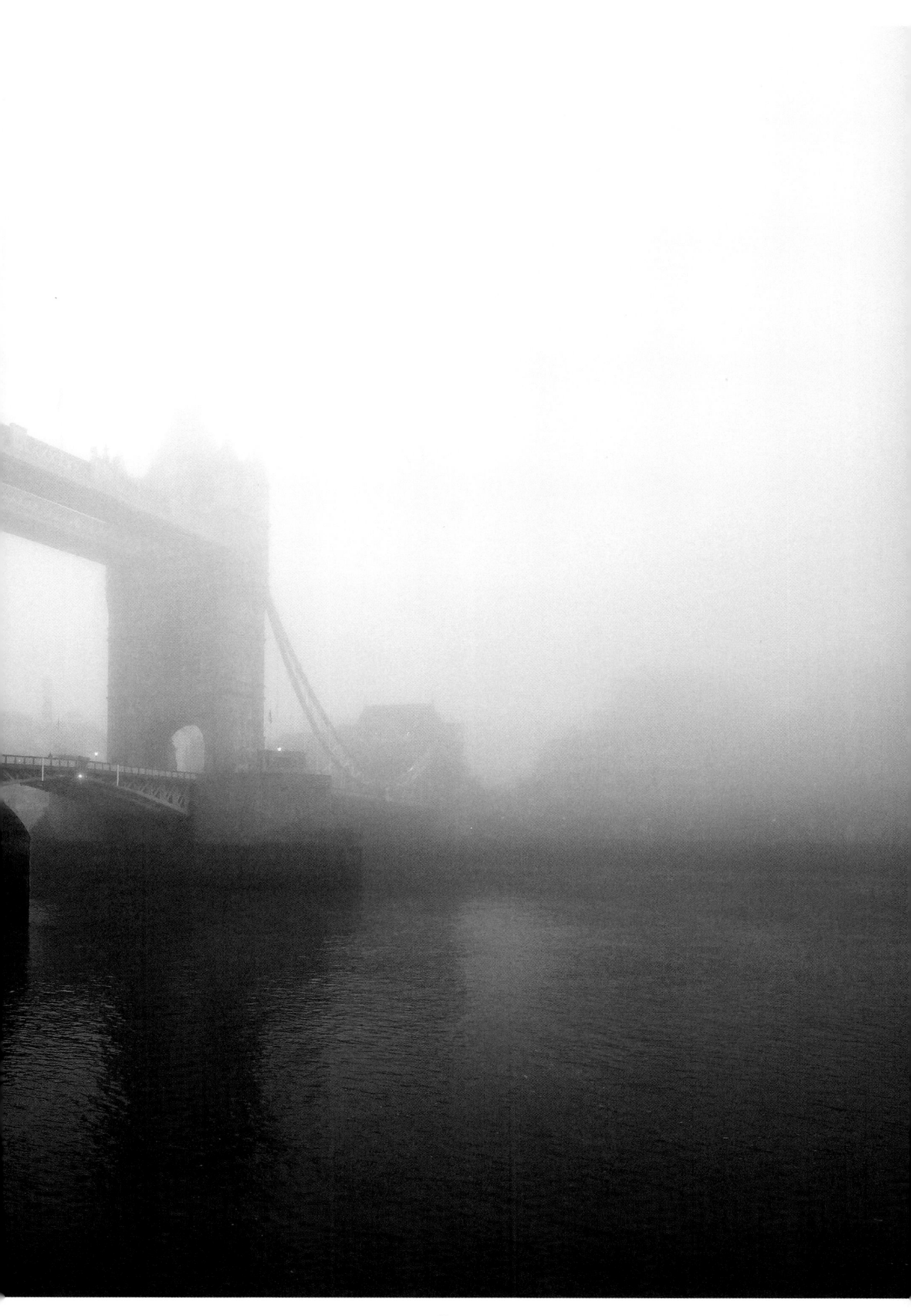

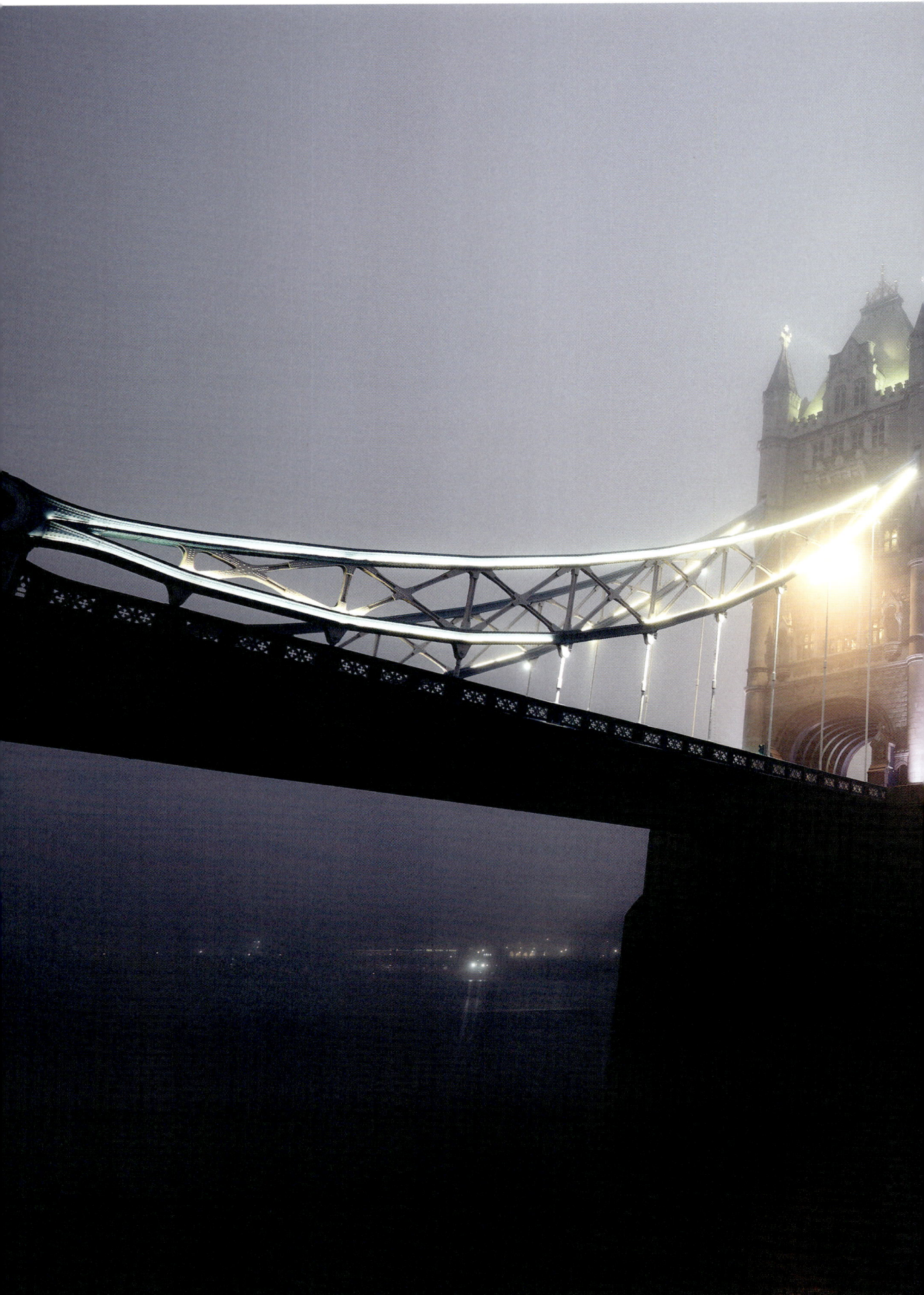

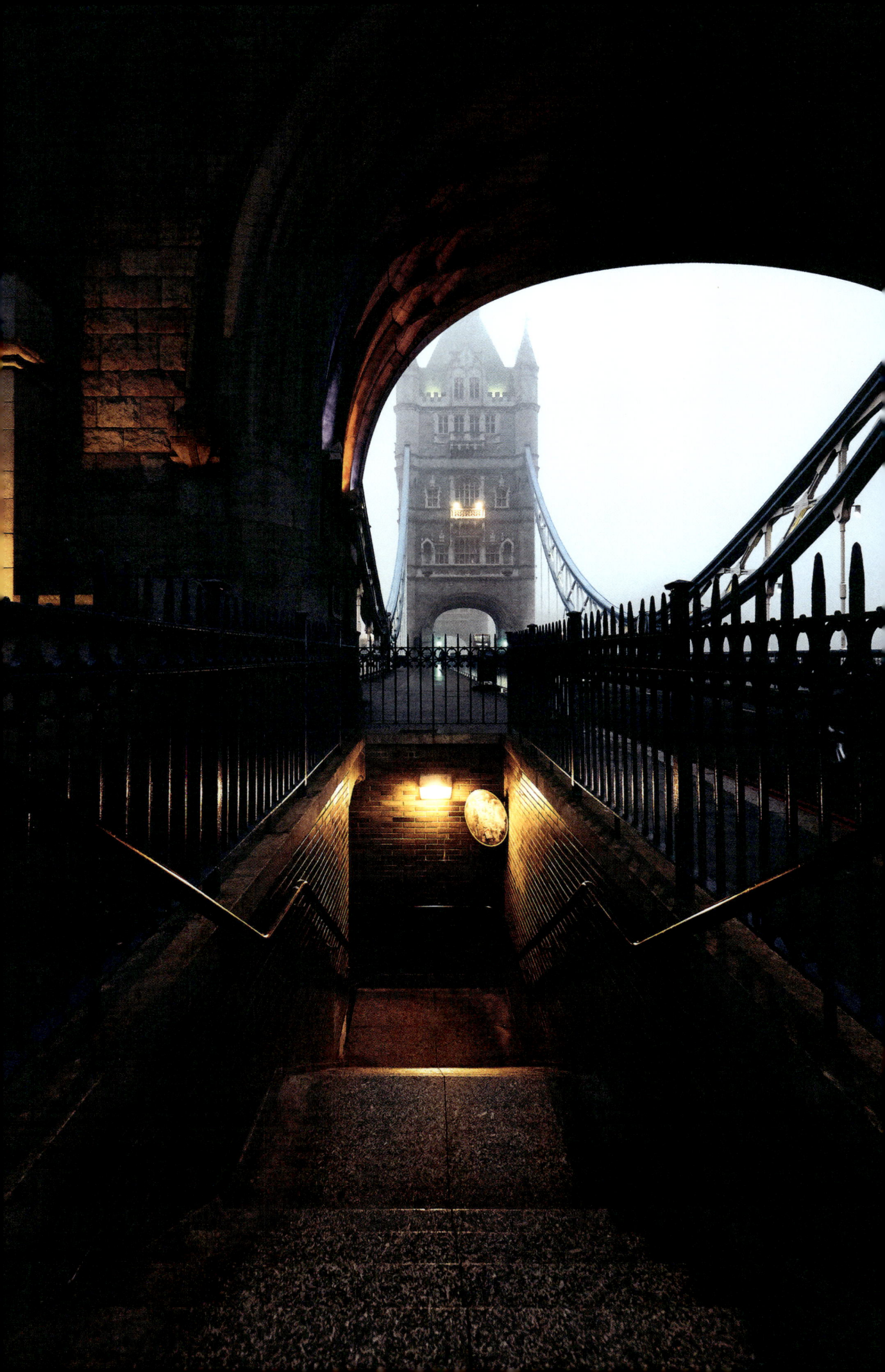

I really wanted to document what I was seeing, so that's where my passion came from.

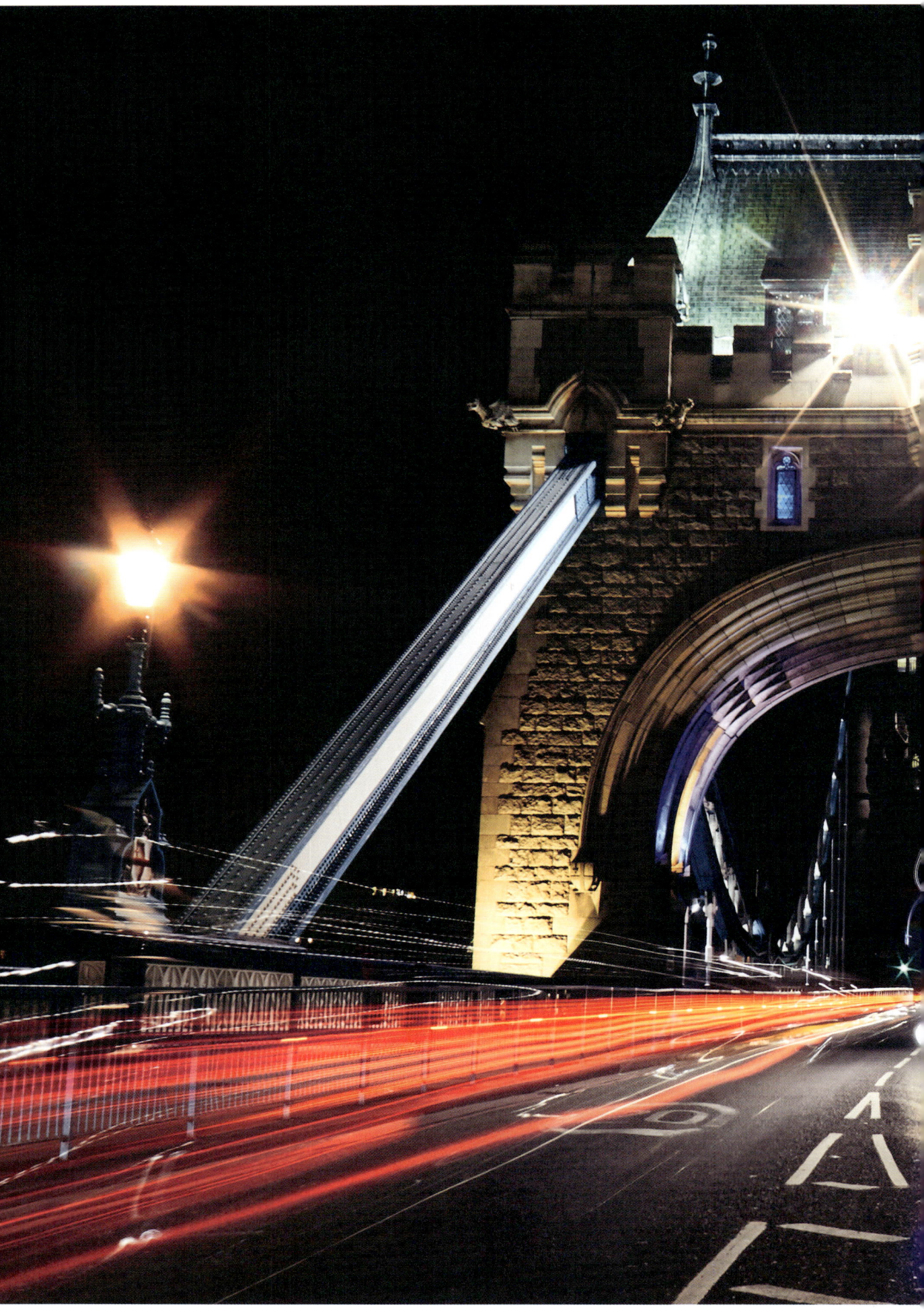

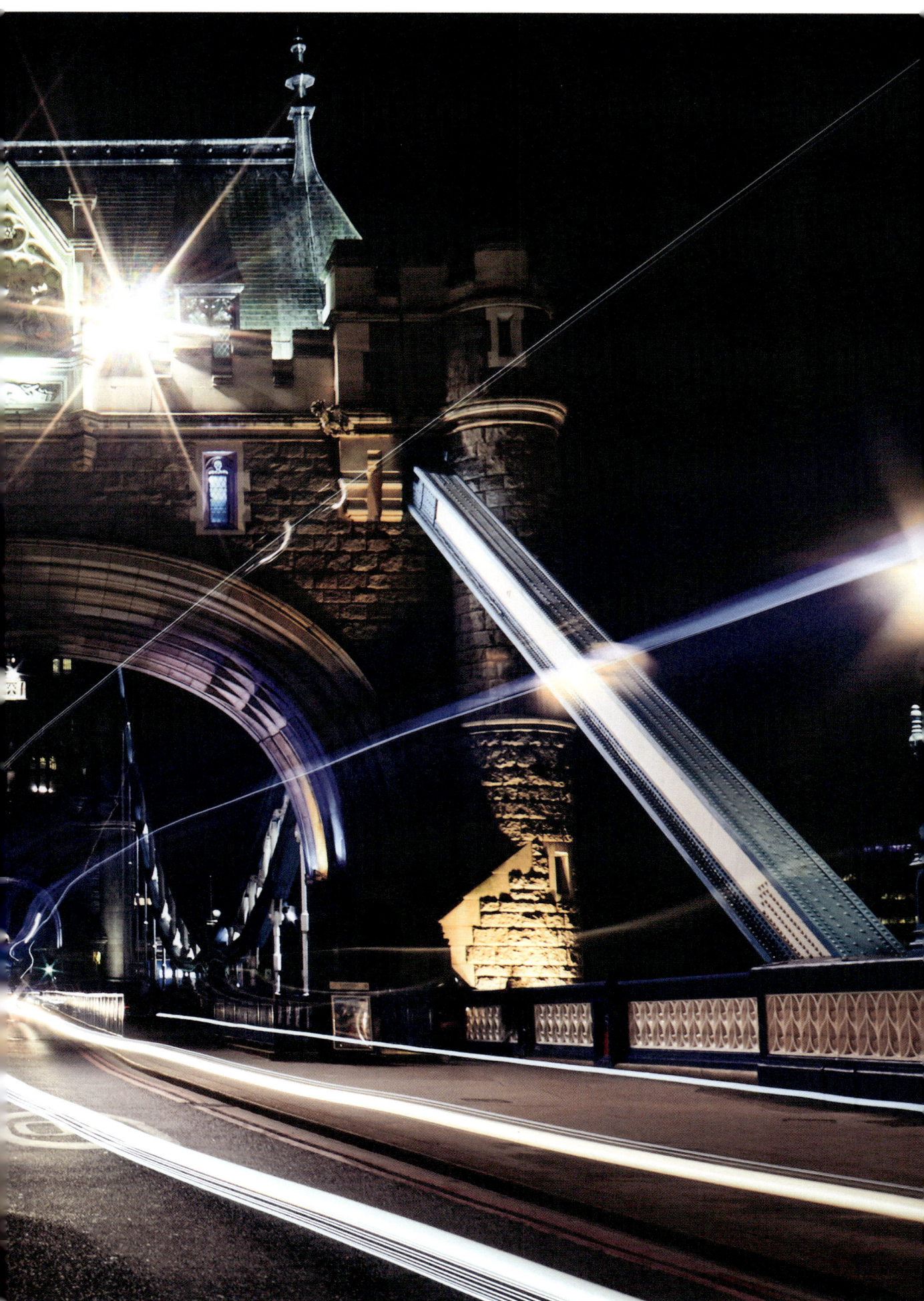

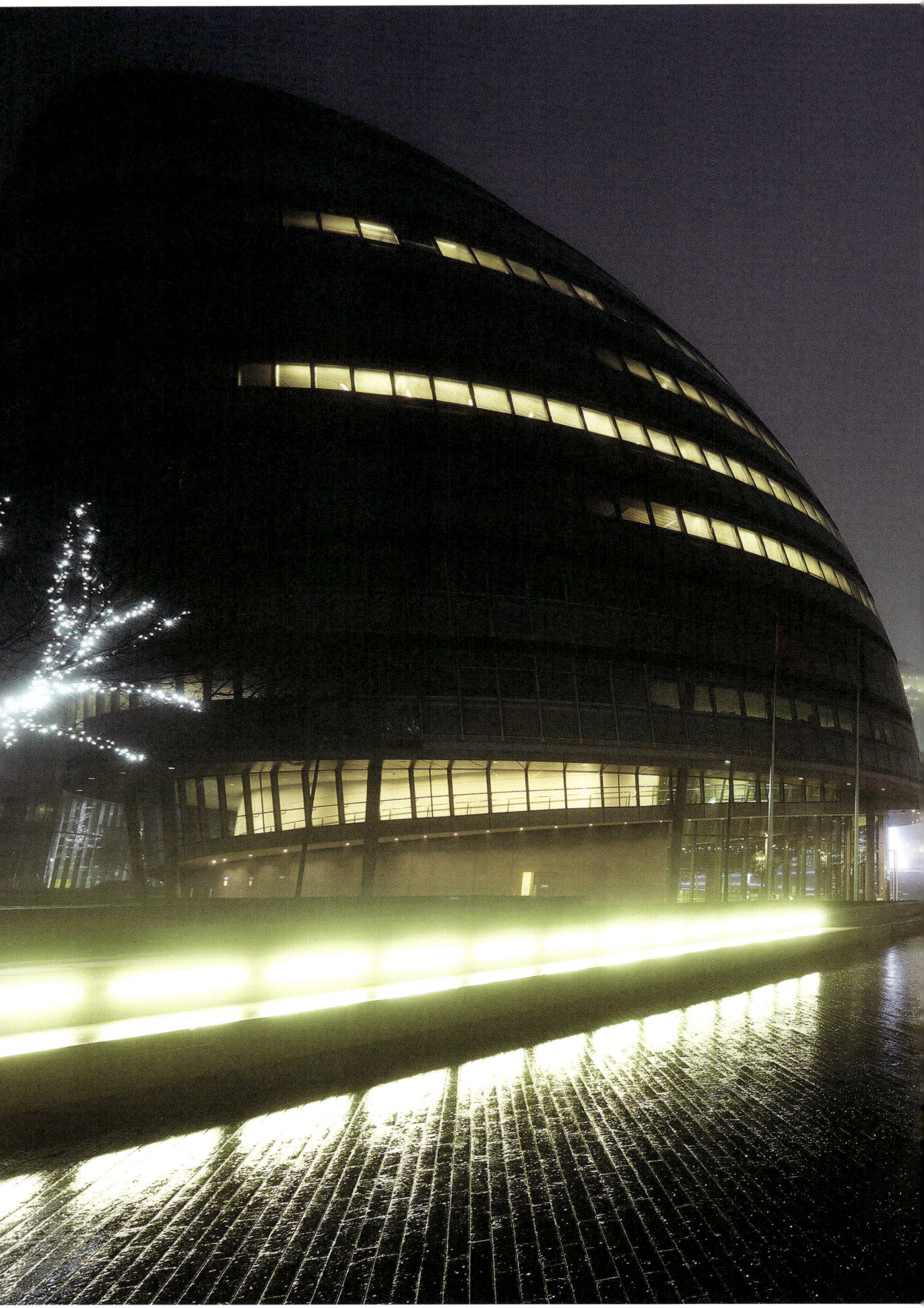

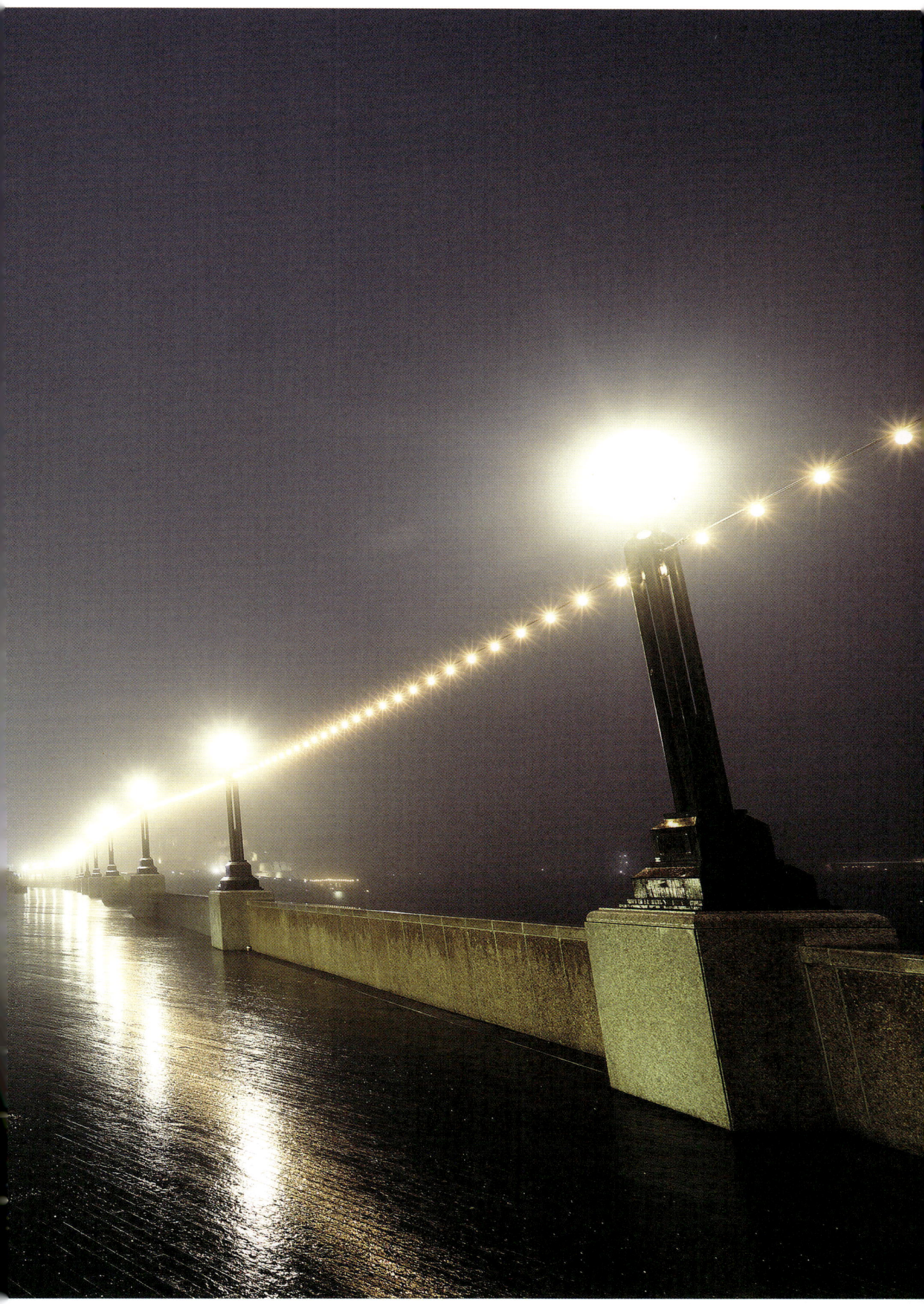

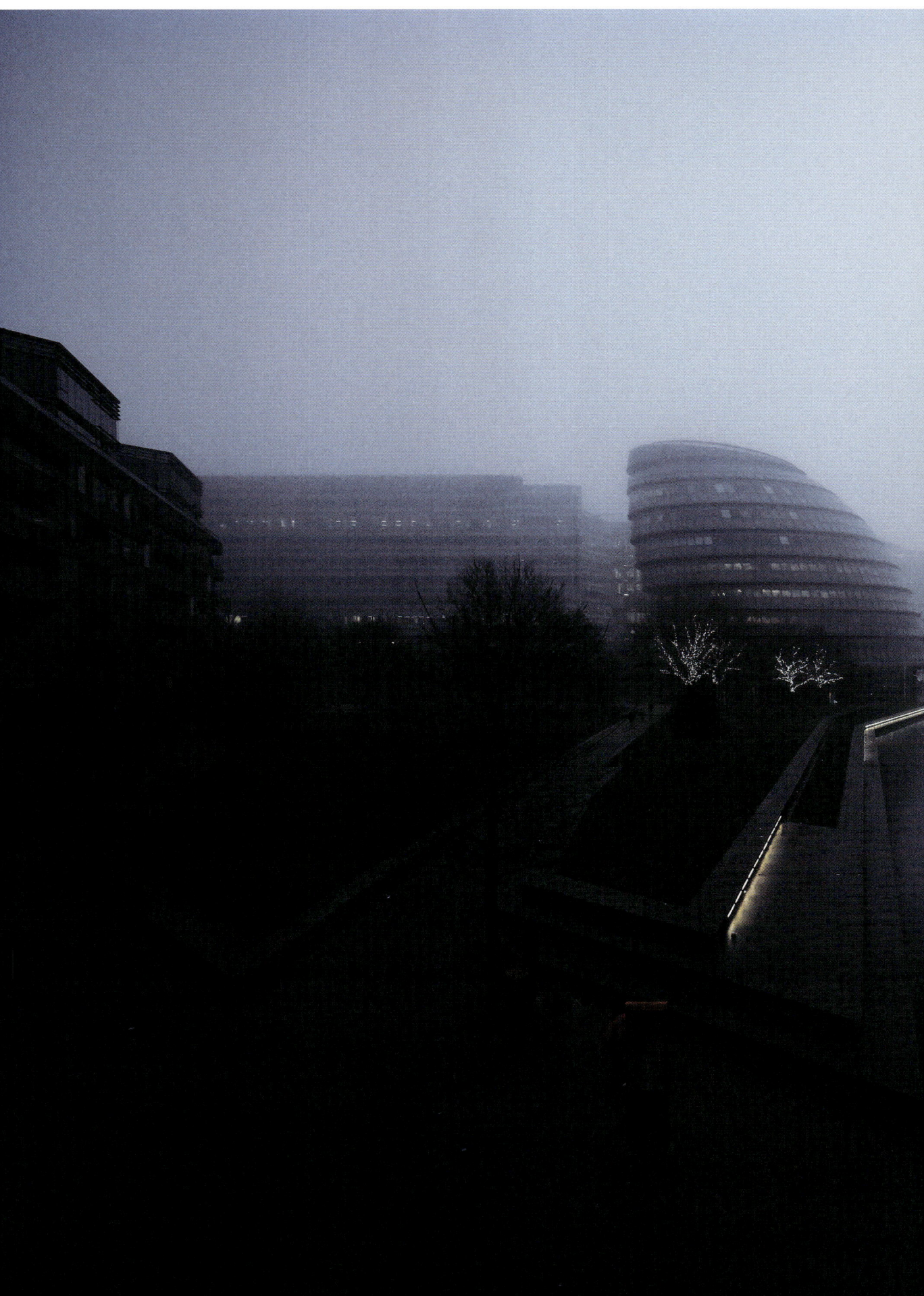

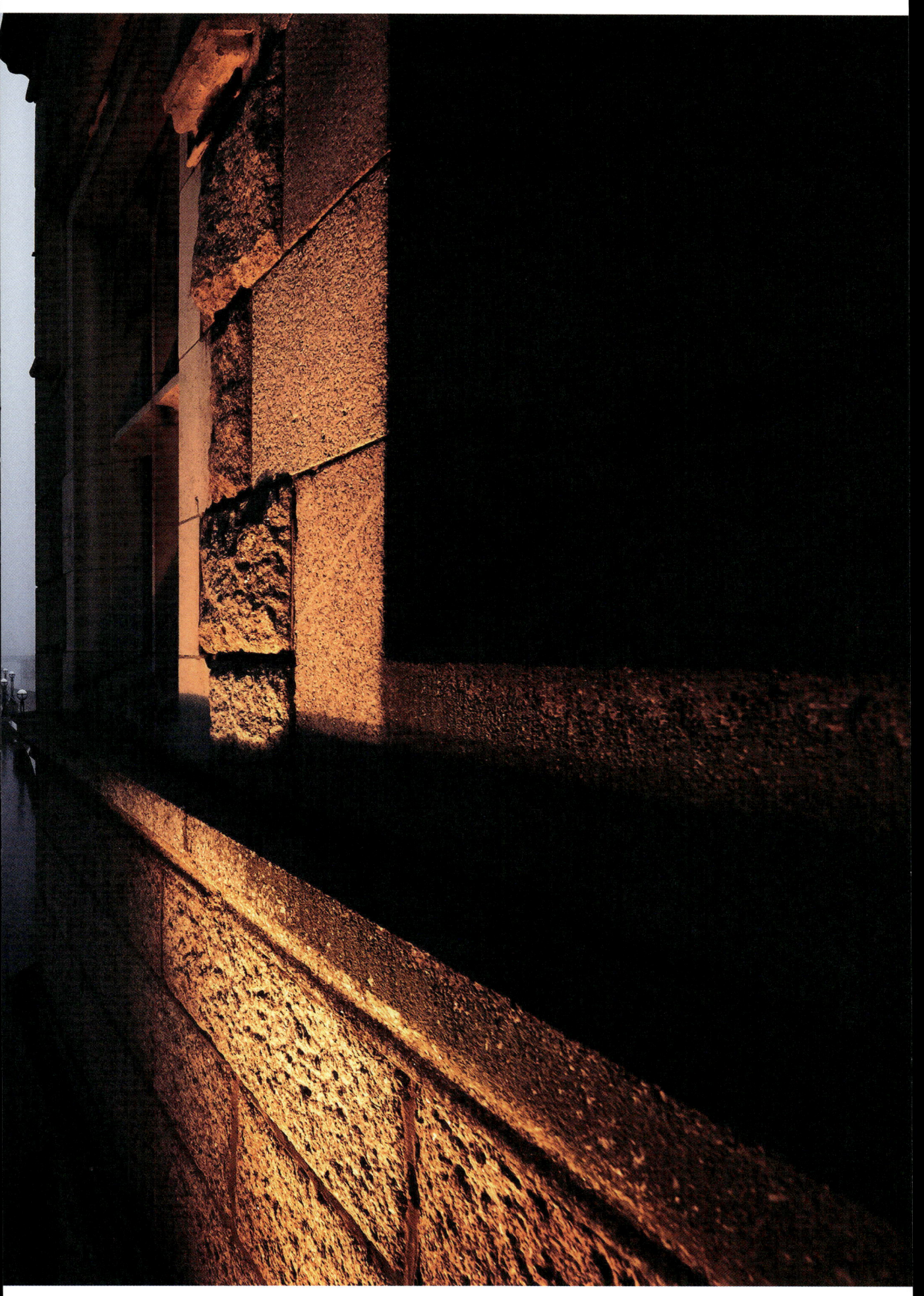

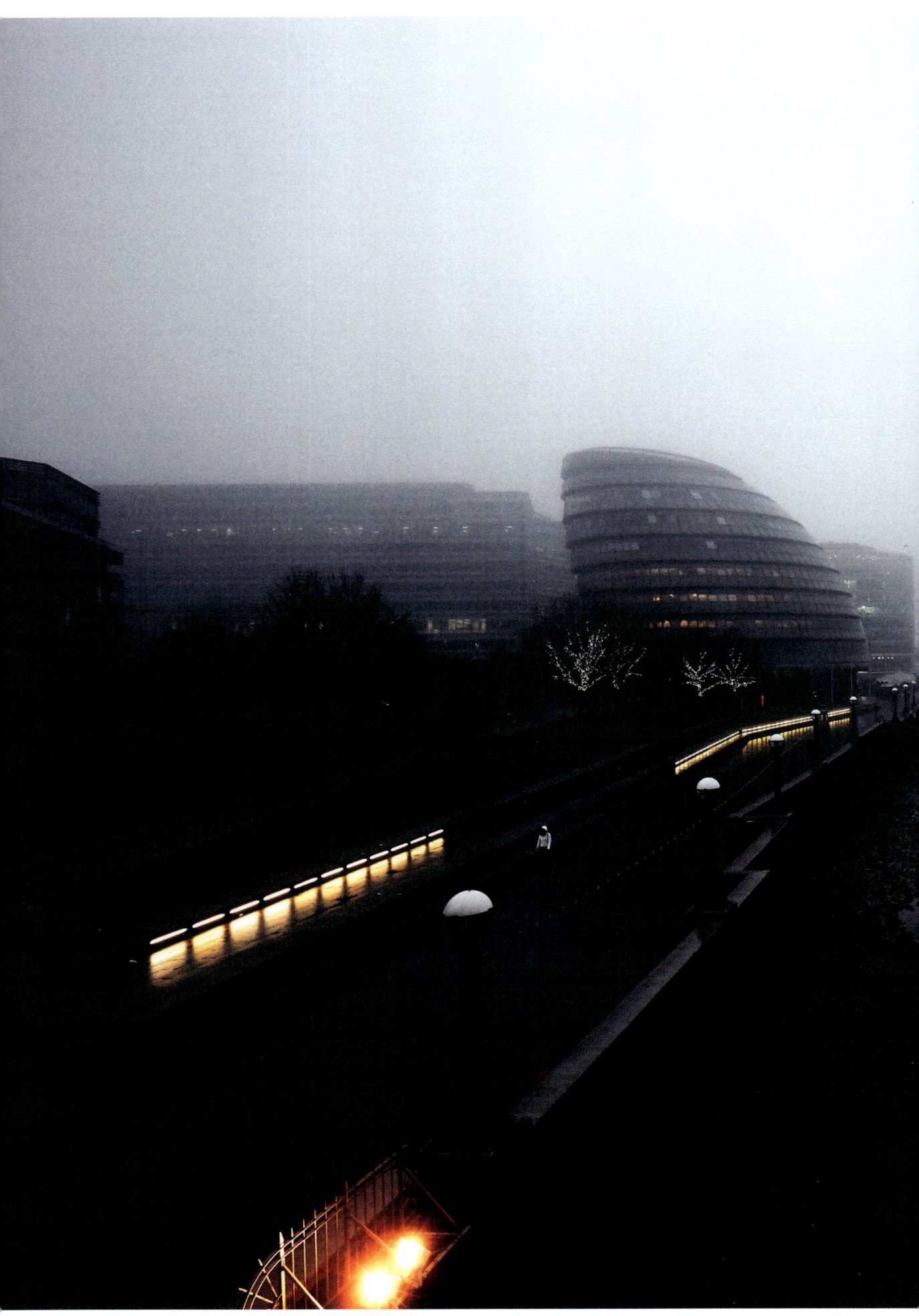

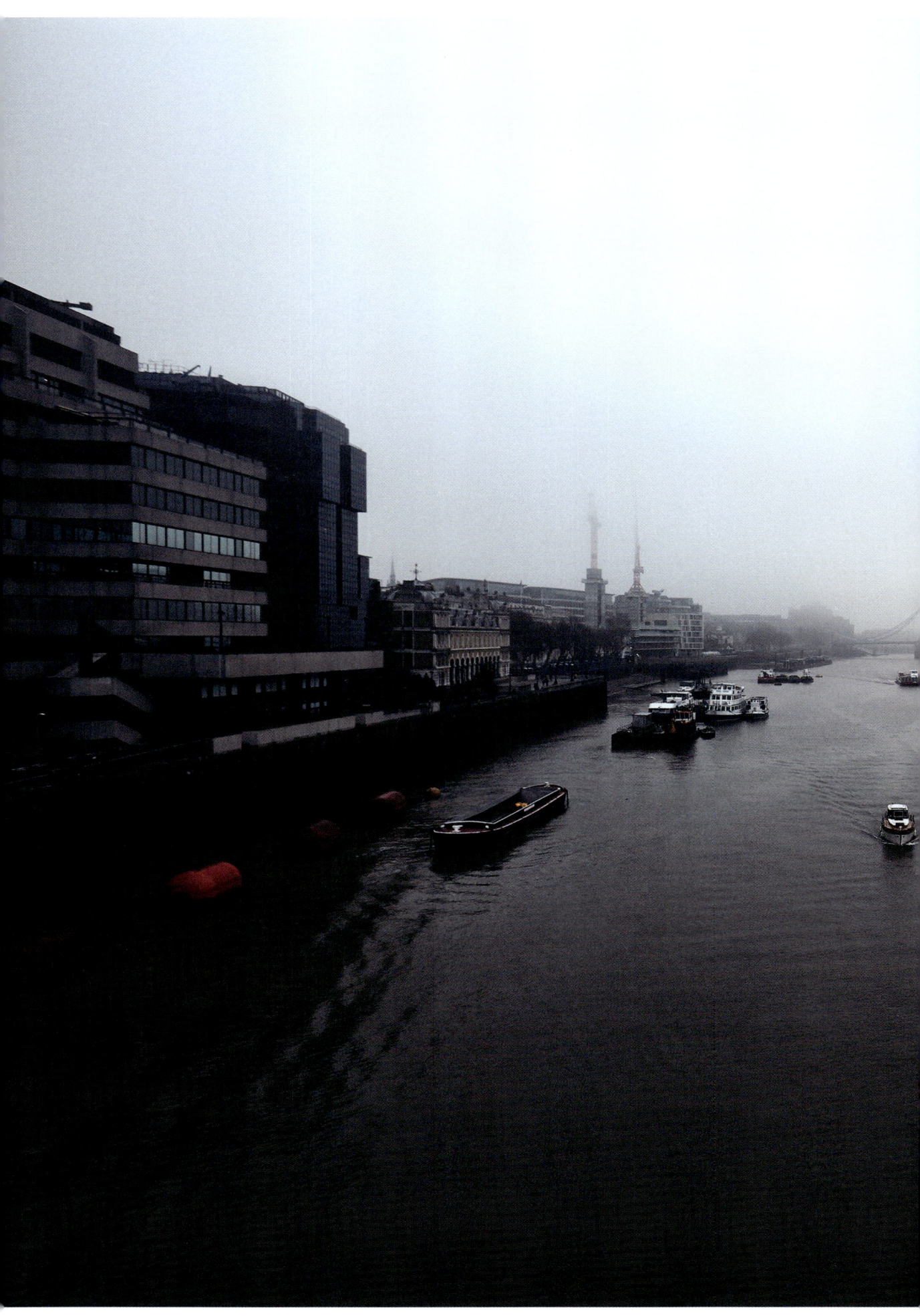

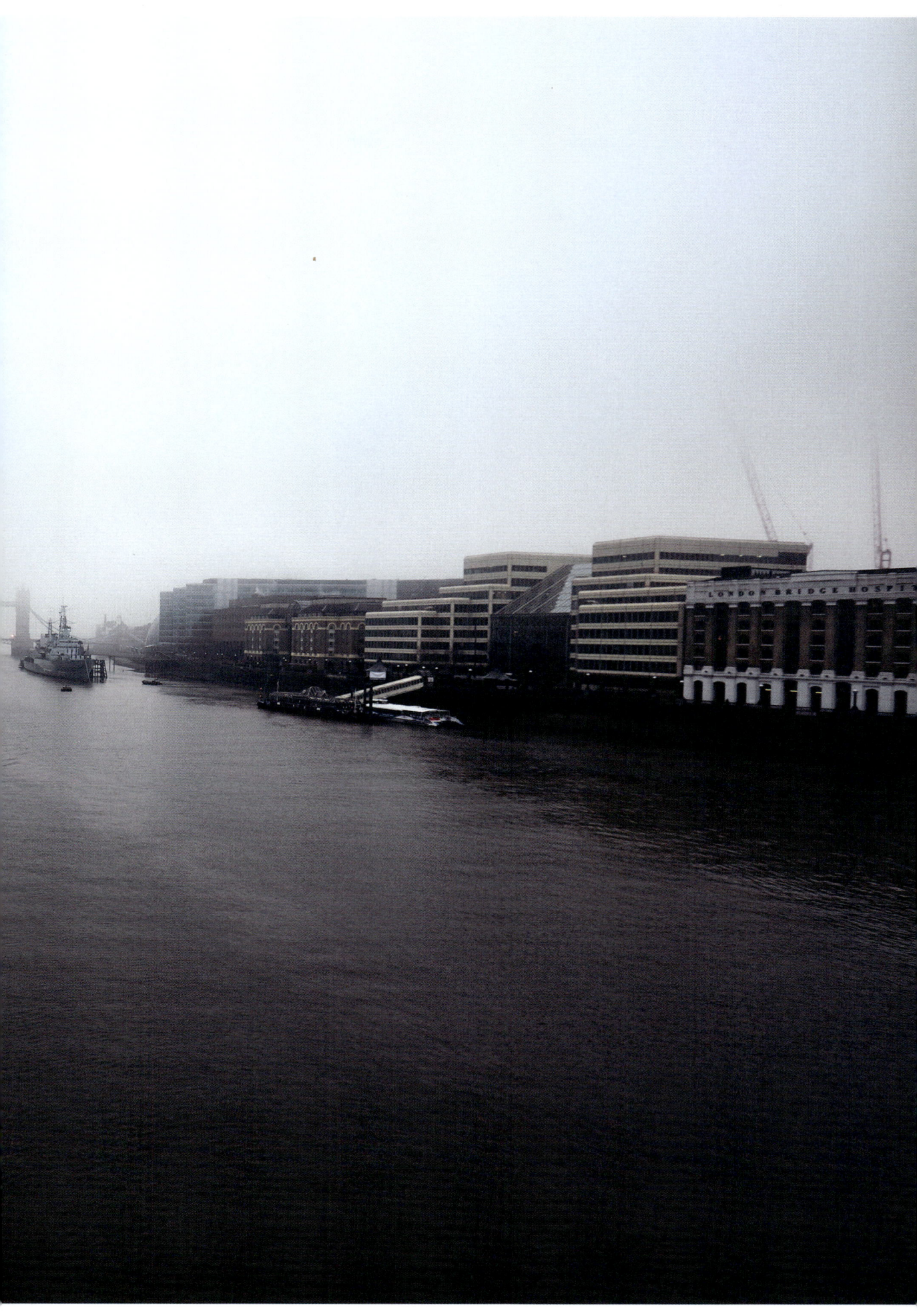

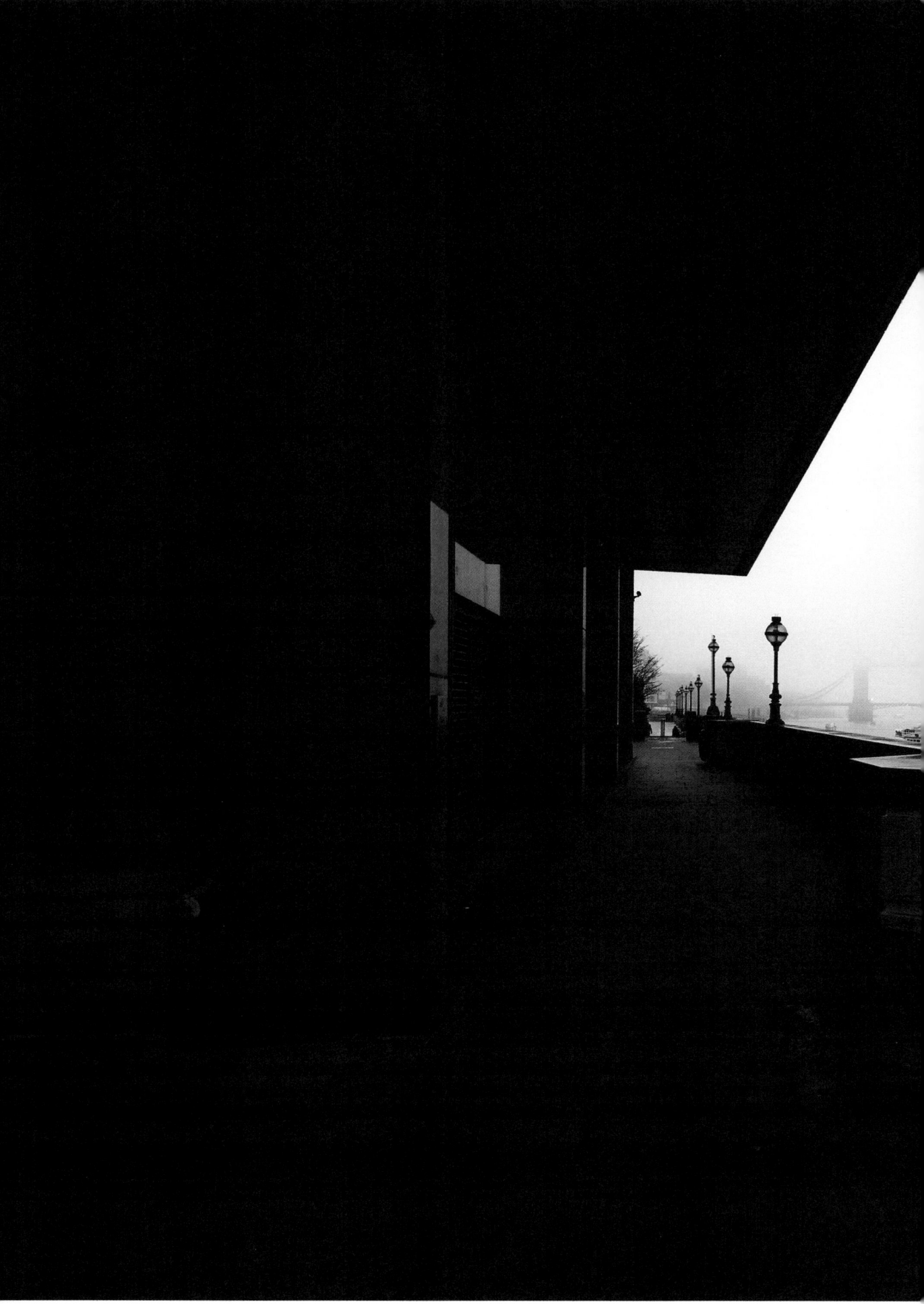

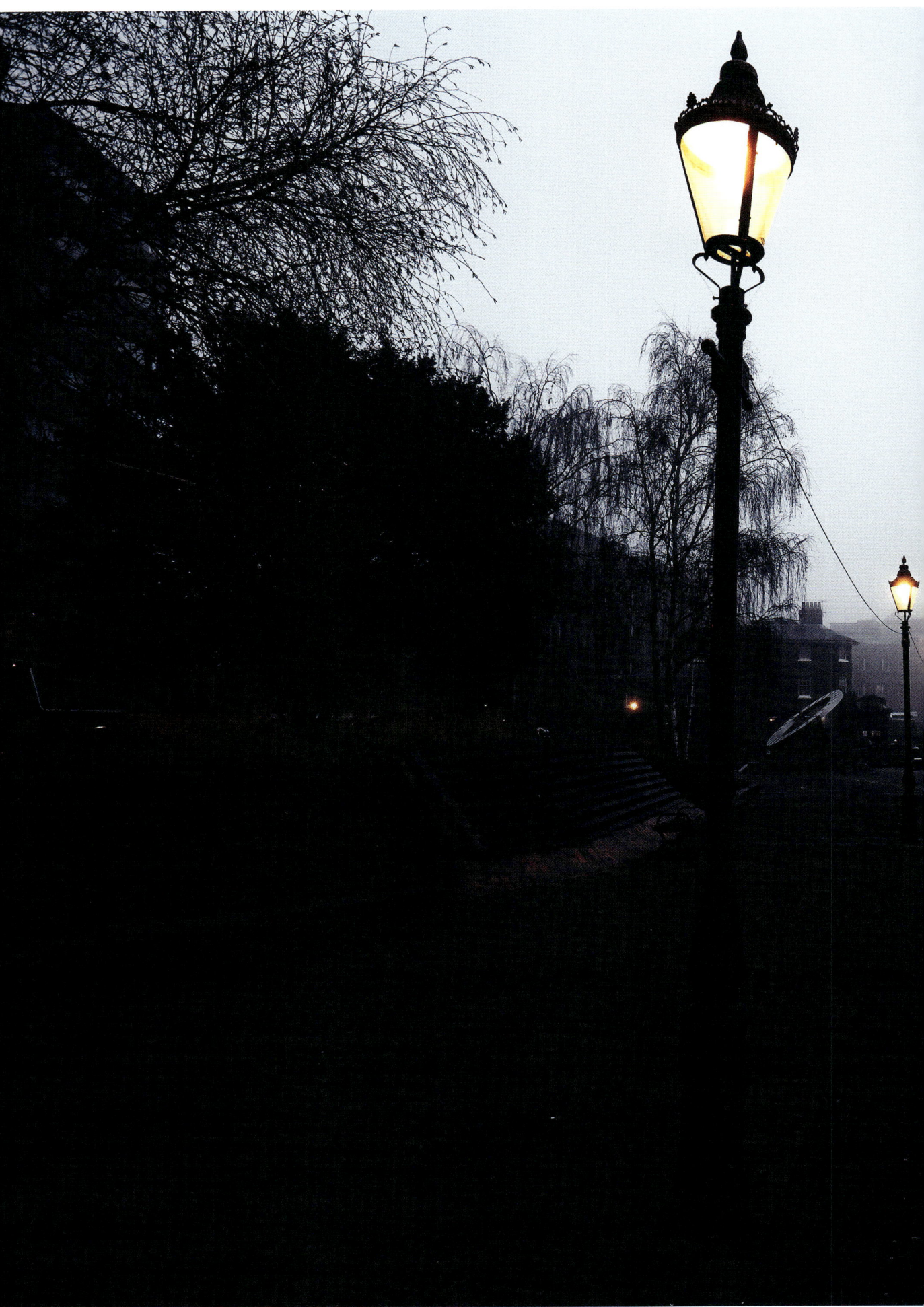

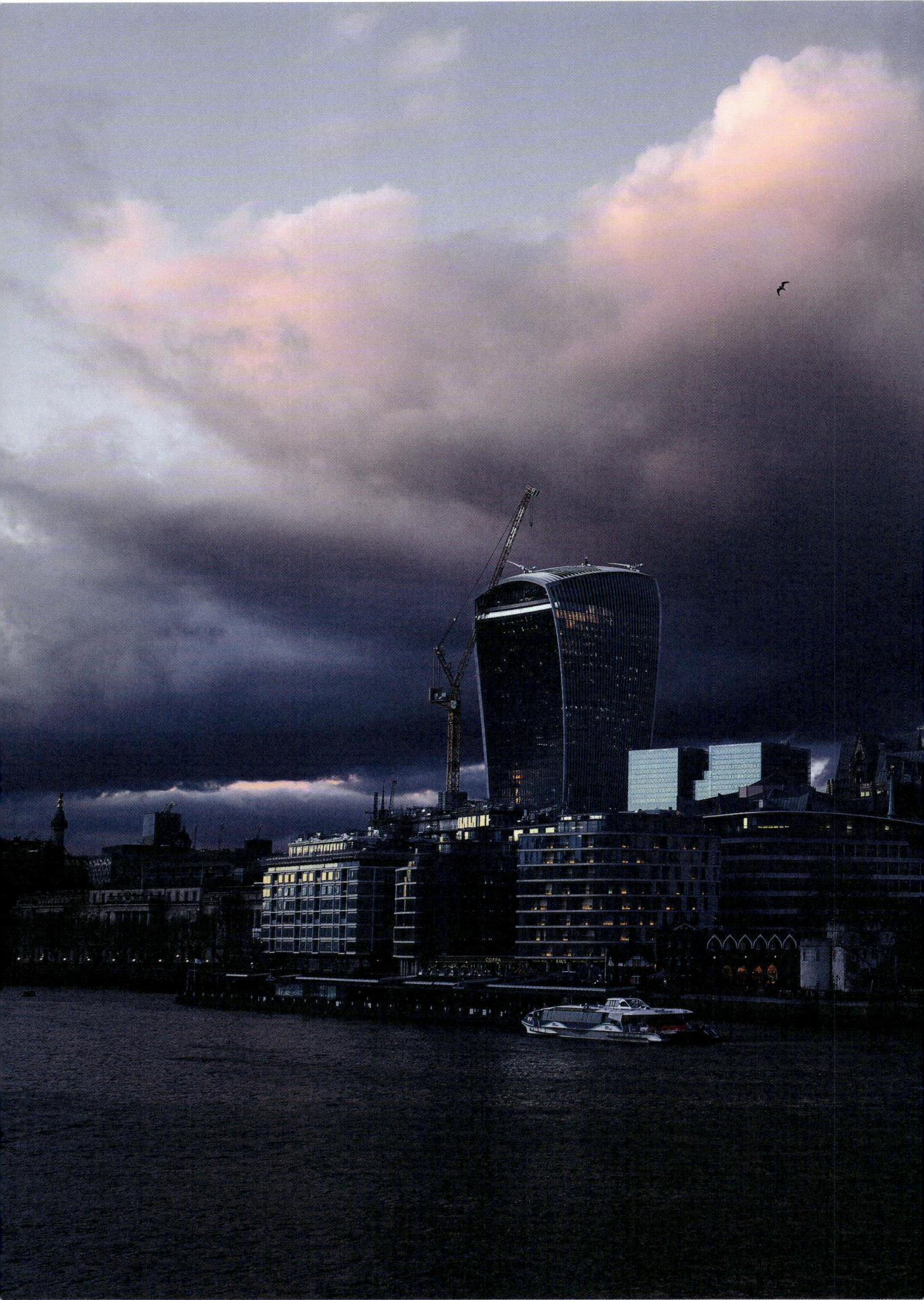

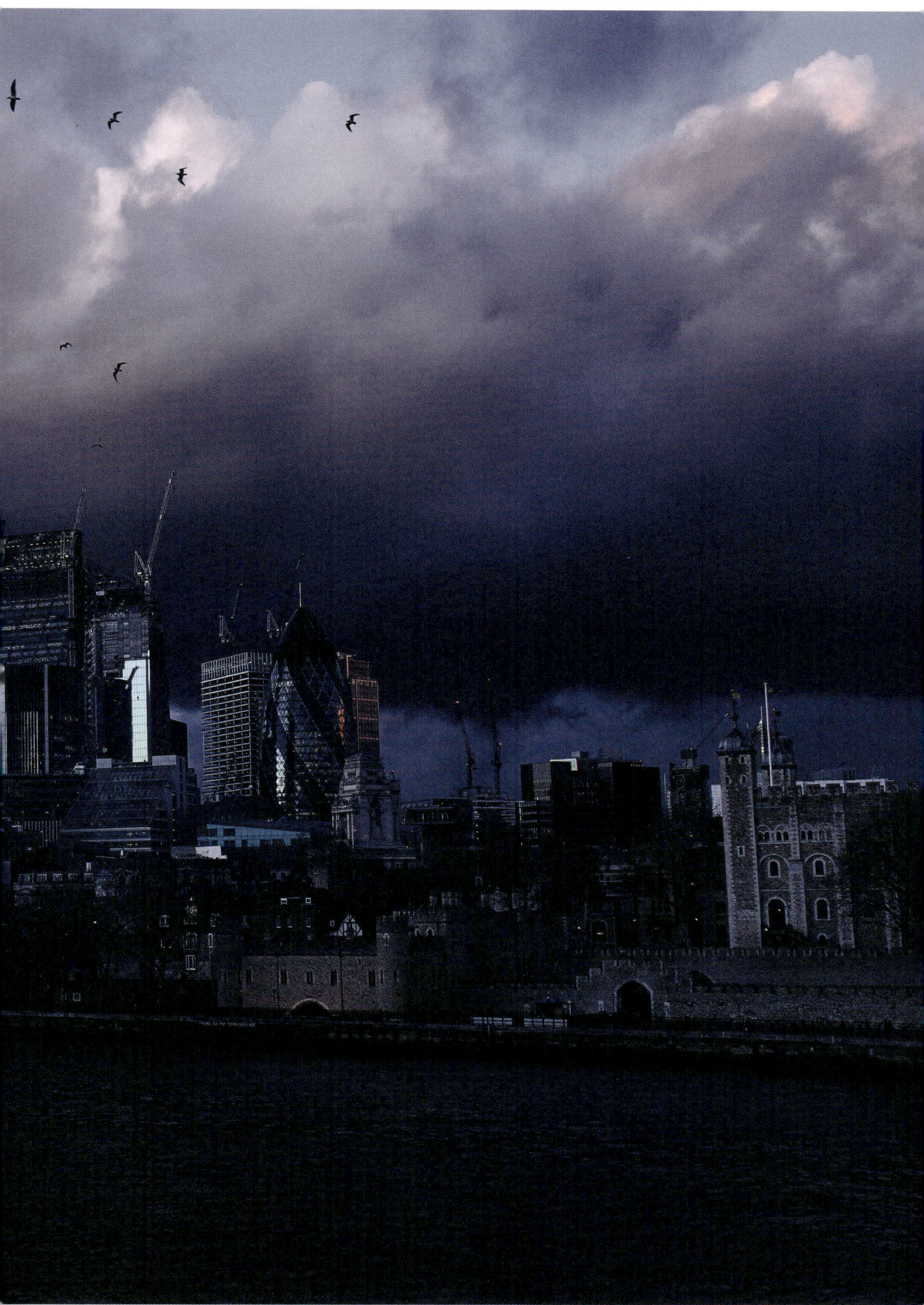

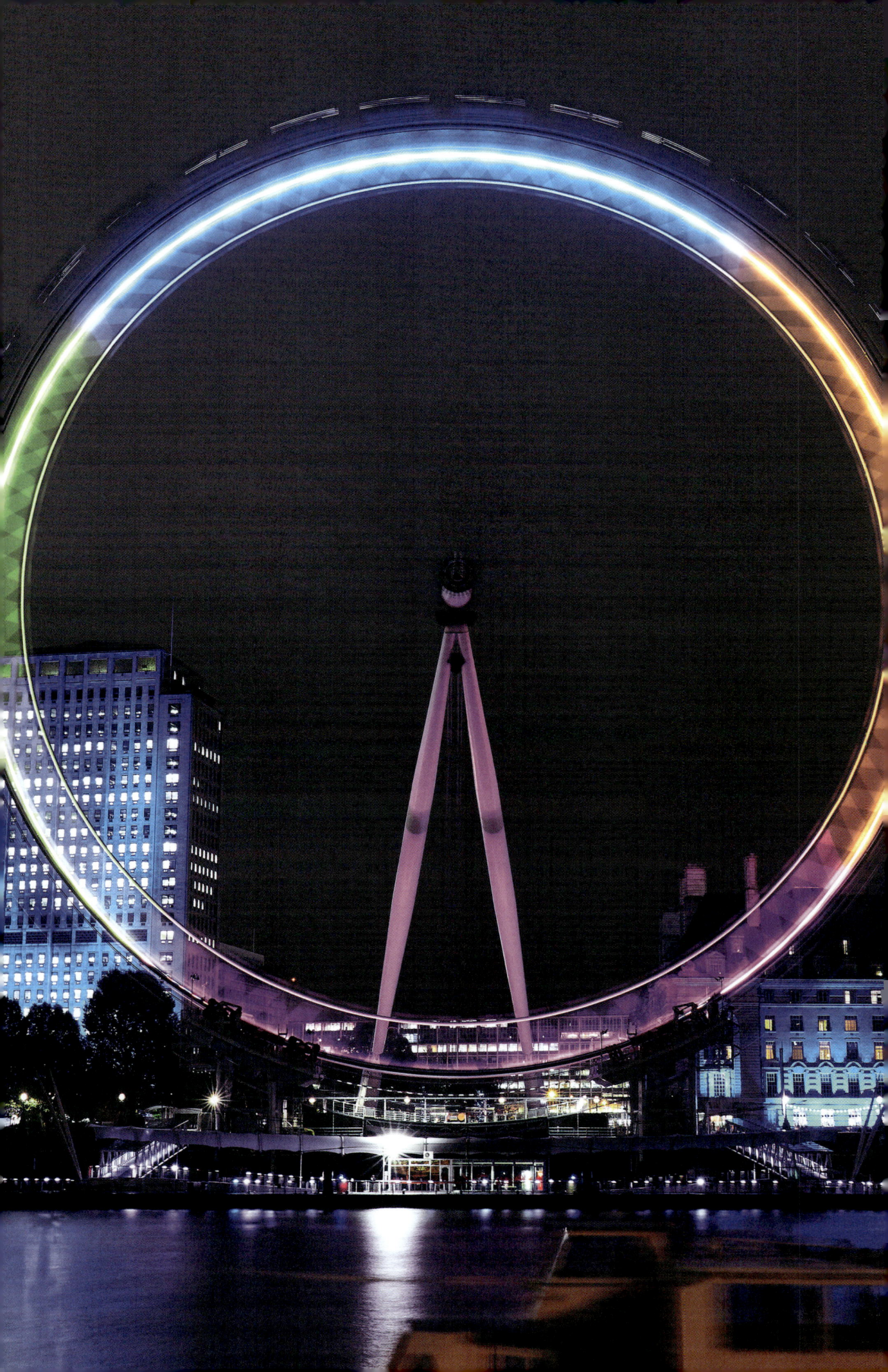

I love the London night life. It's when I feel the most alive. As darkness sweeps away life's distractions, I become deeply in touch with my creative soul.

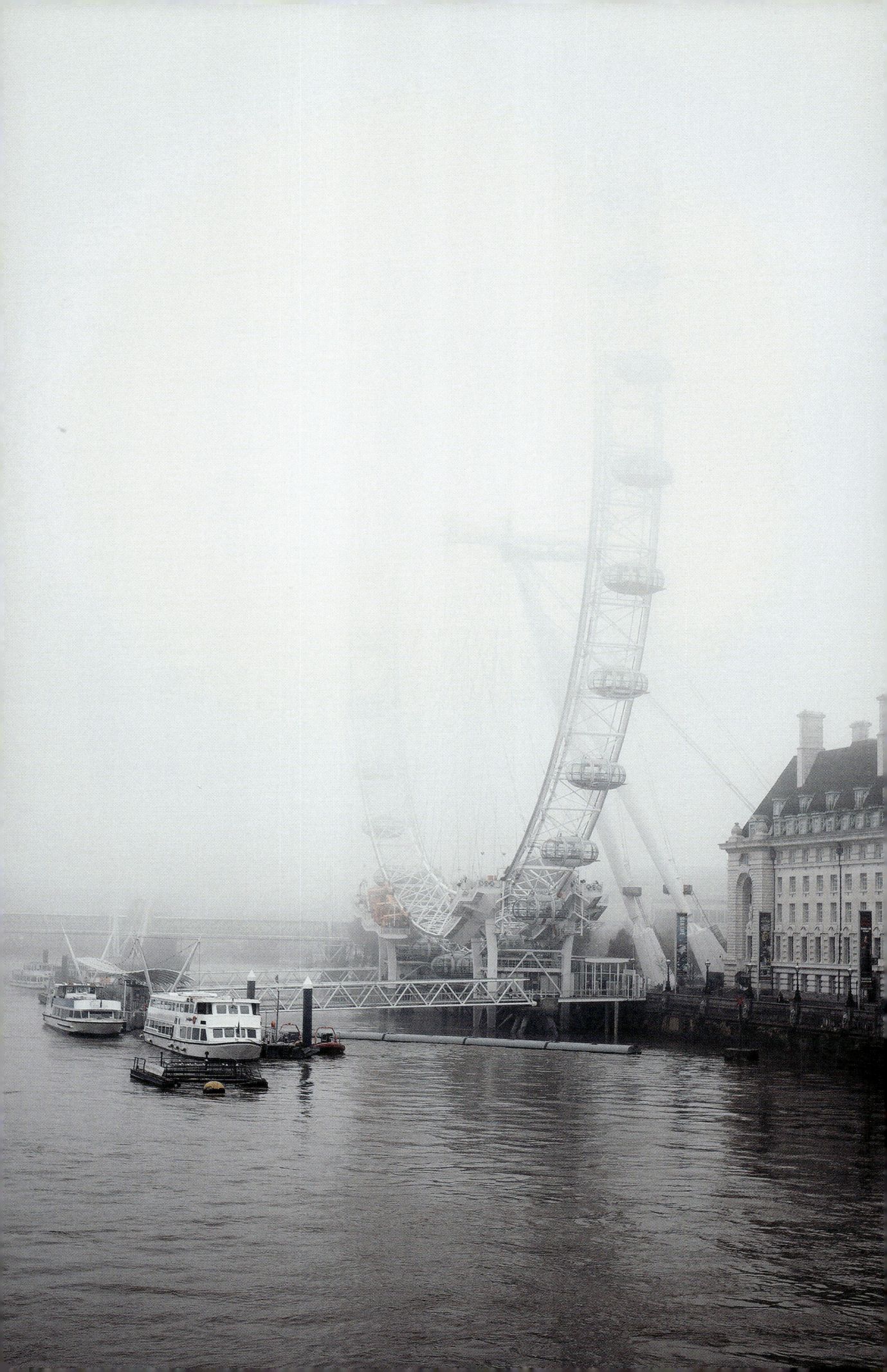

After capturing it, that moment in an image will last forever.

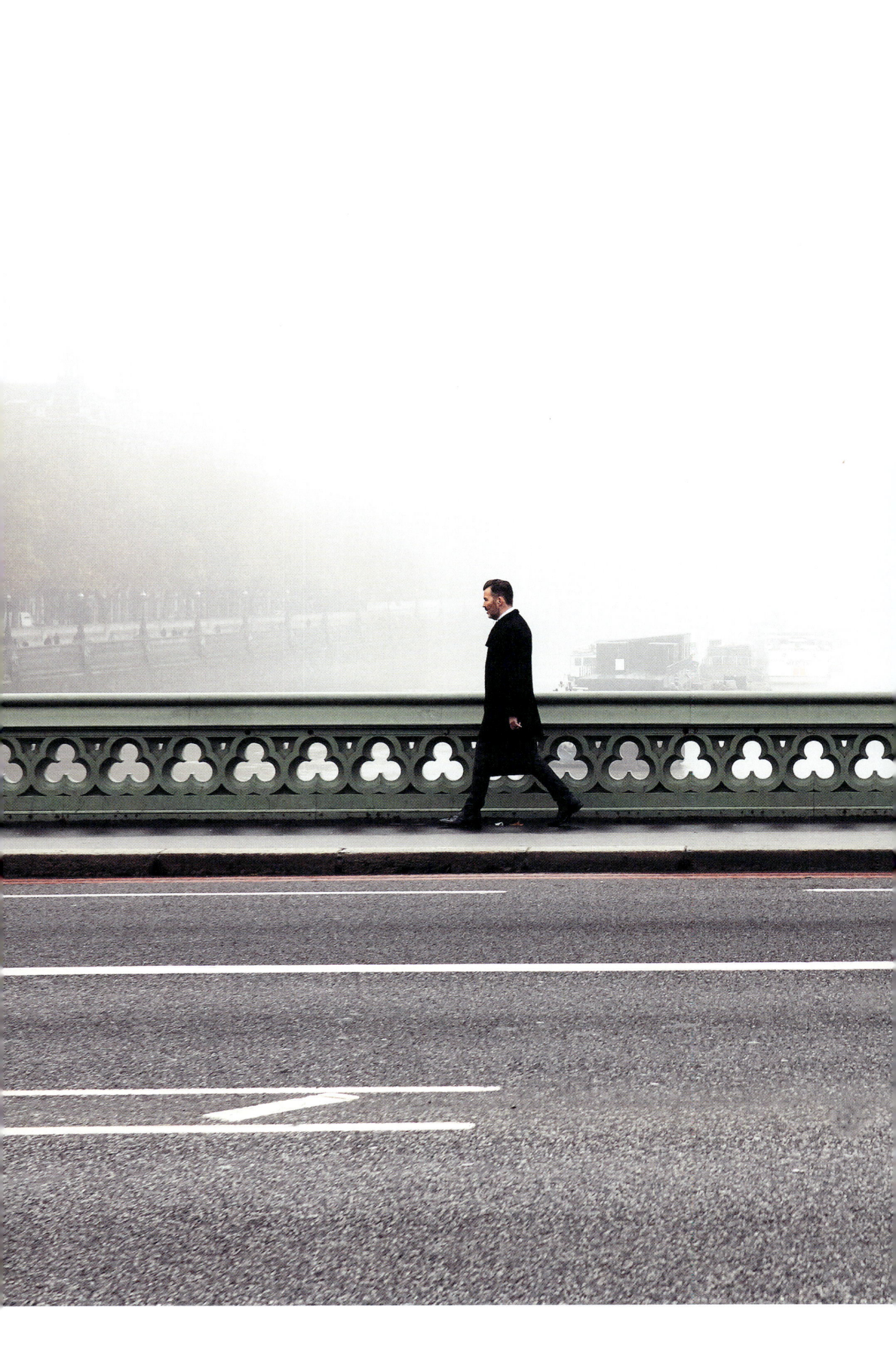

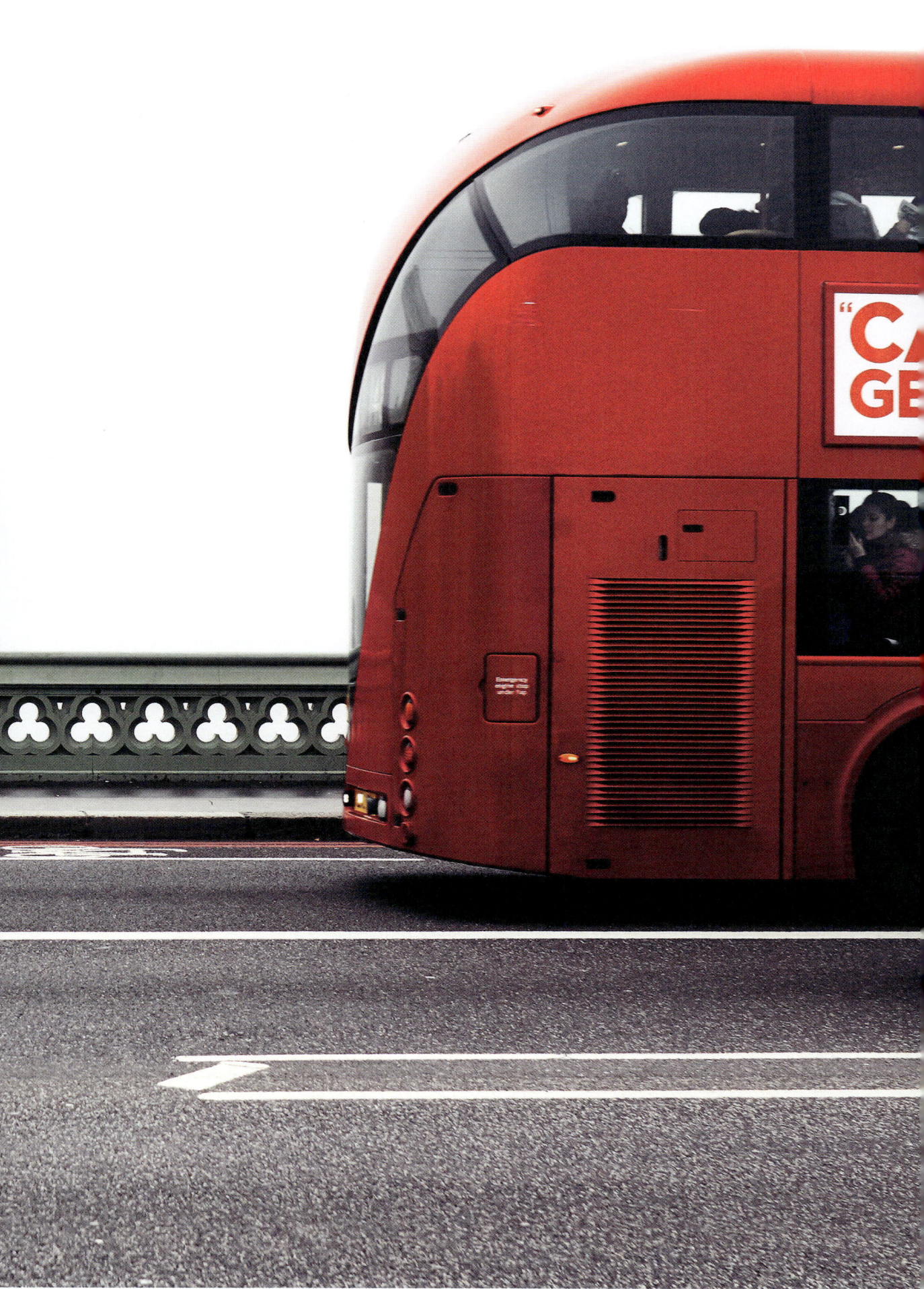

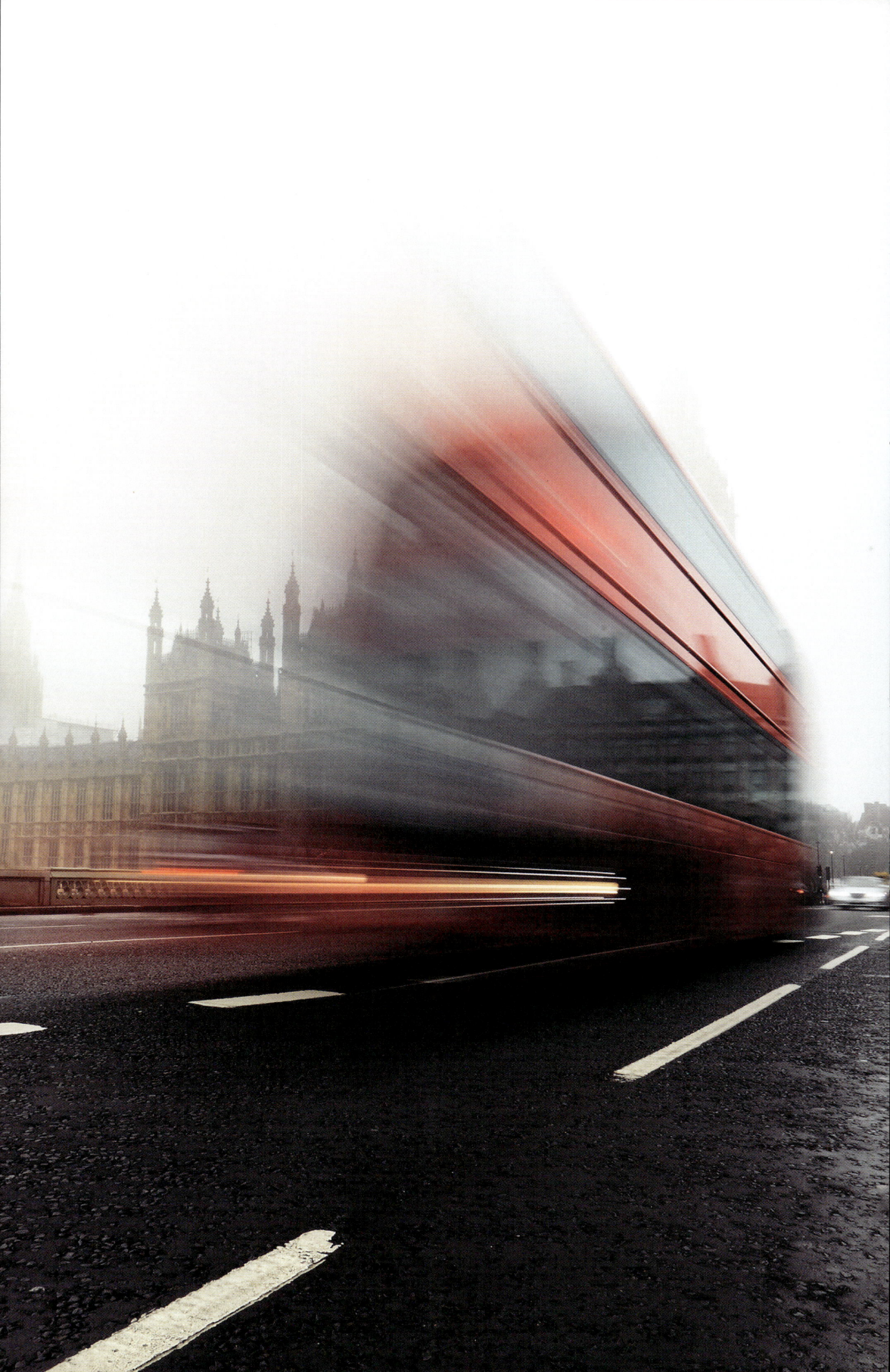

I have always believed that it is easier to succeed at something you love doing than at something you don't.

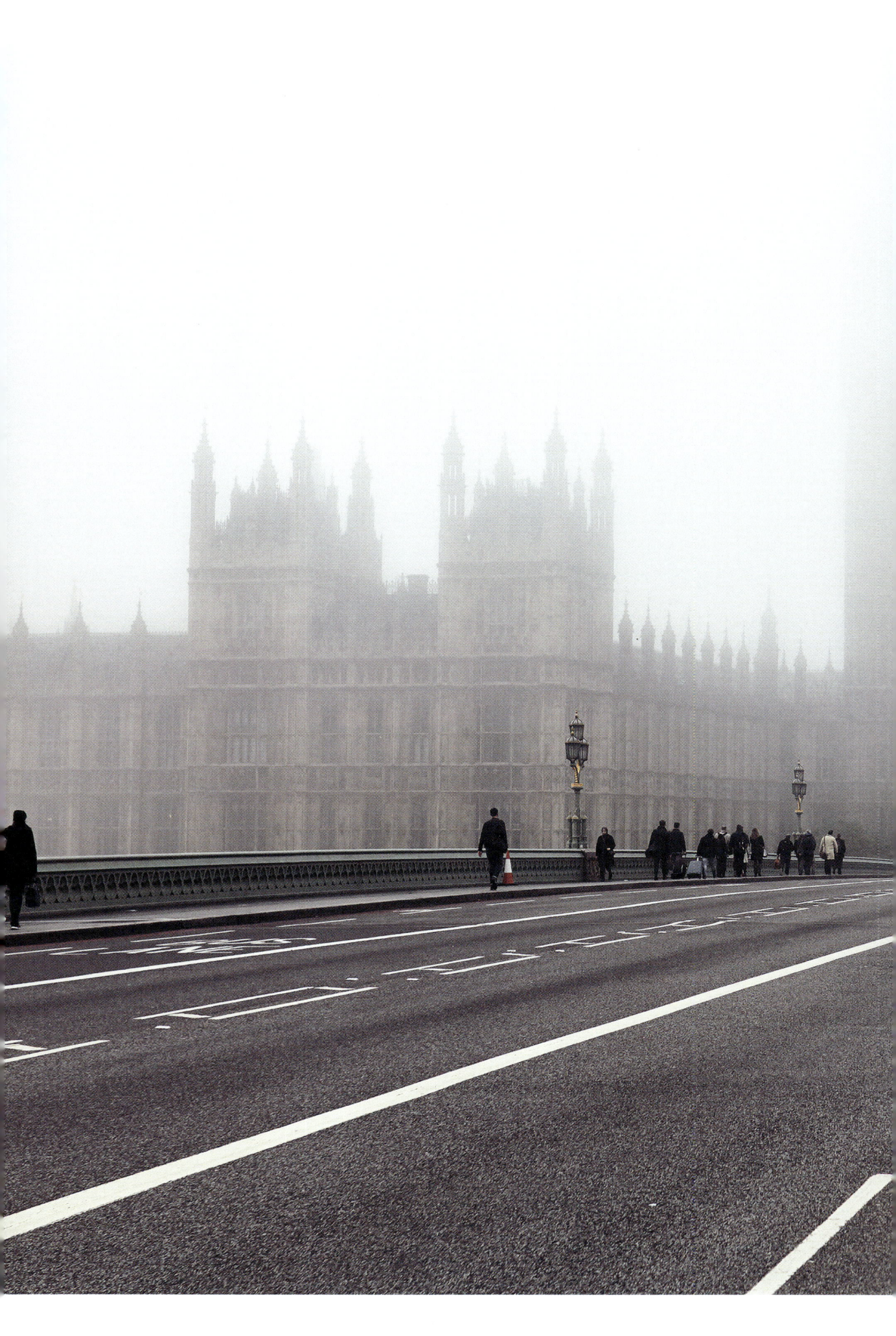

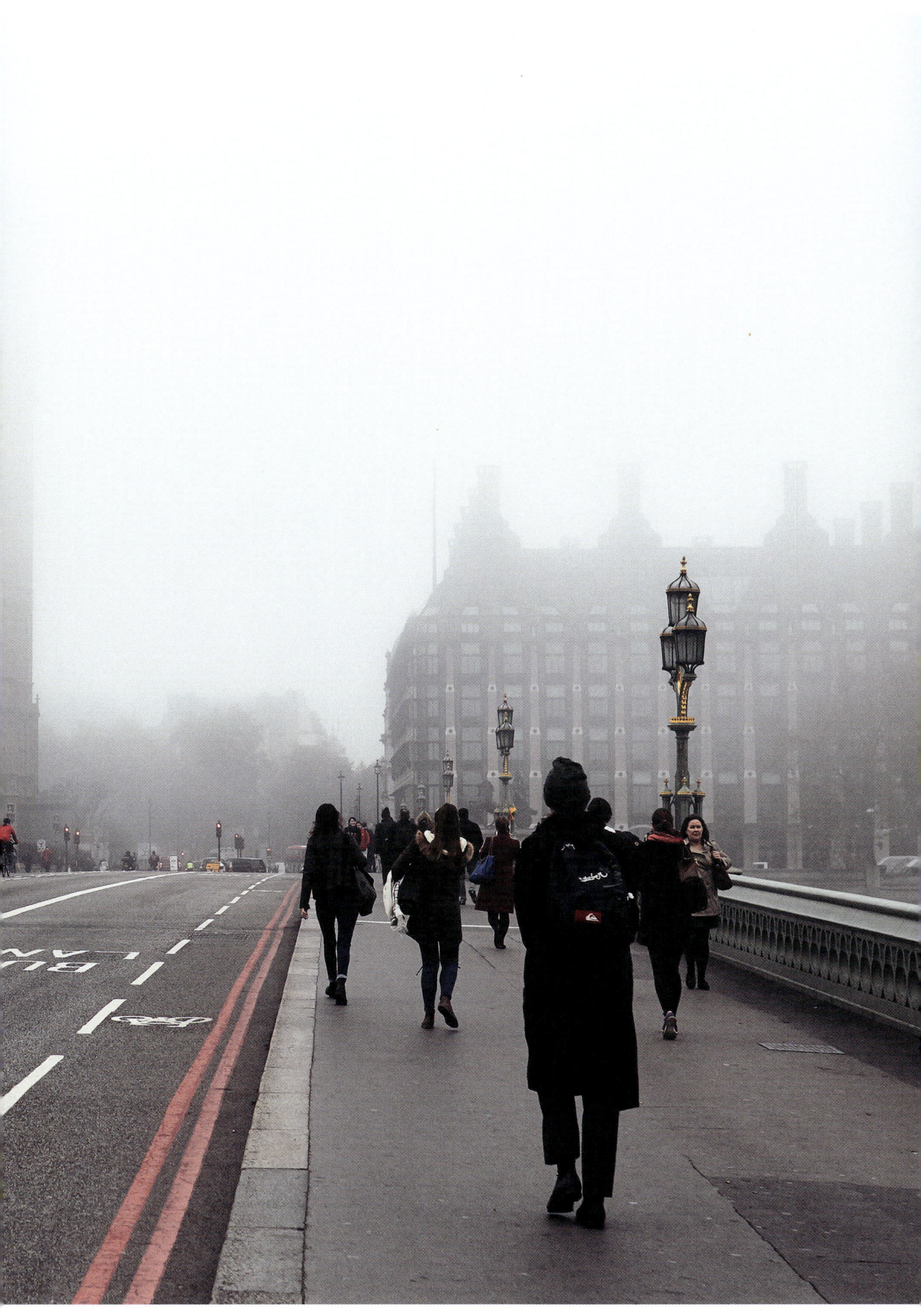

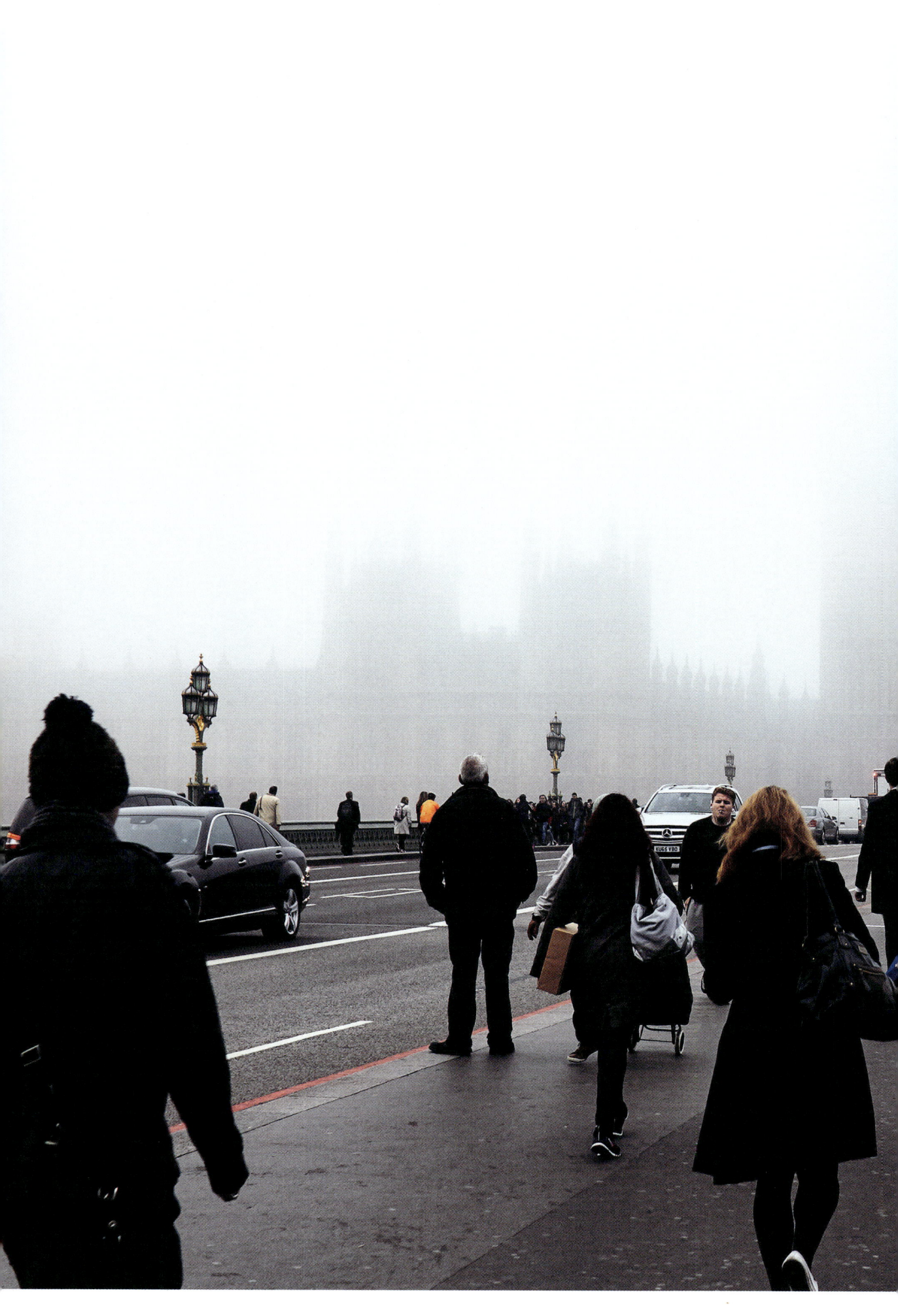

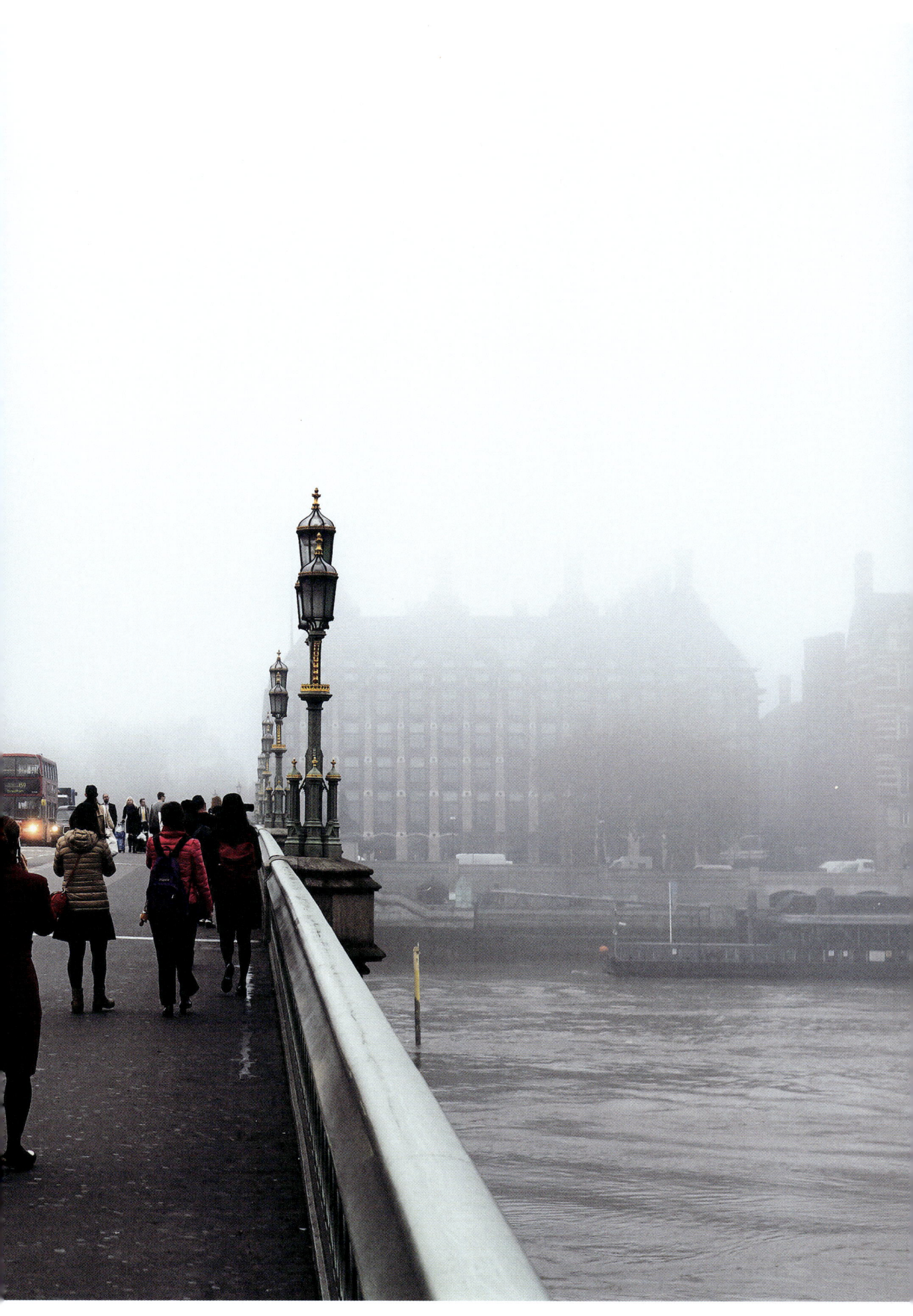

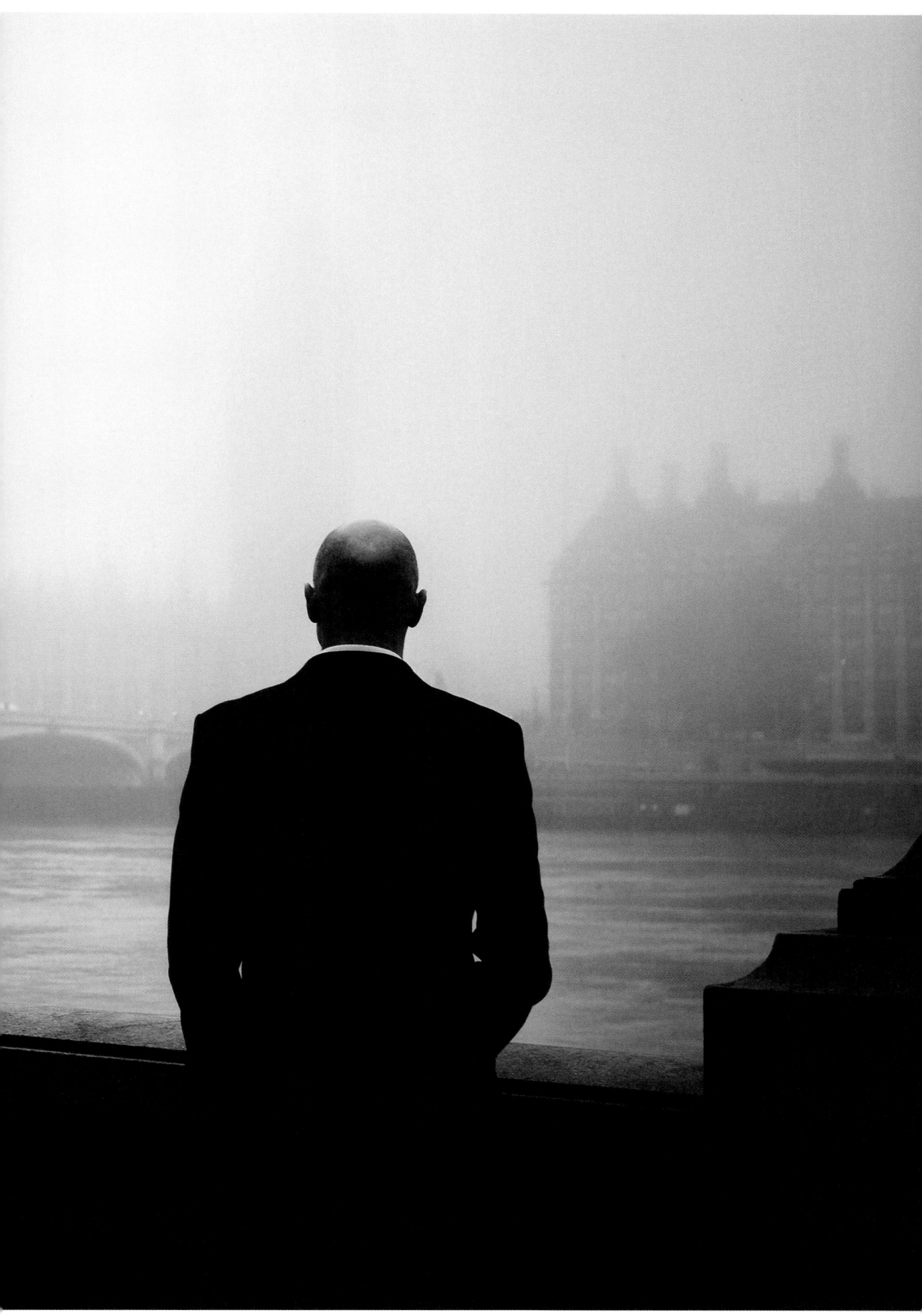

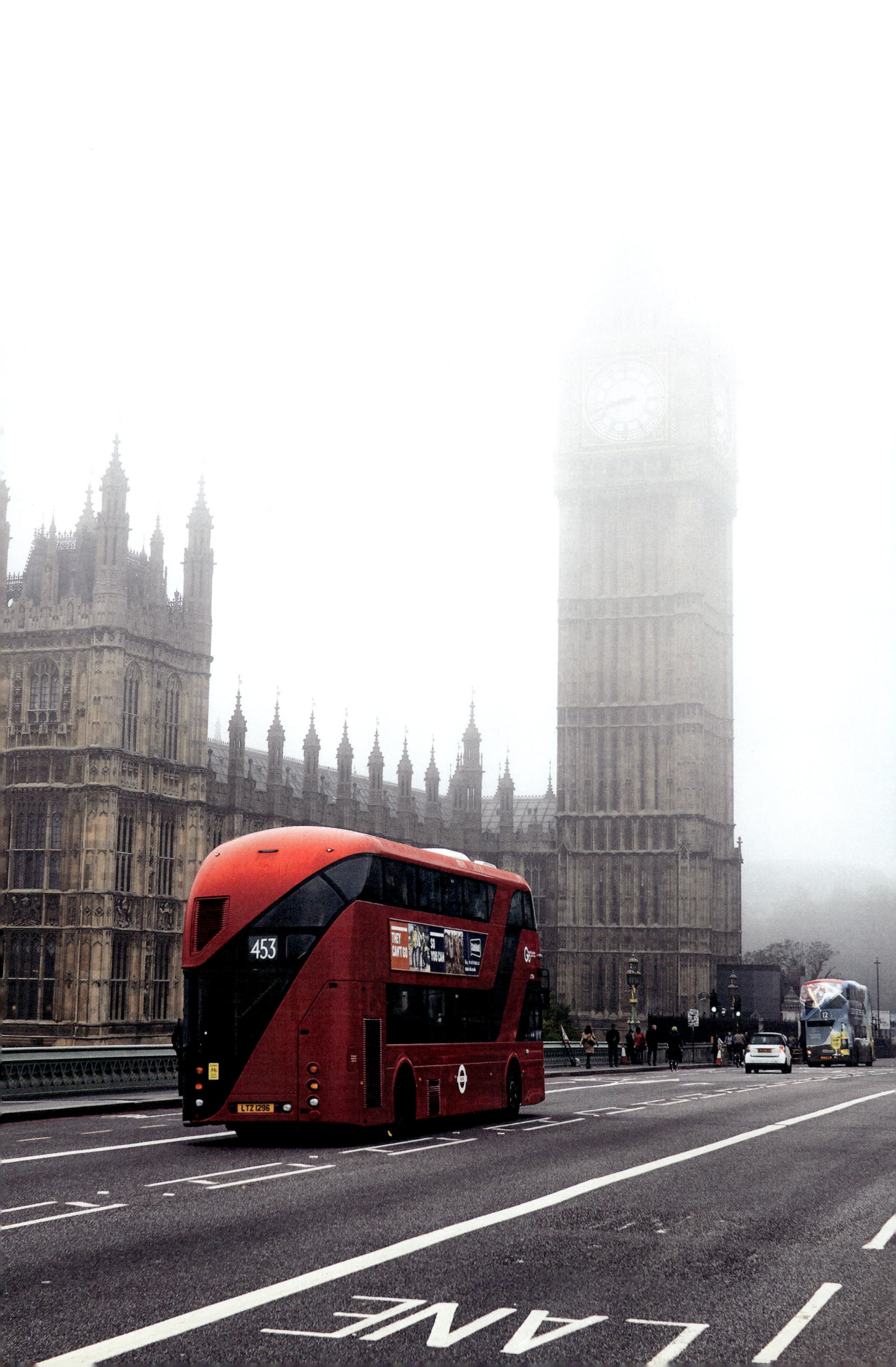

Taking photos allows me to express myself through a medium that simultaneously documents moments in time. In essence, it's my creative, visual diary.

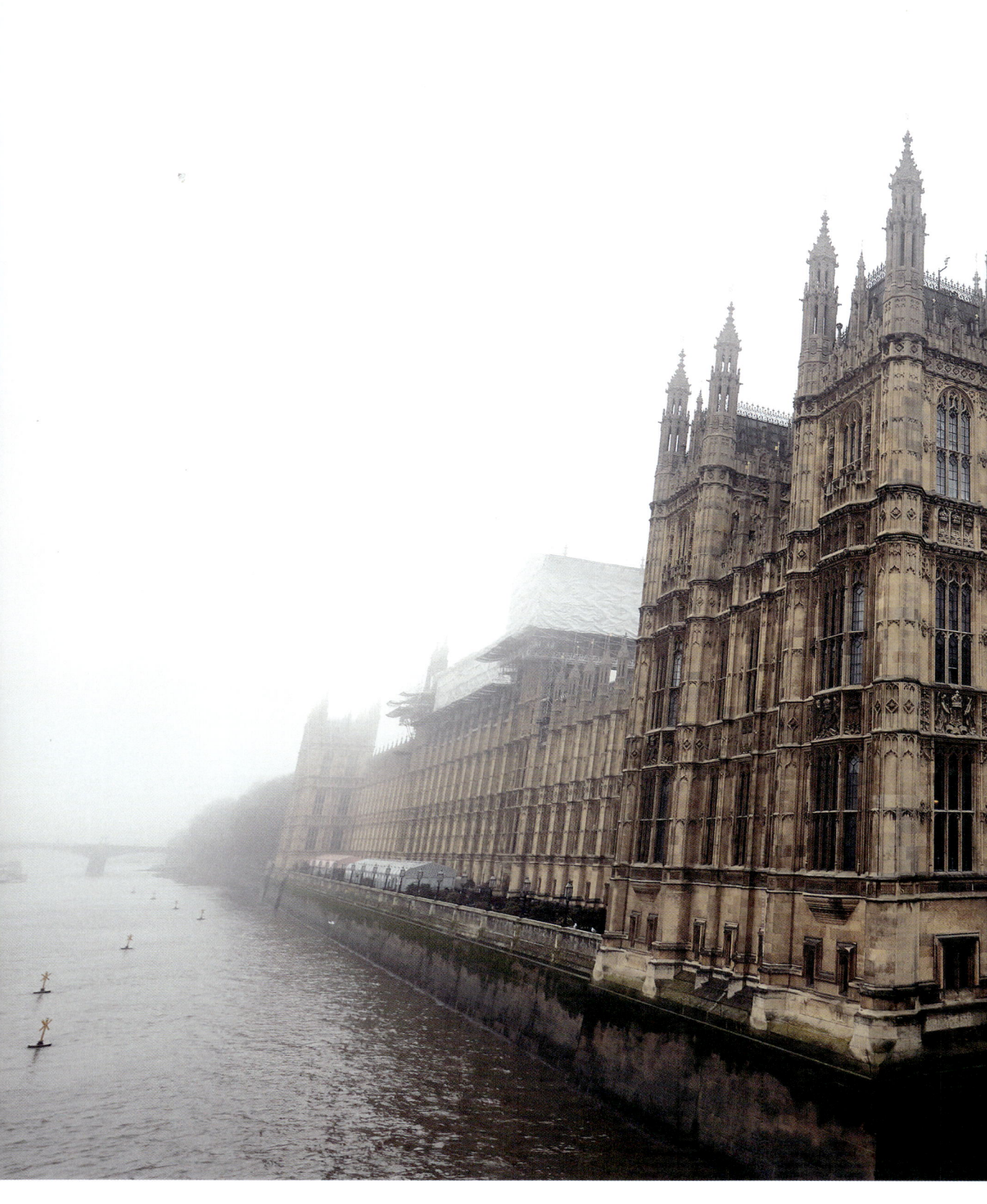

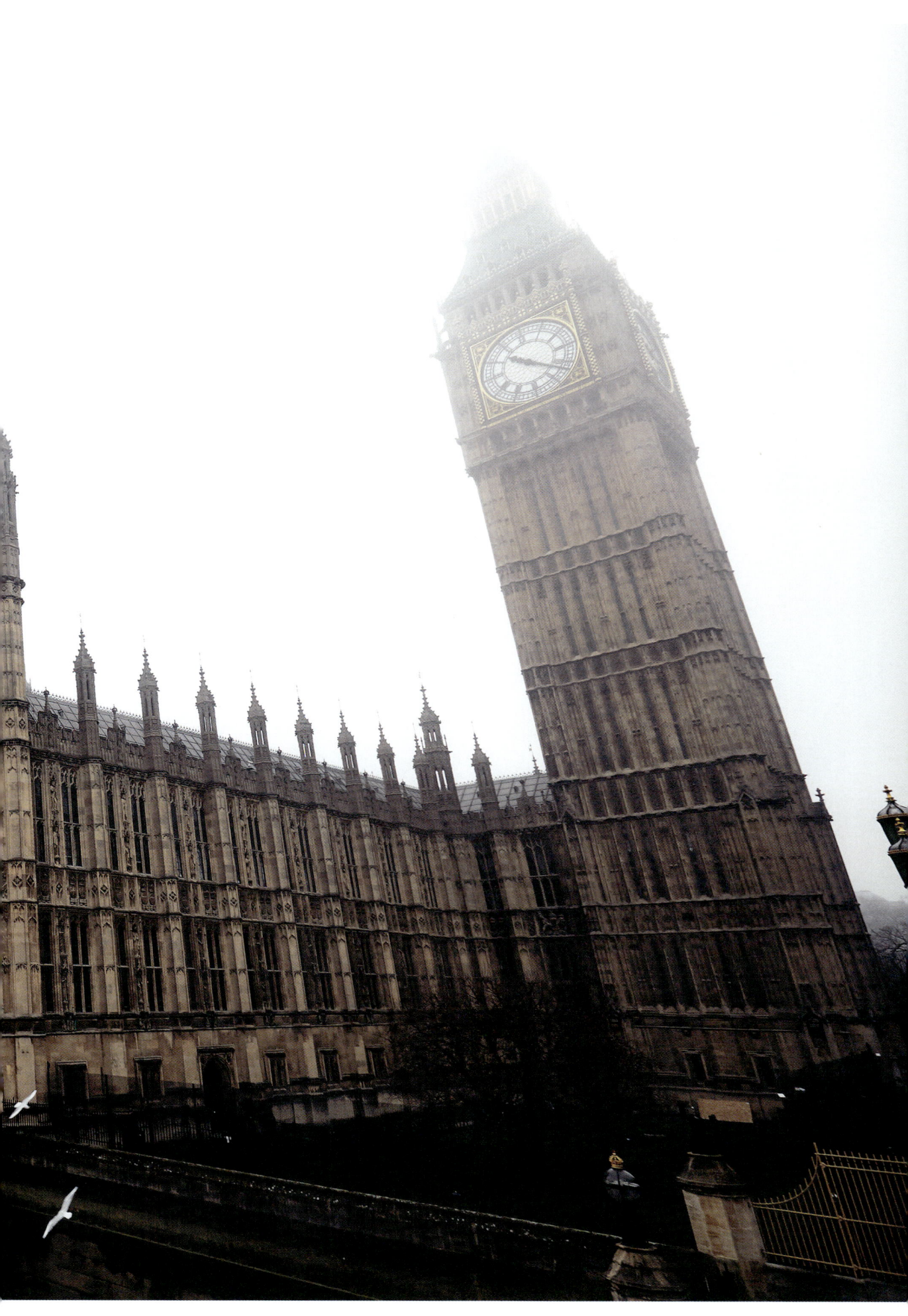

This city is wildly overwhelming. Its architecture is sharp with contrast. The architecture ignites my soul.

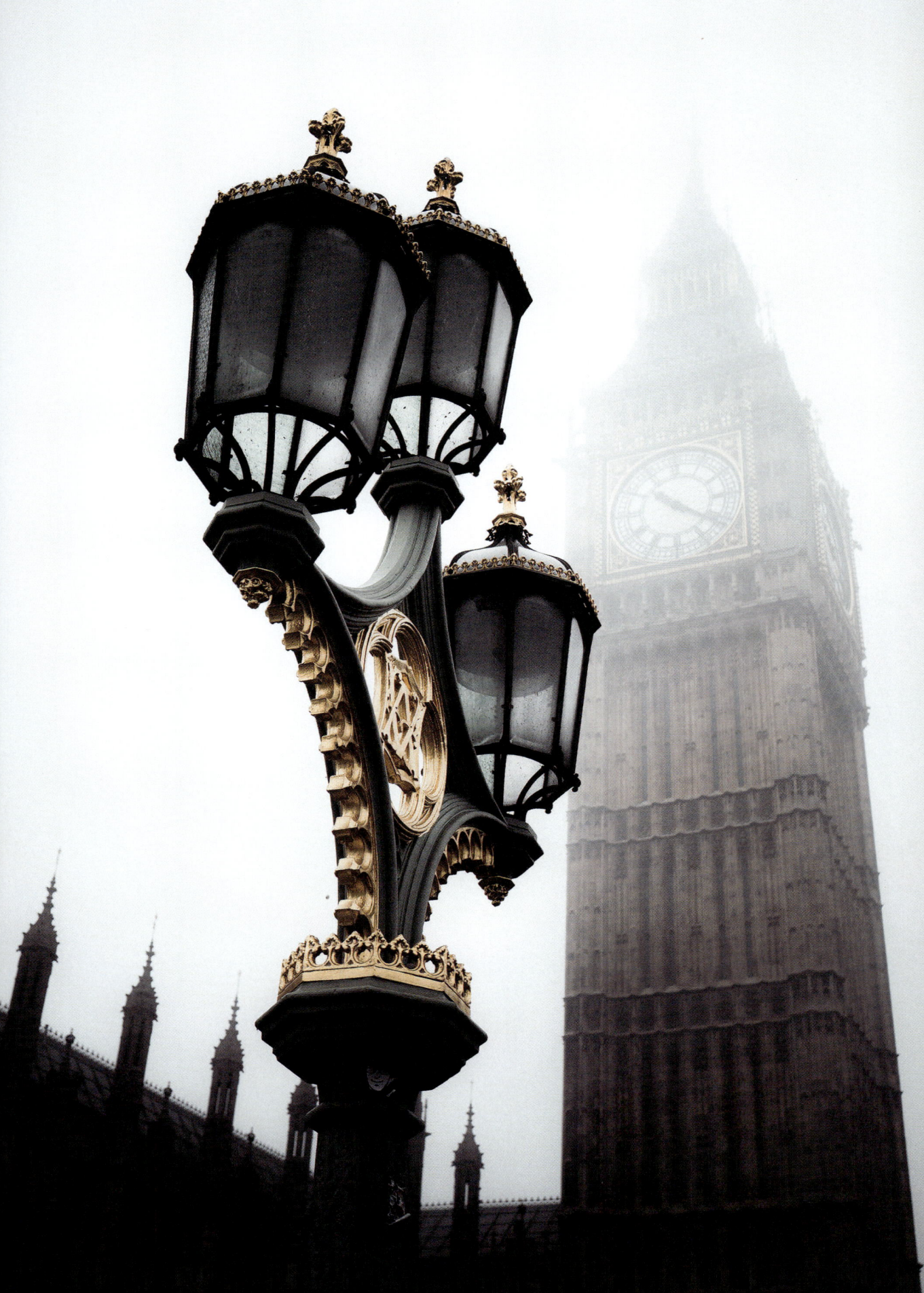

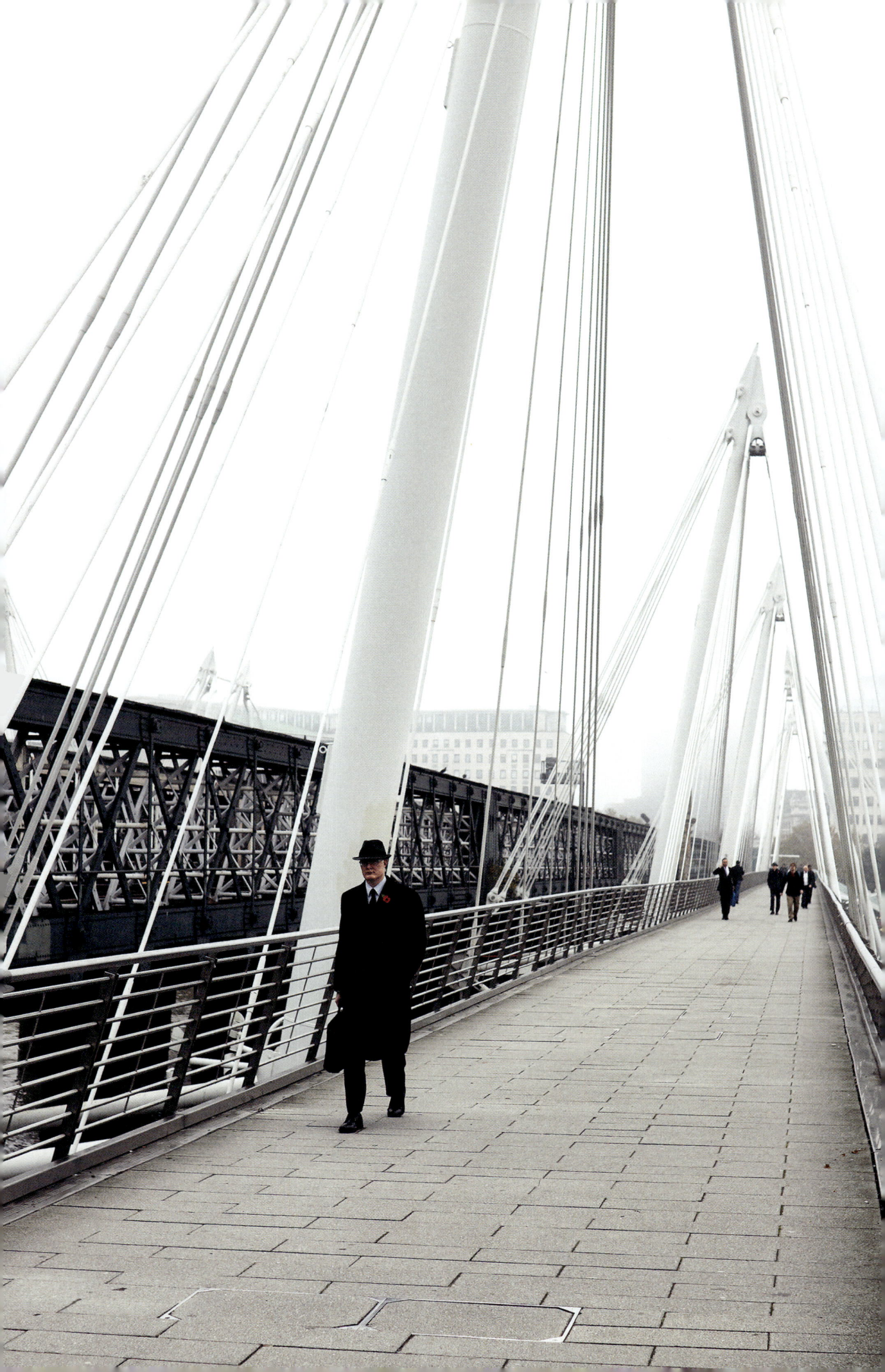

There are so many visually different places to shoot street photography in London. That diversity is what I love so much.

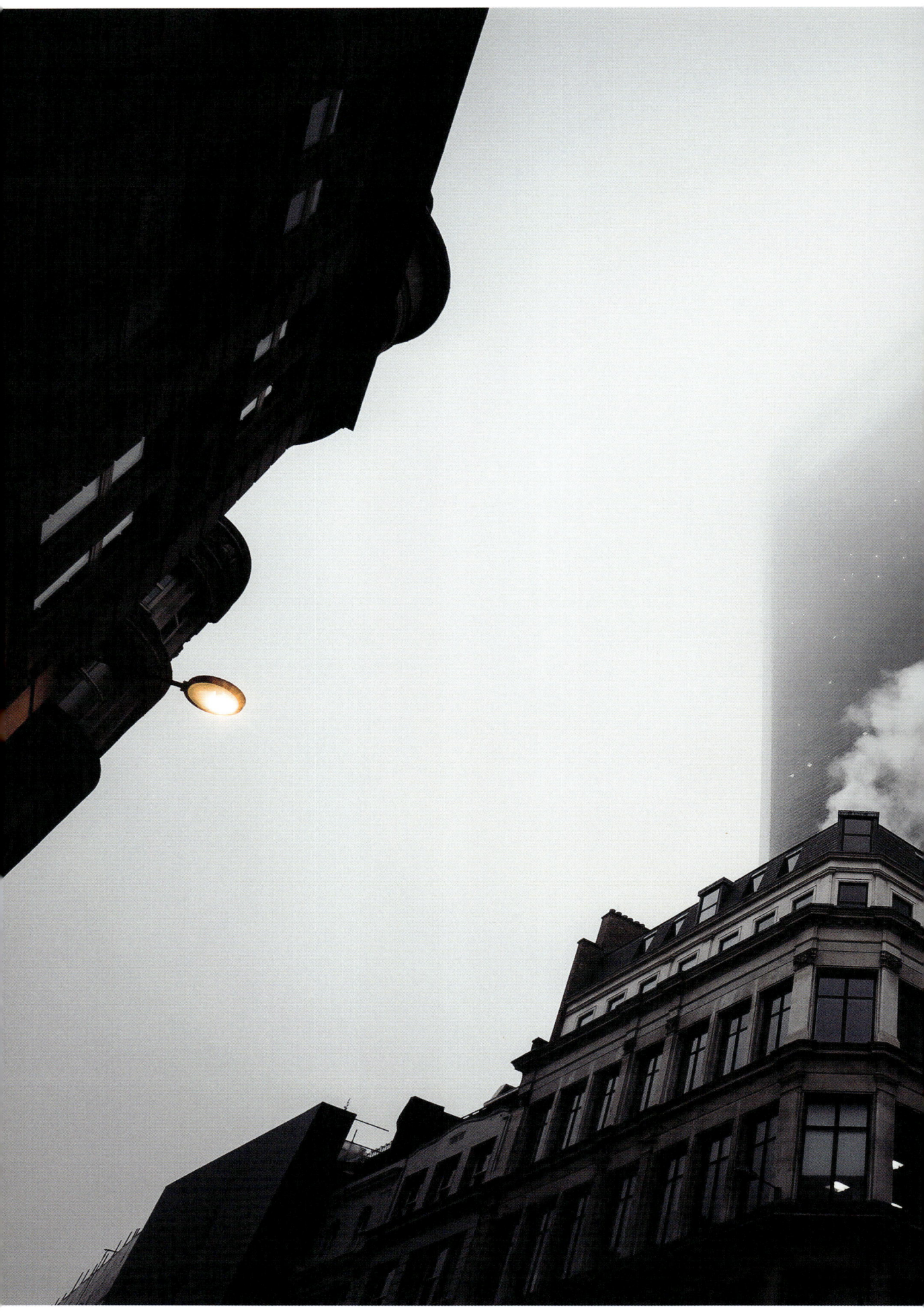

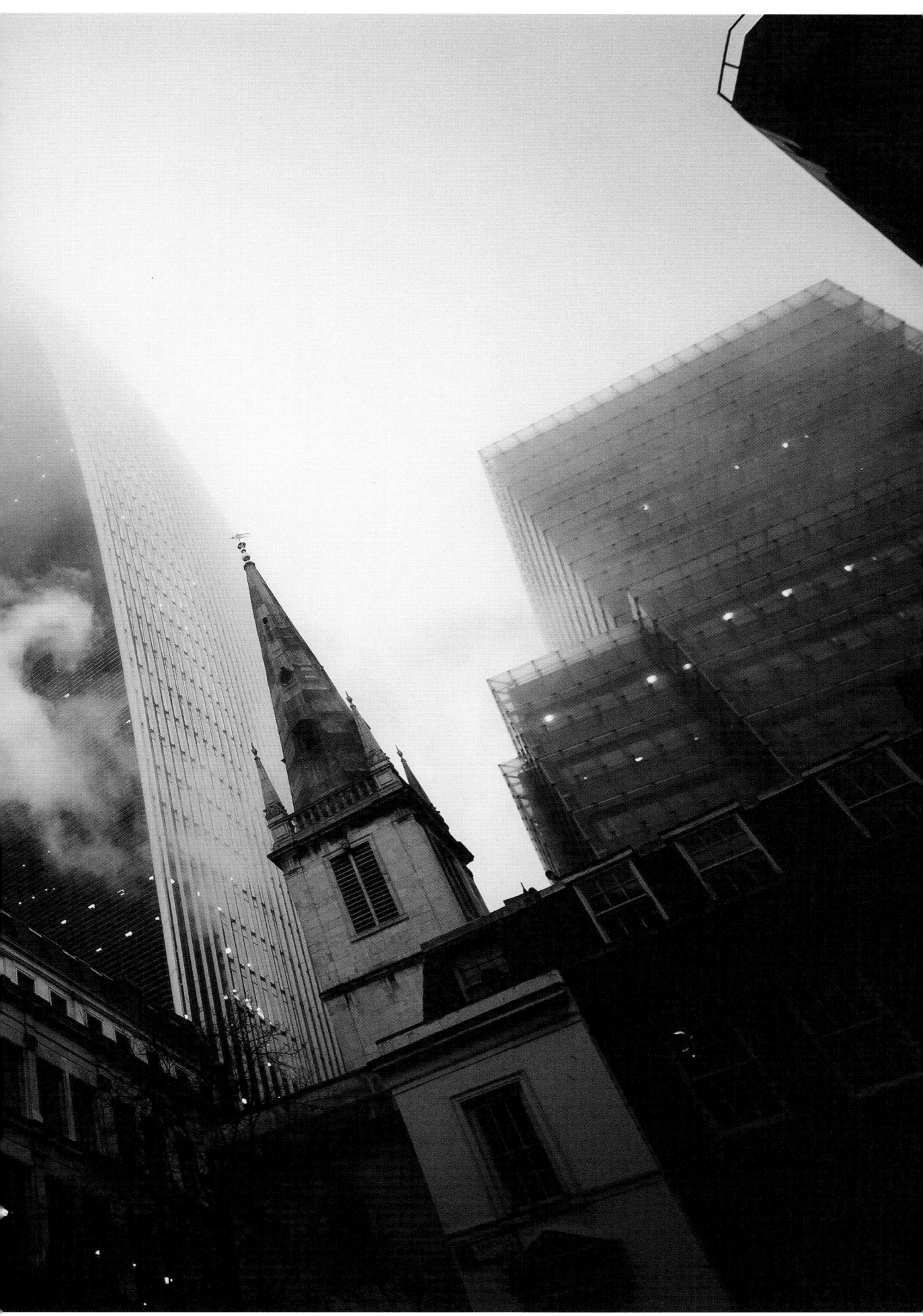

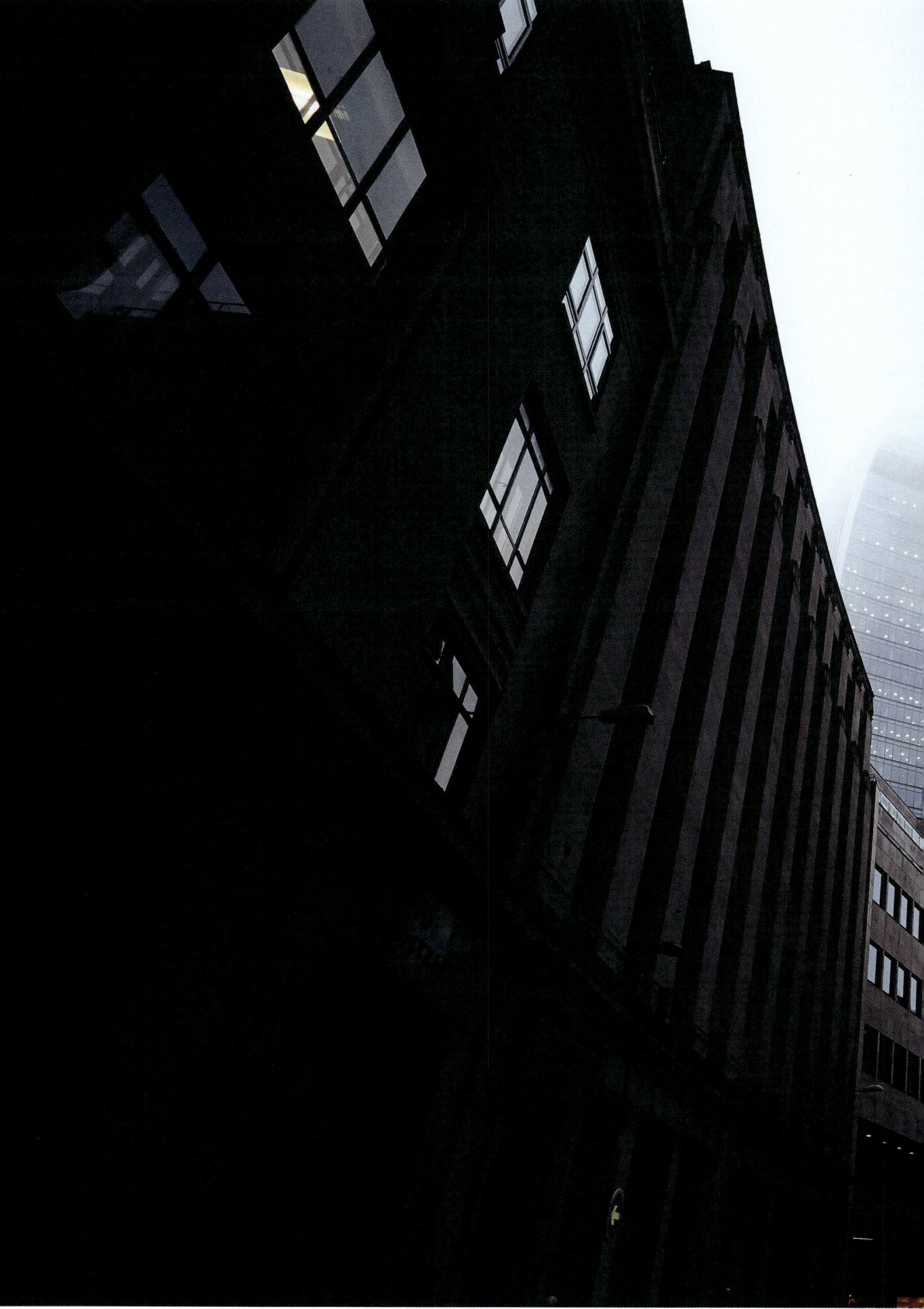

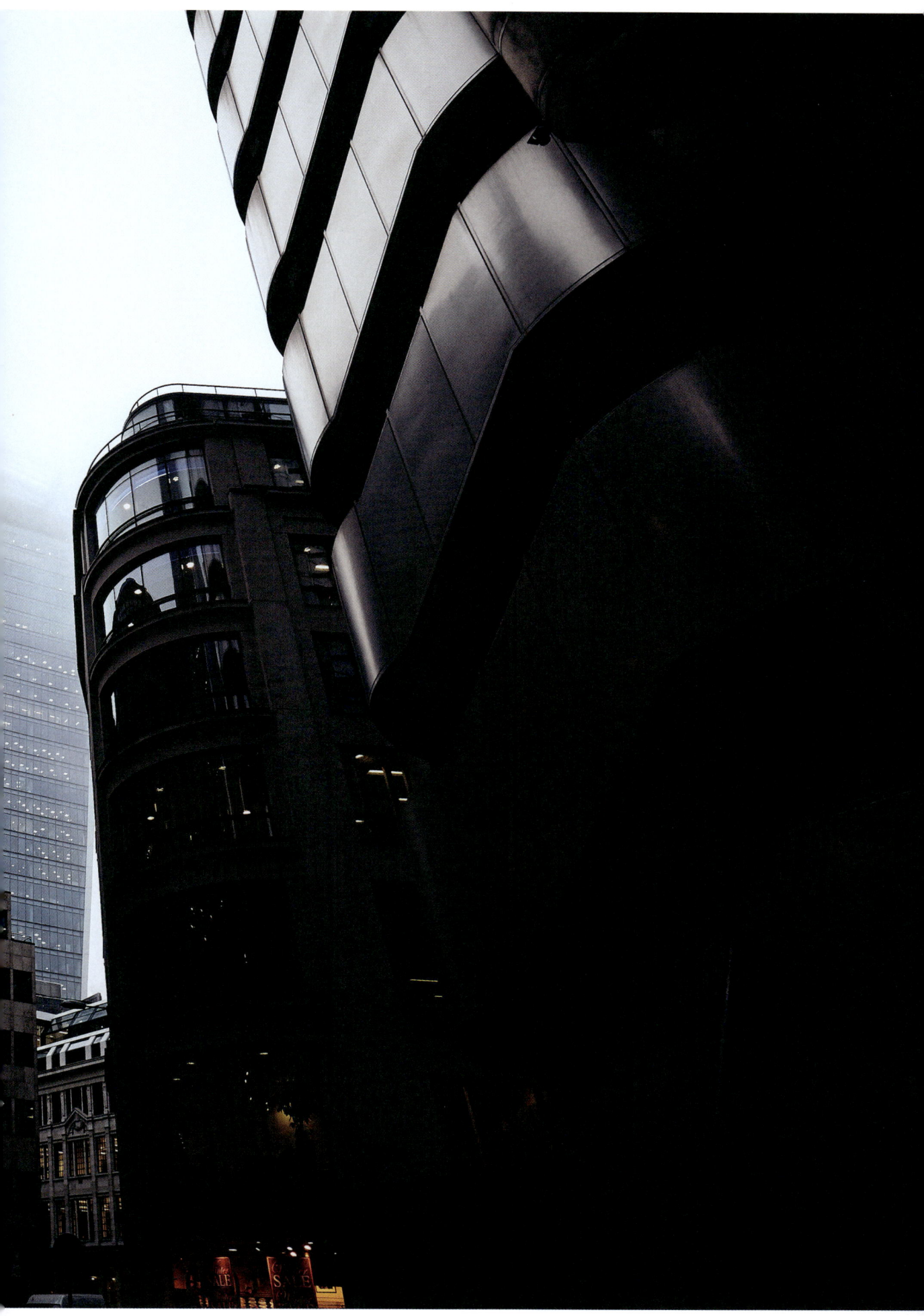

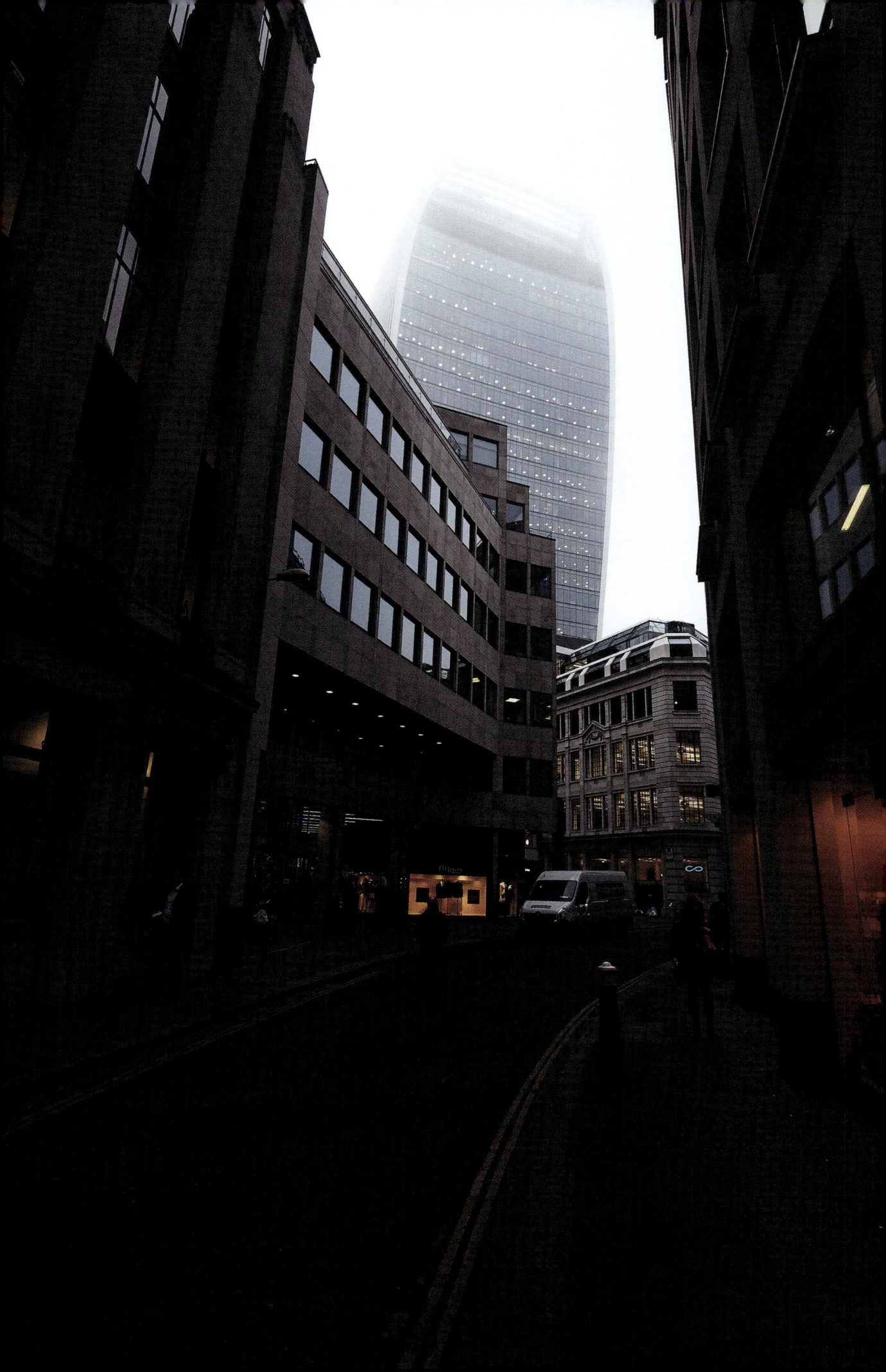

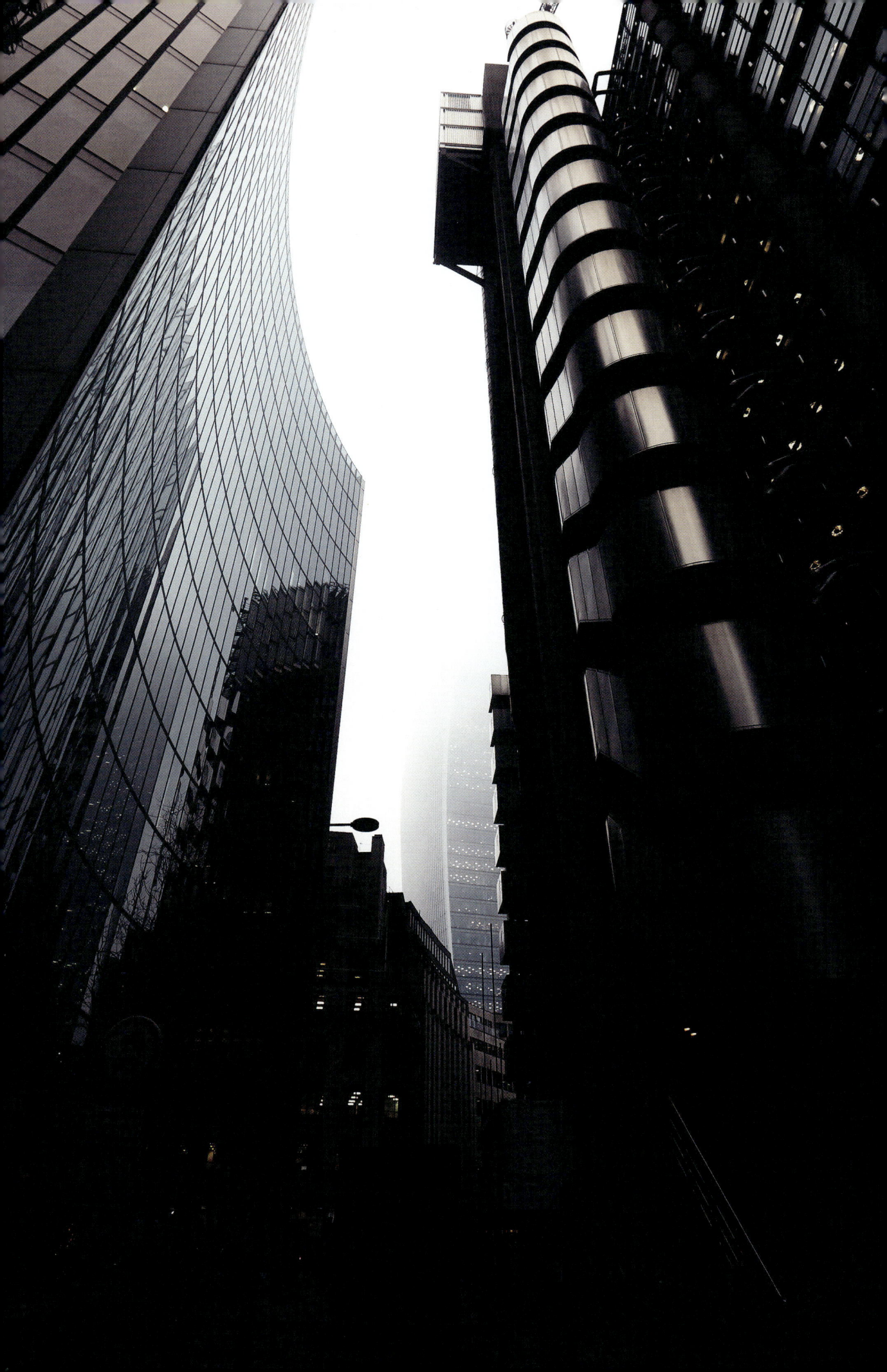

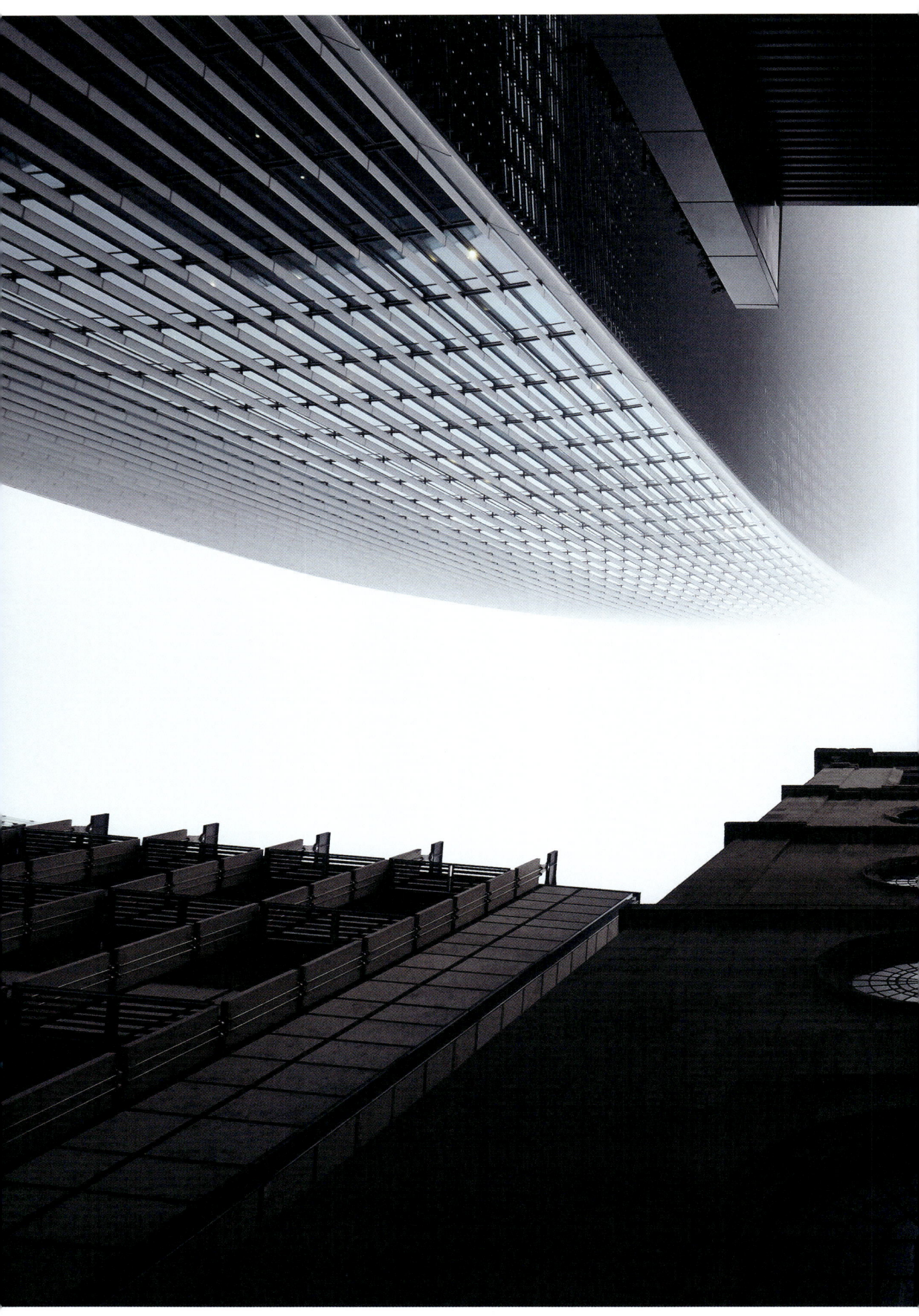

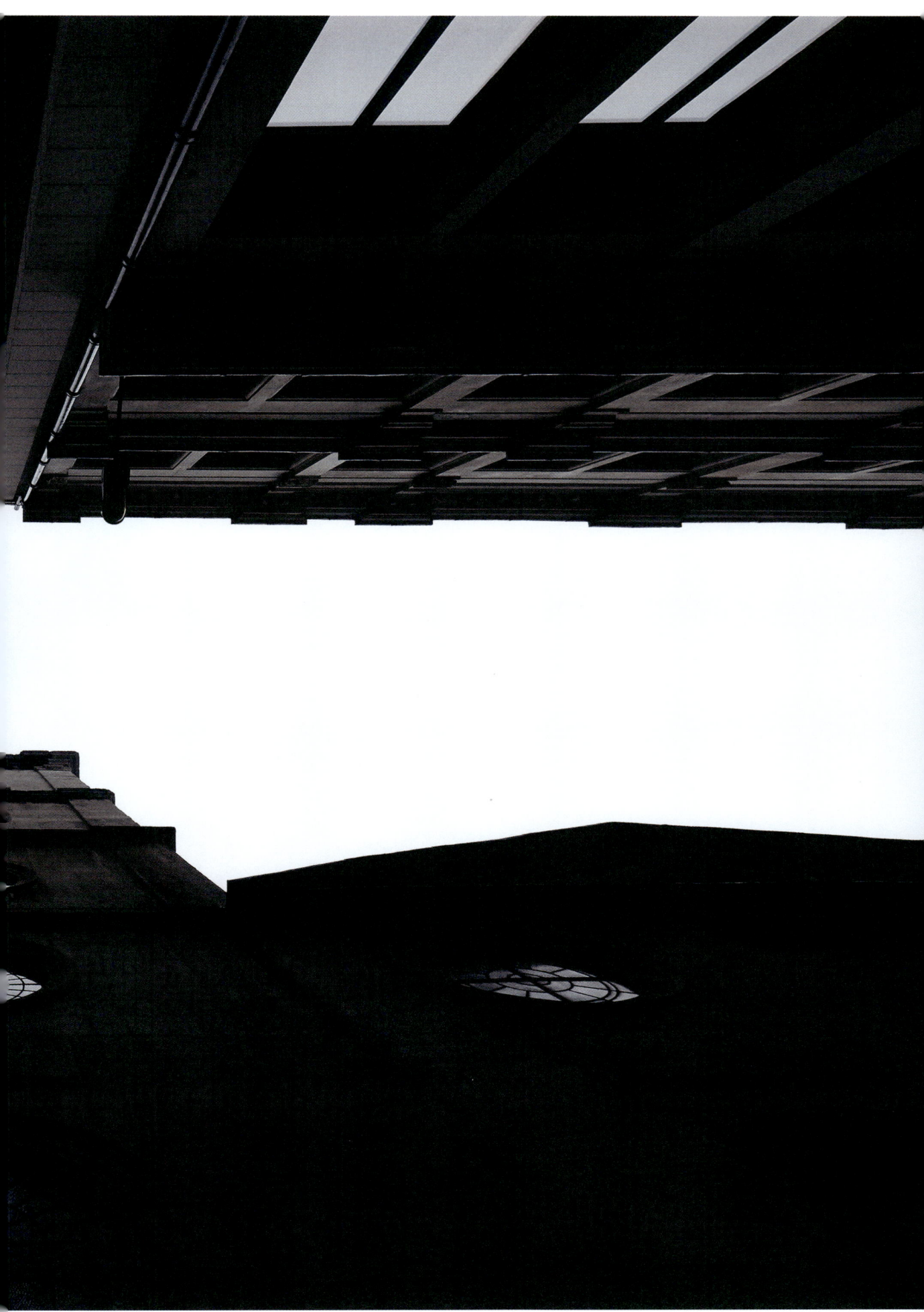

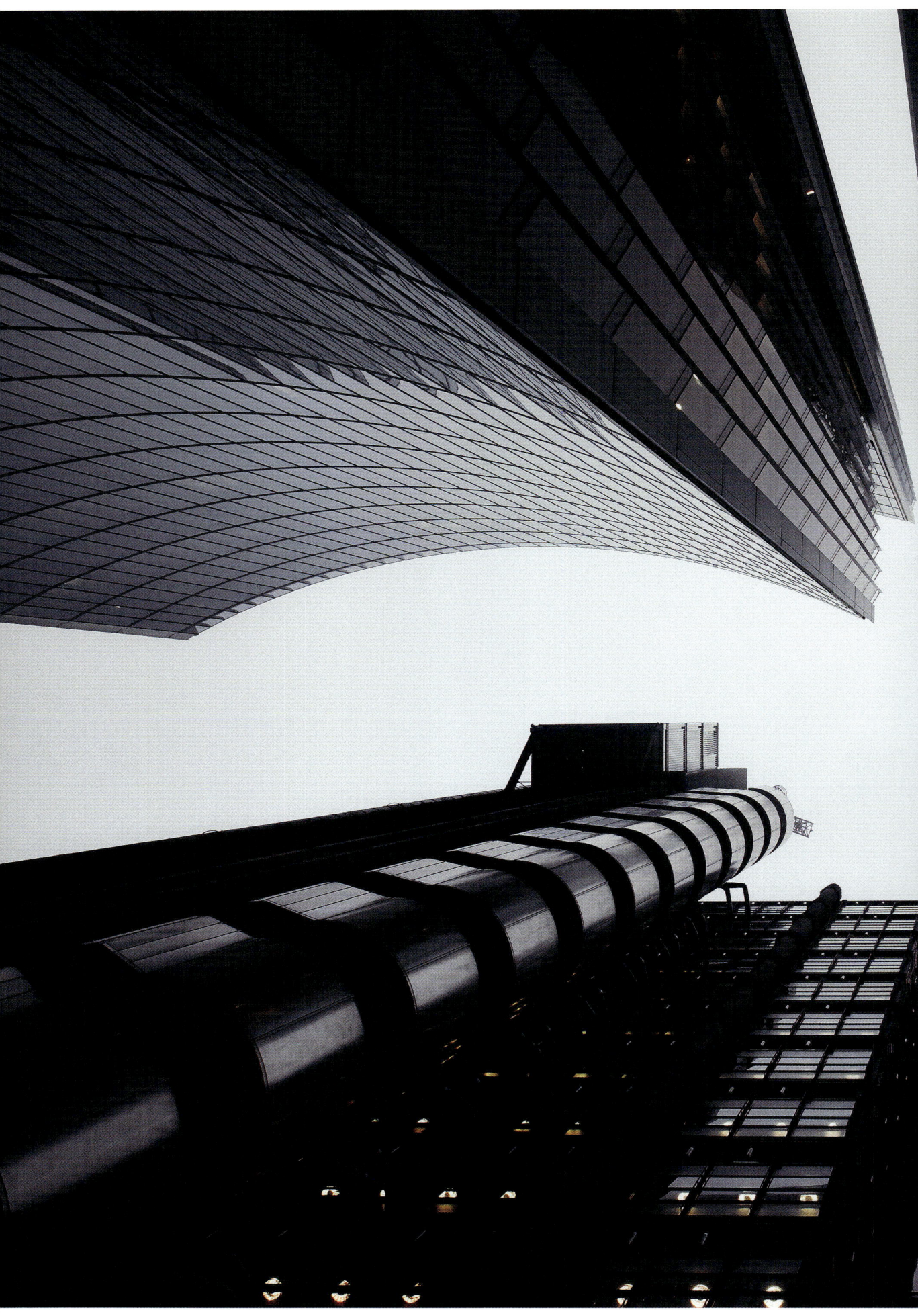

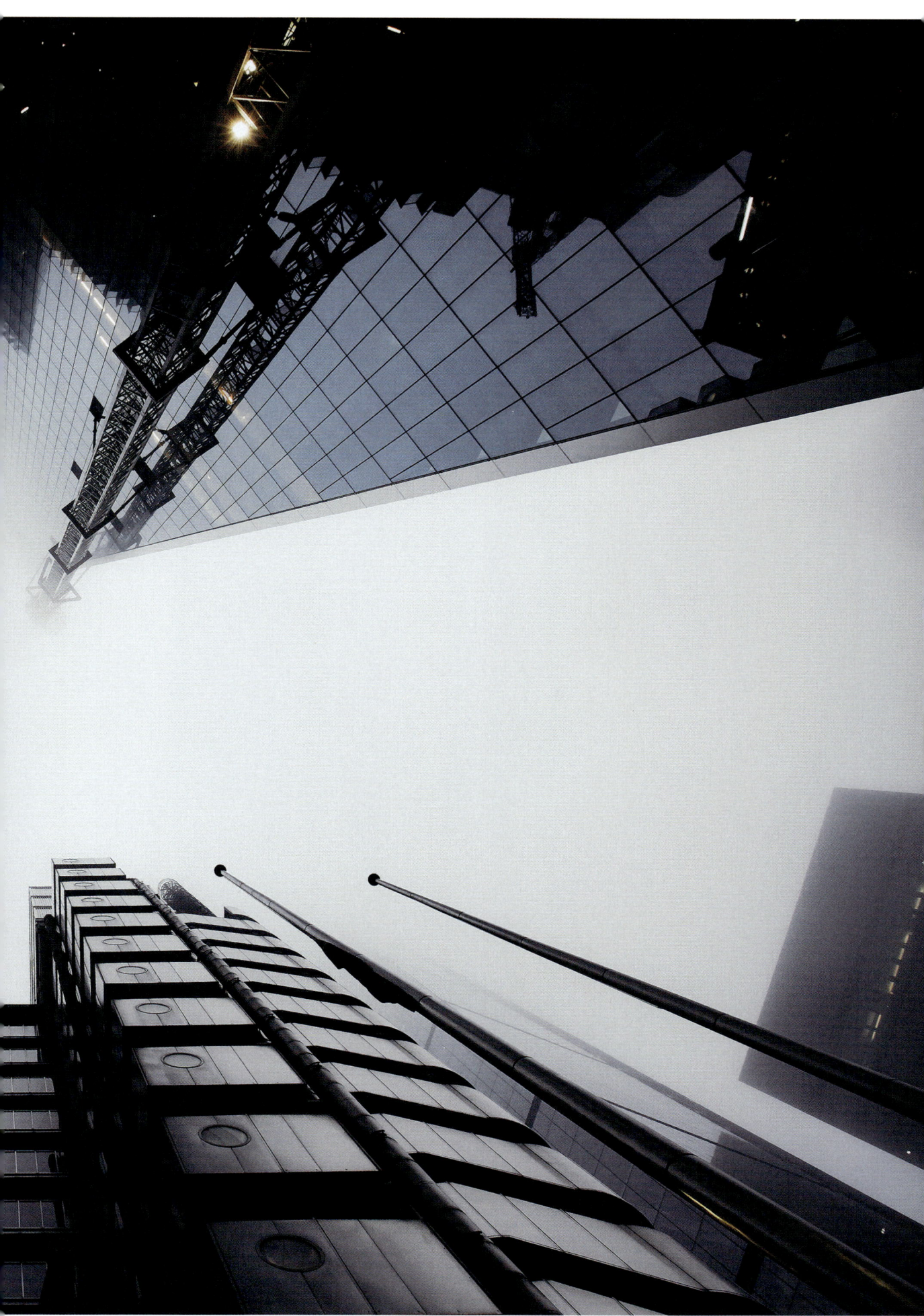

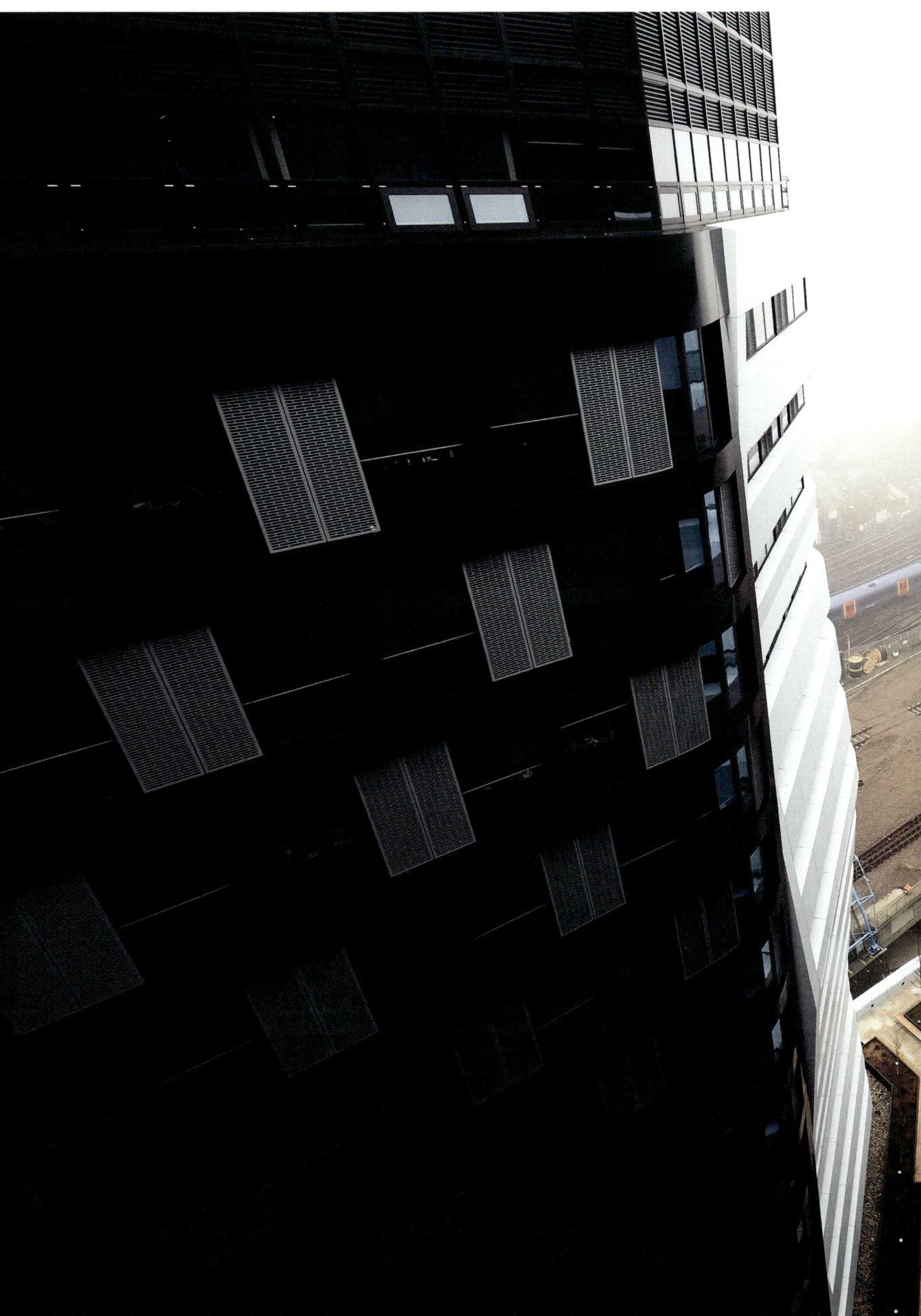

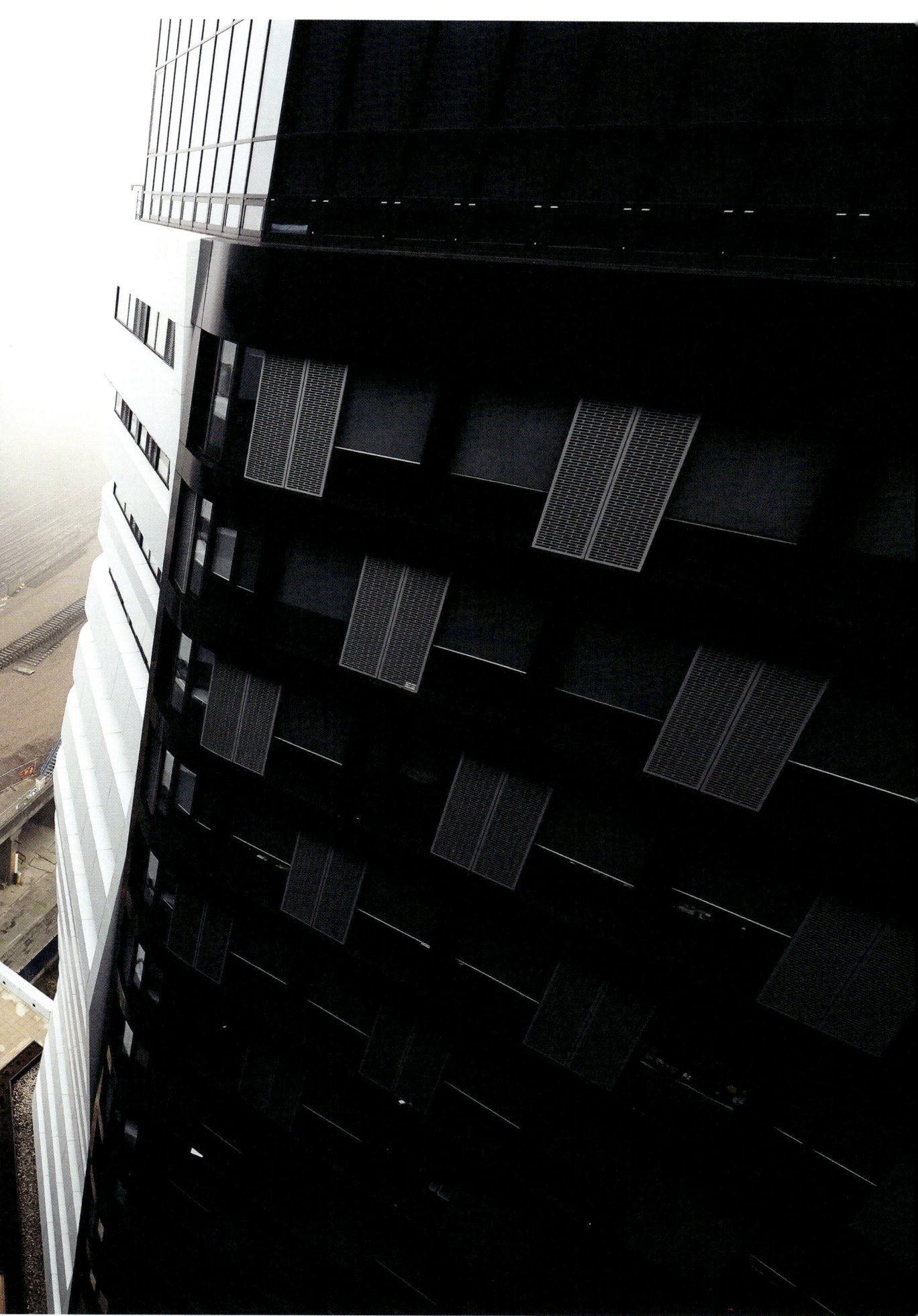

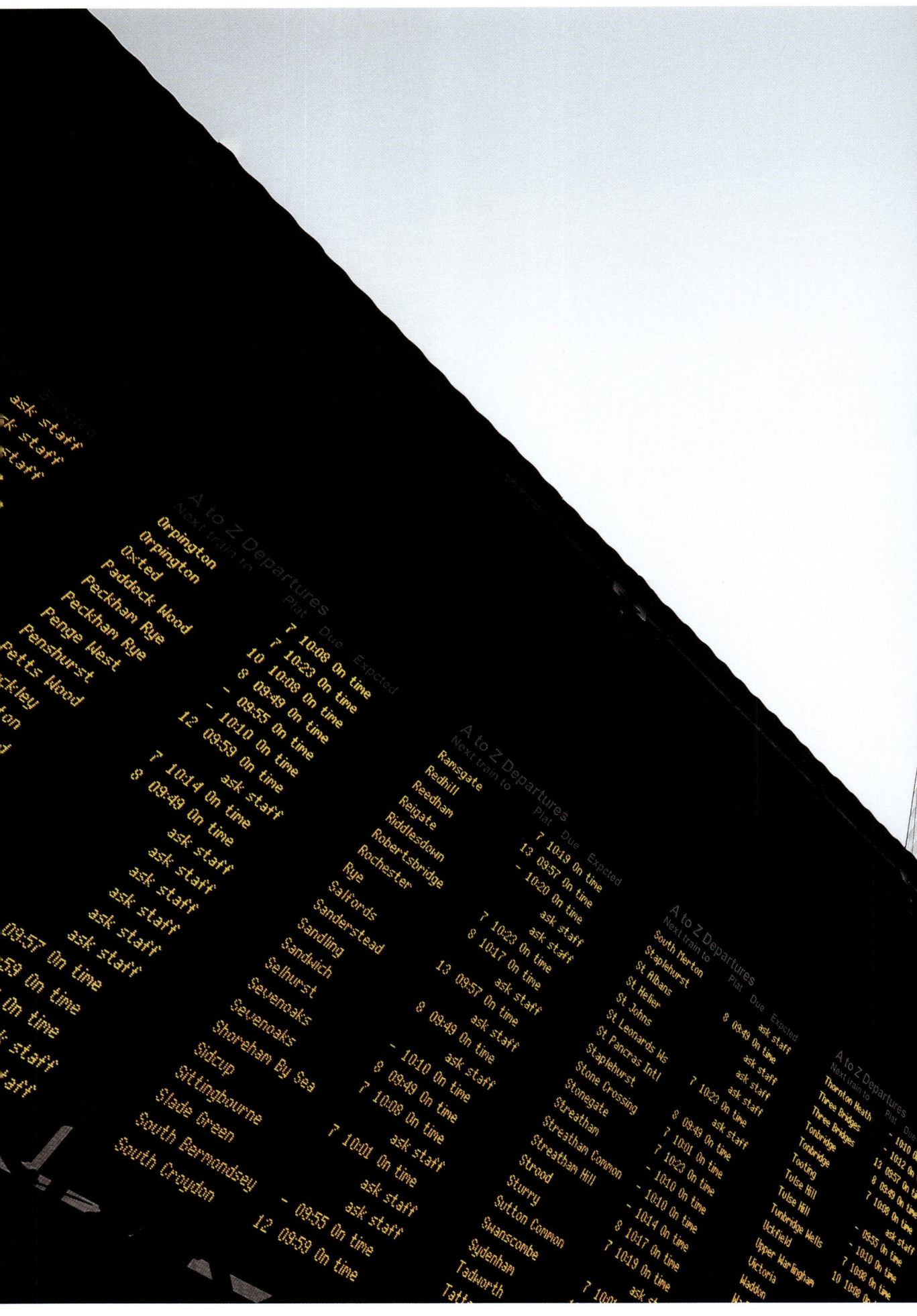

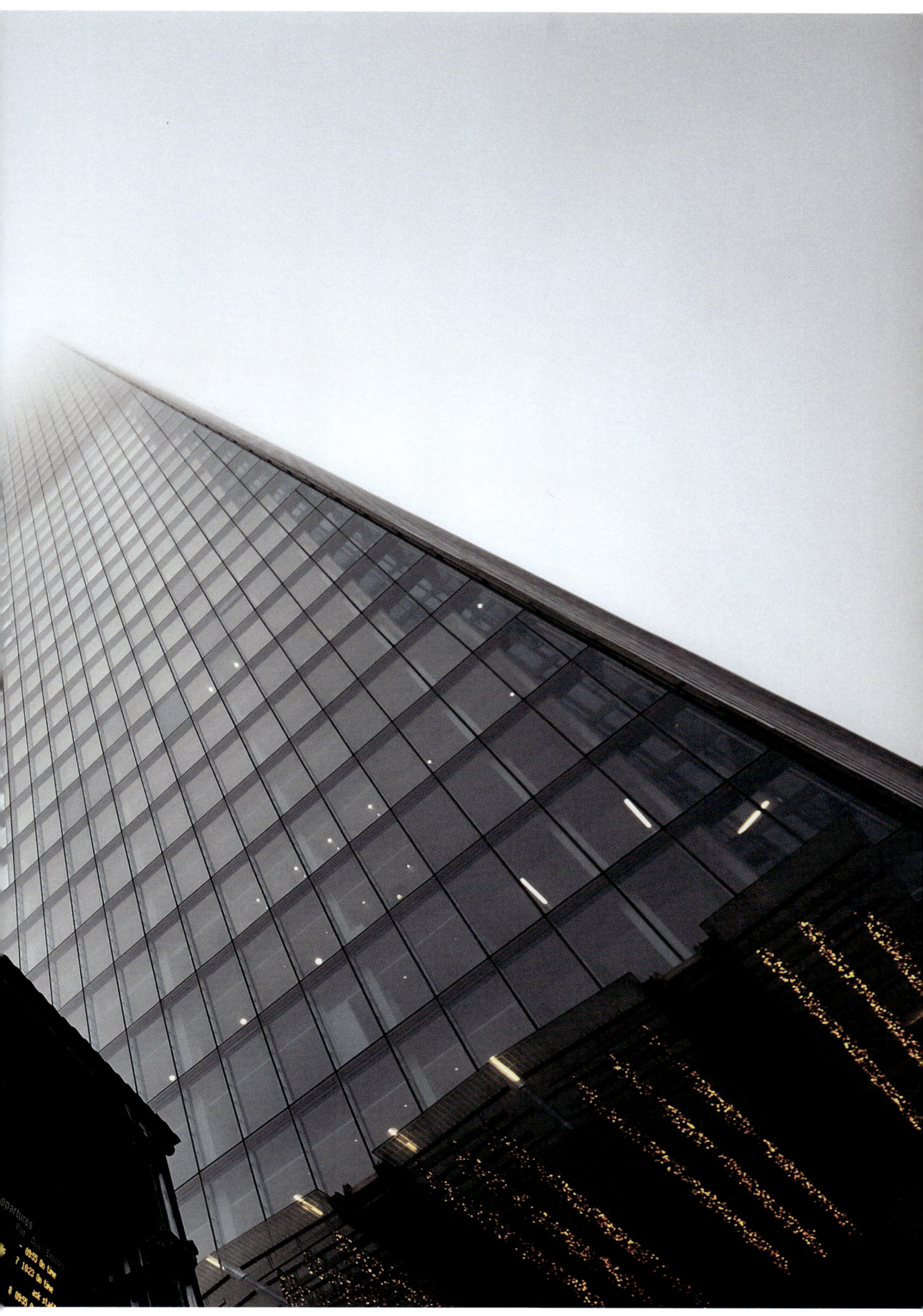

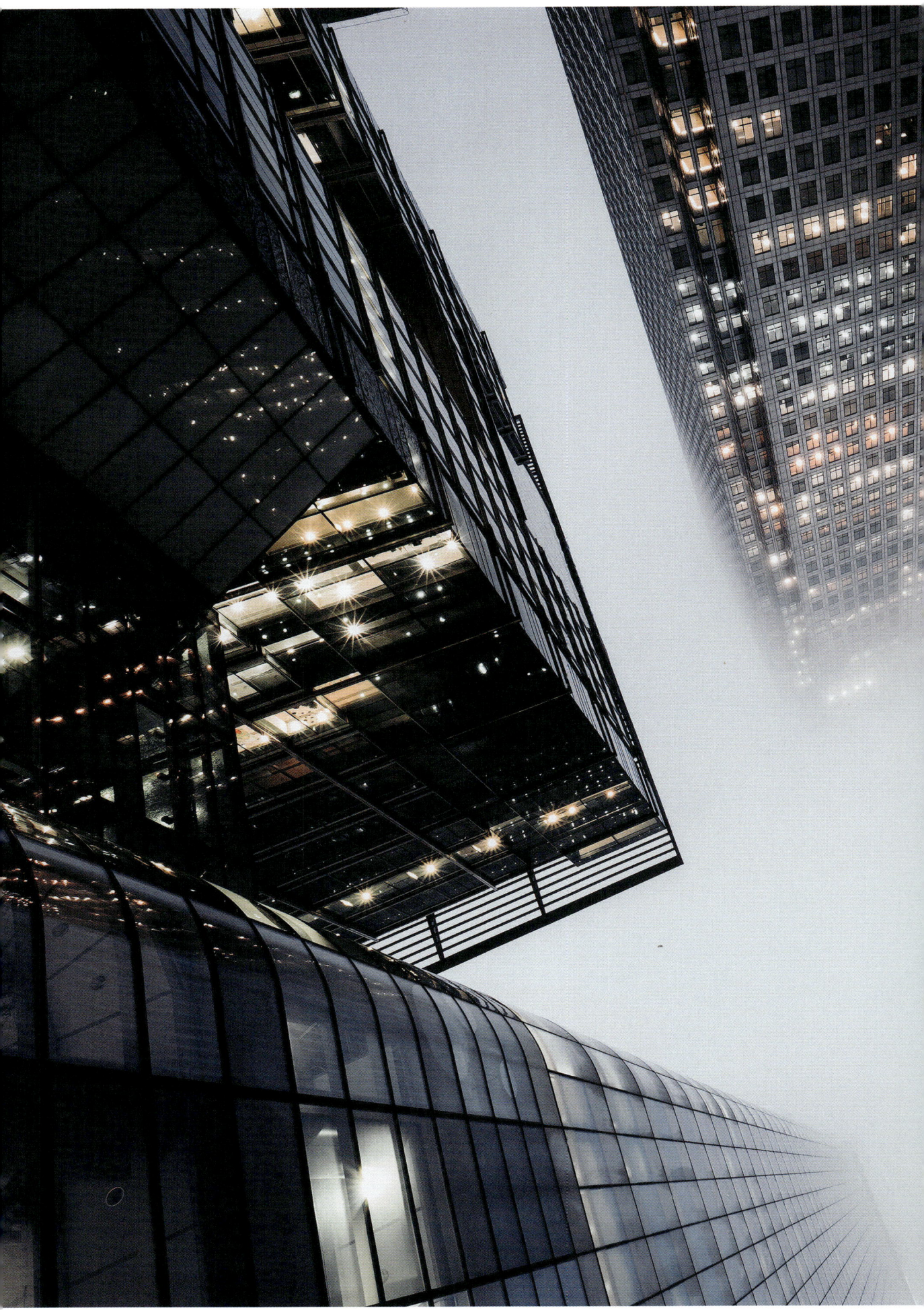

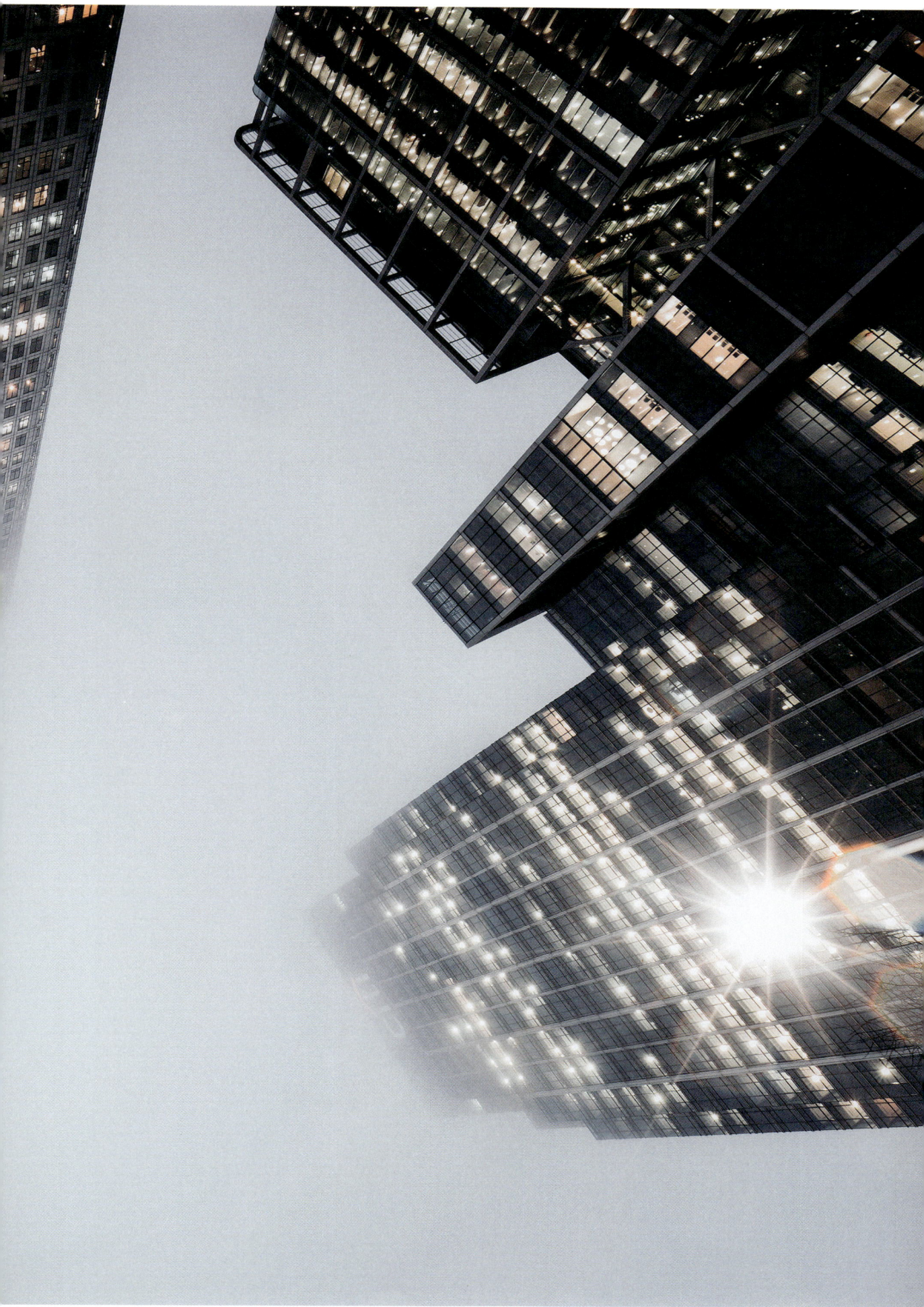

Photography provides me with the ability to process, appreciate and interpret the world around me.

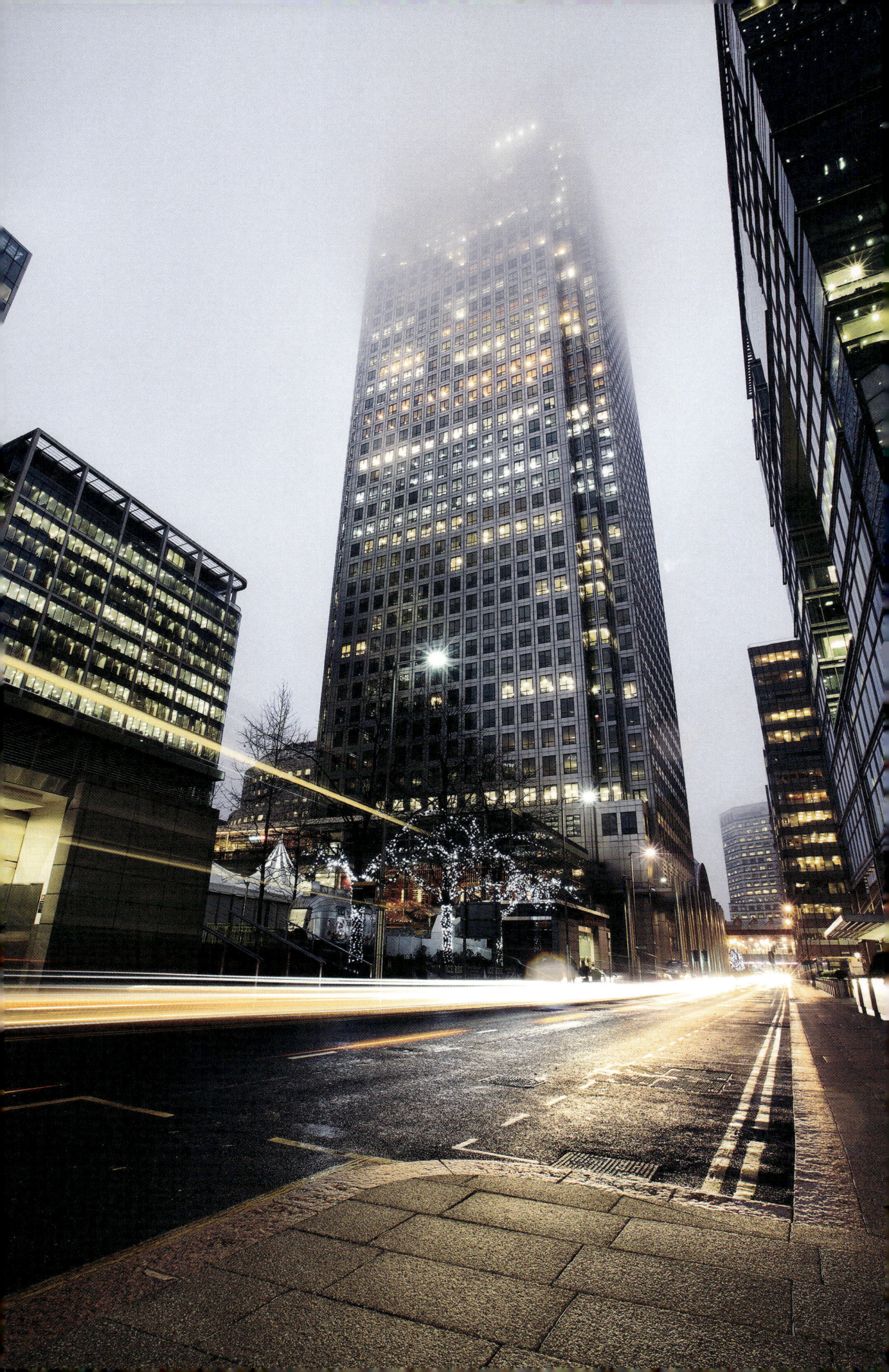

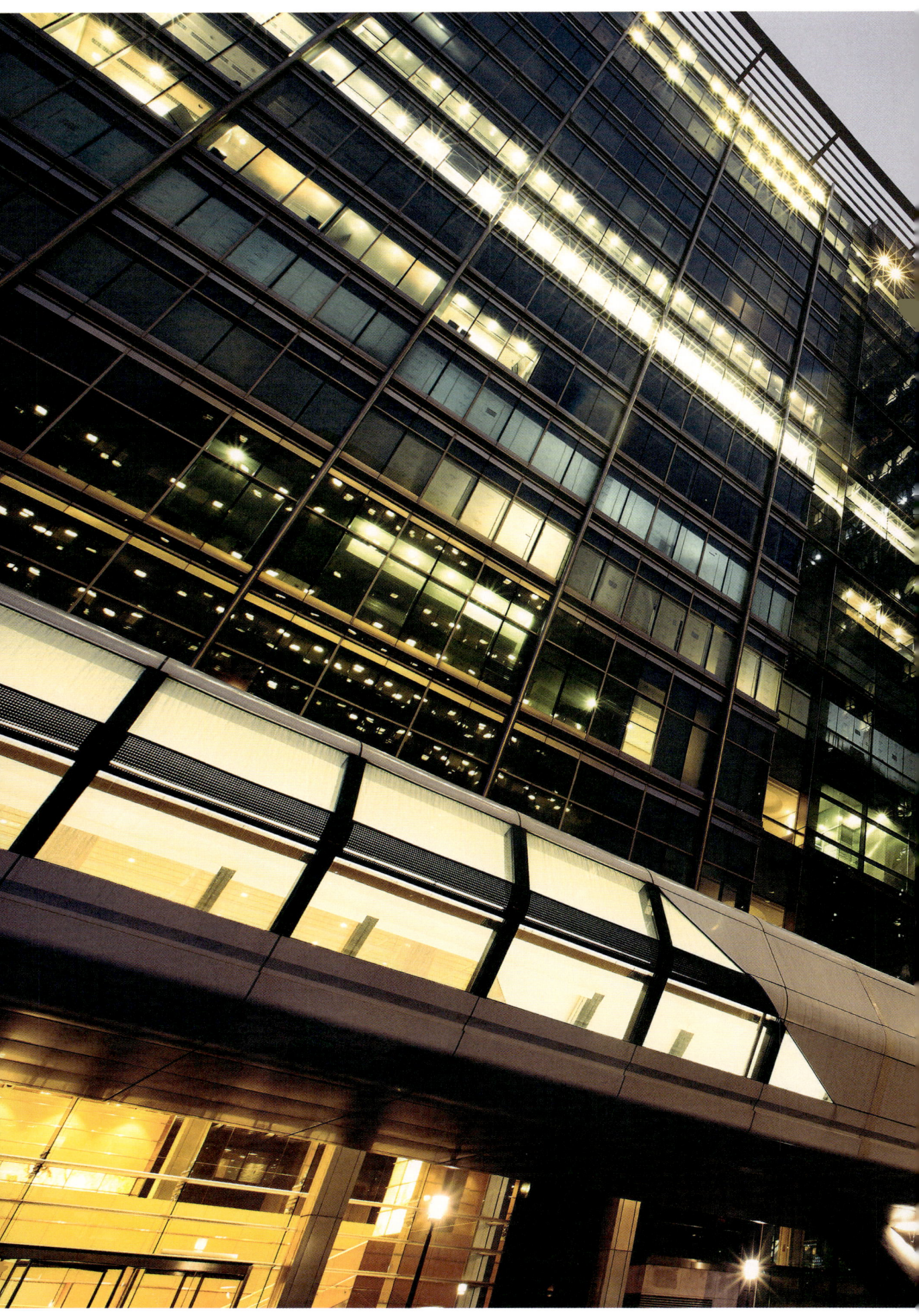

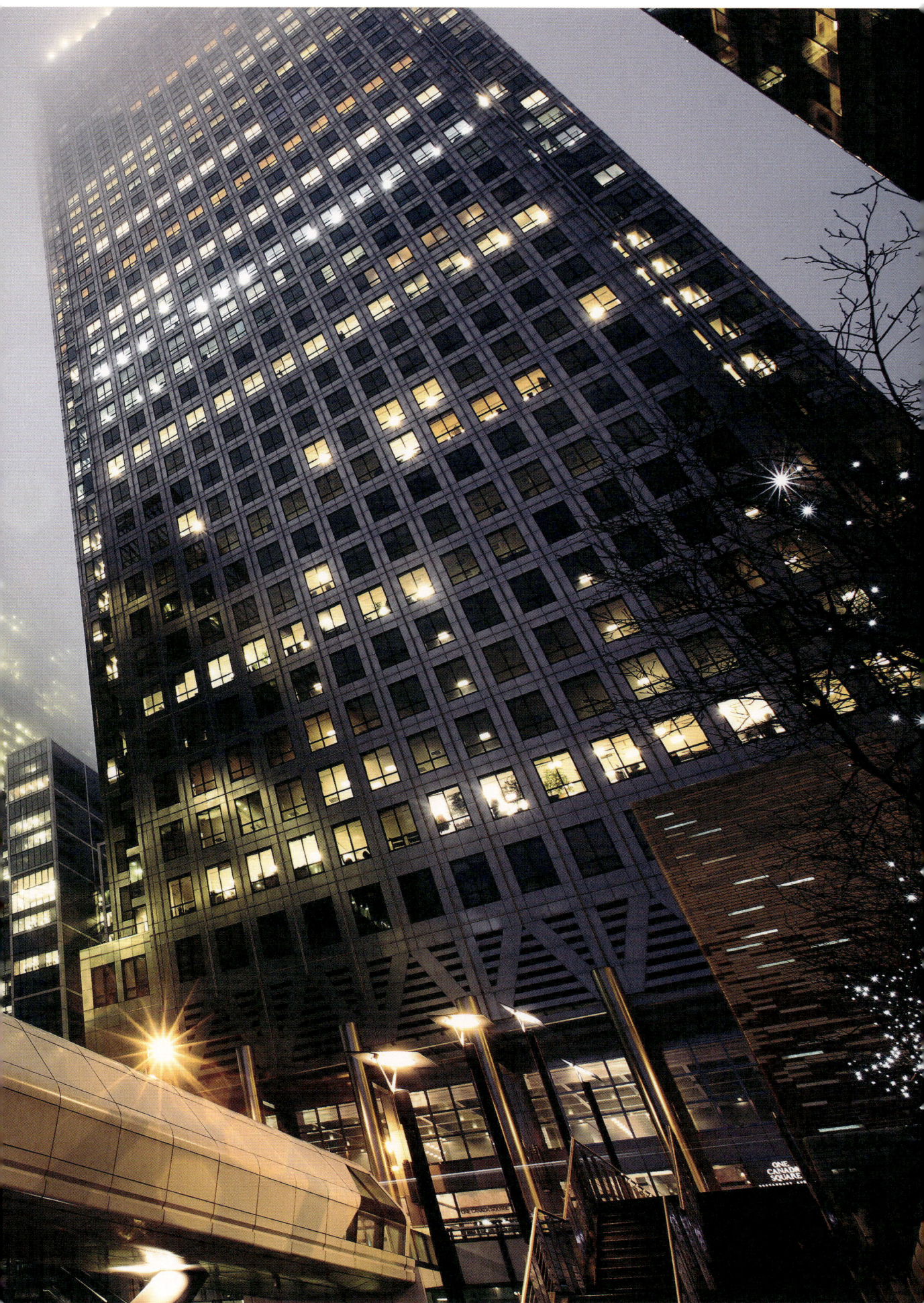

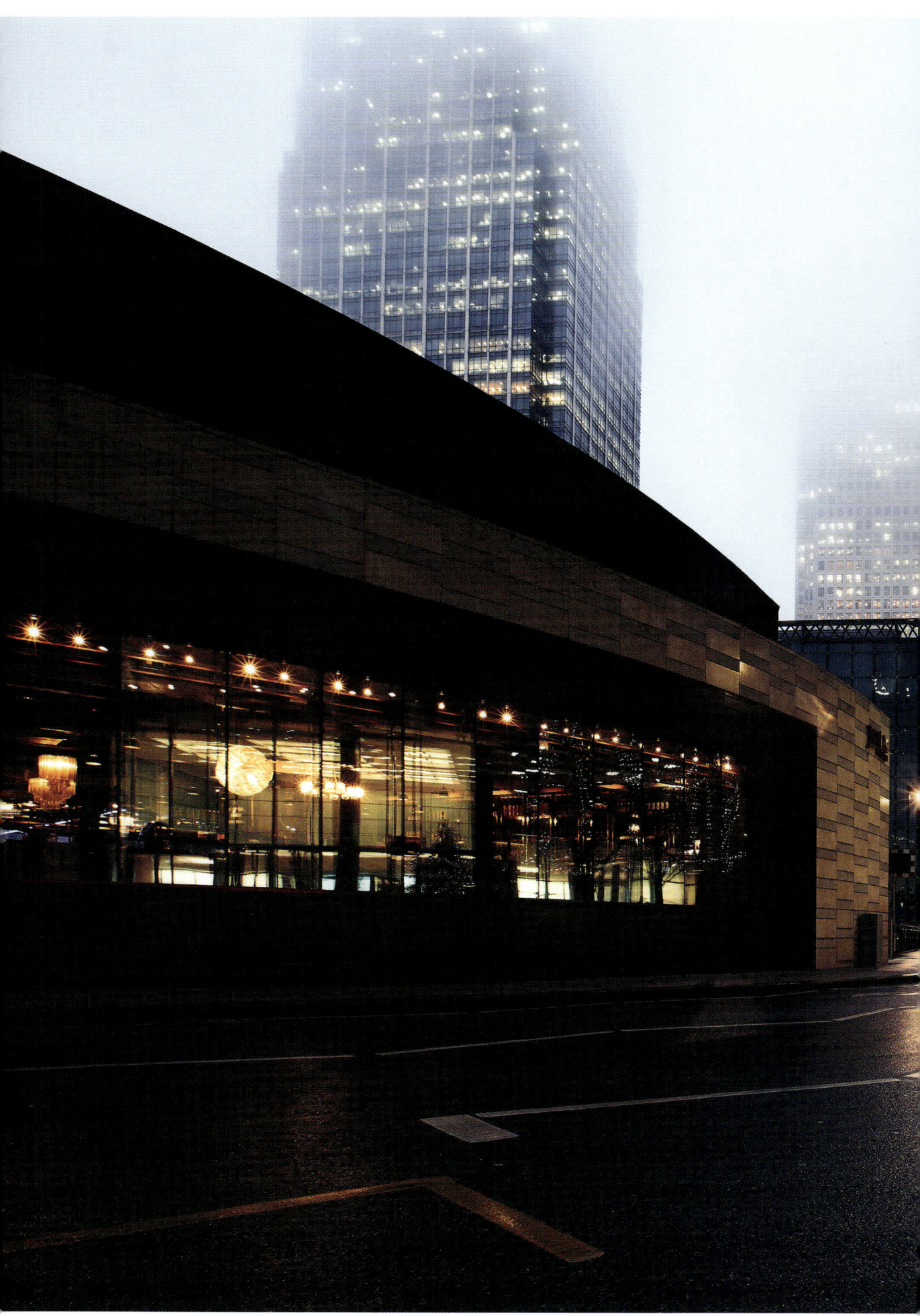

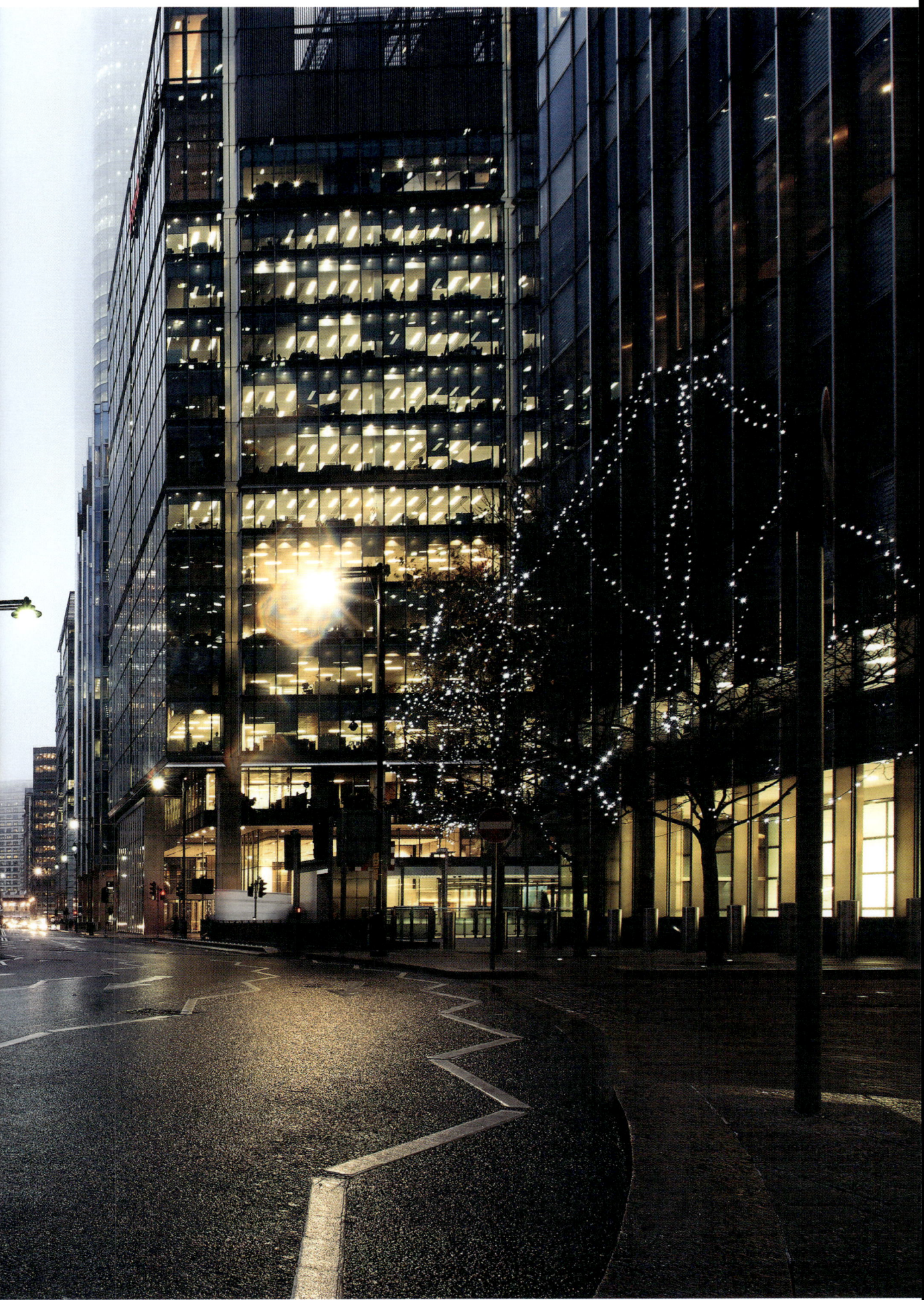

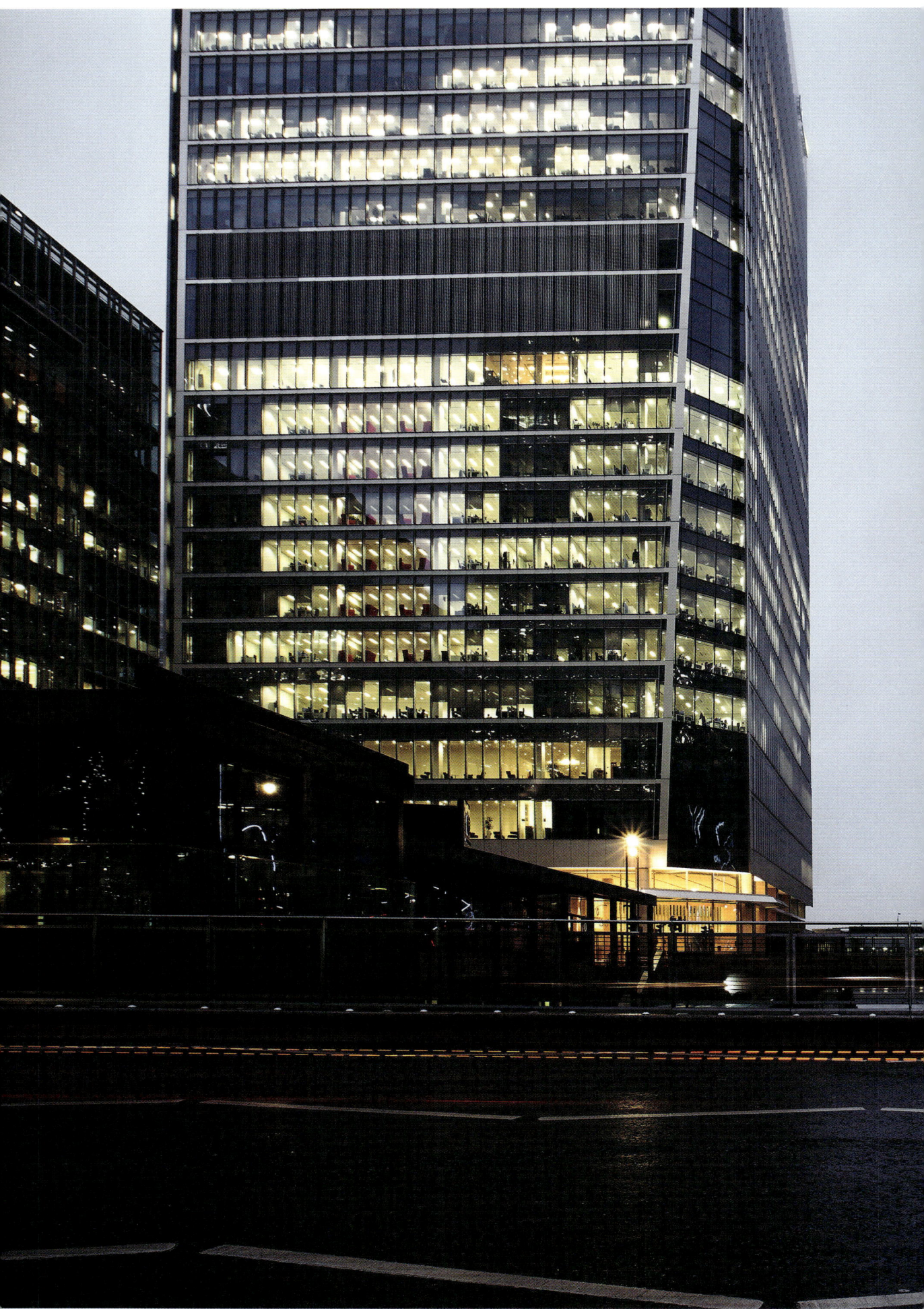

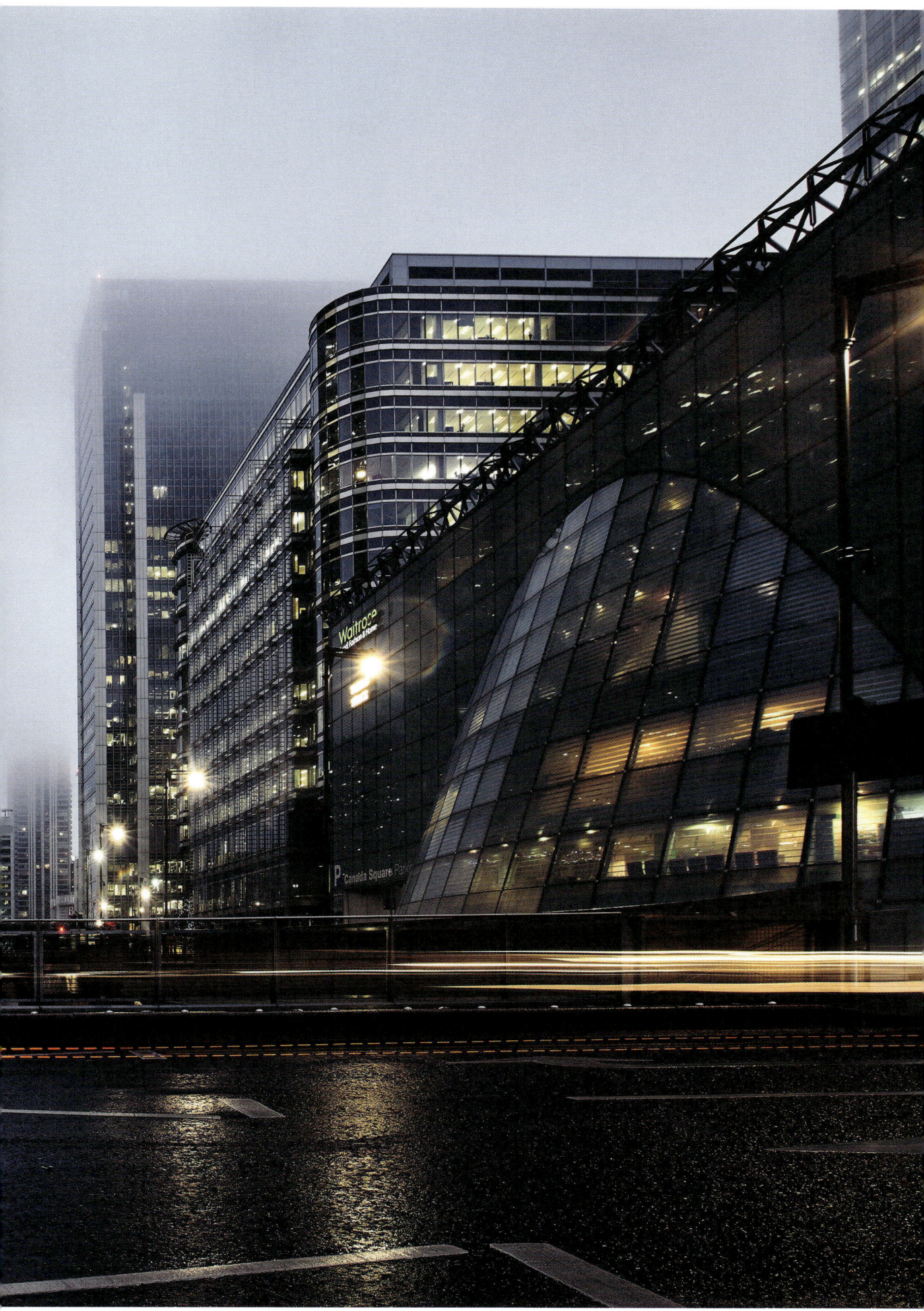

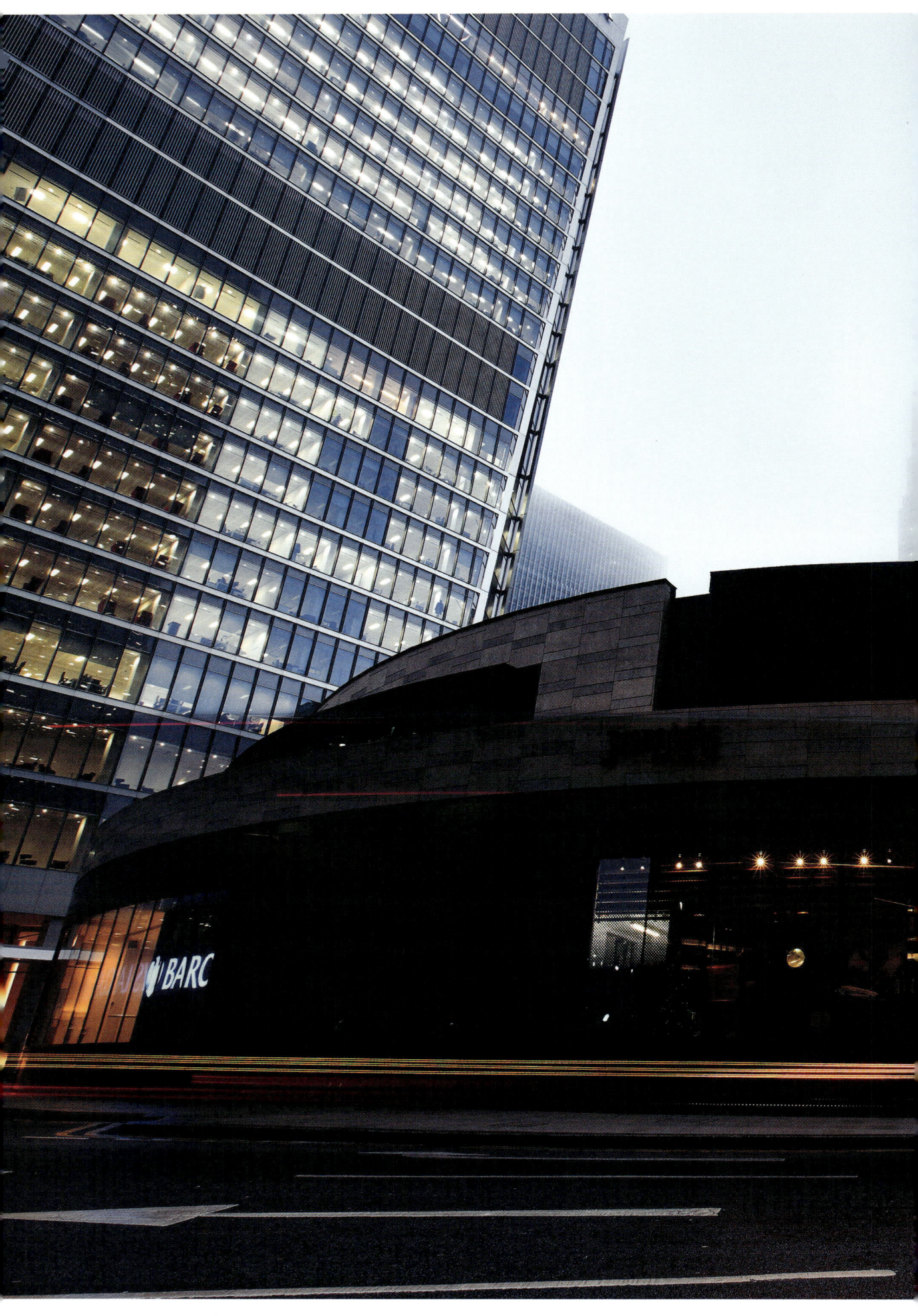

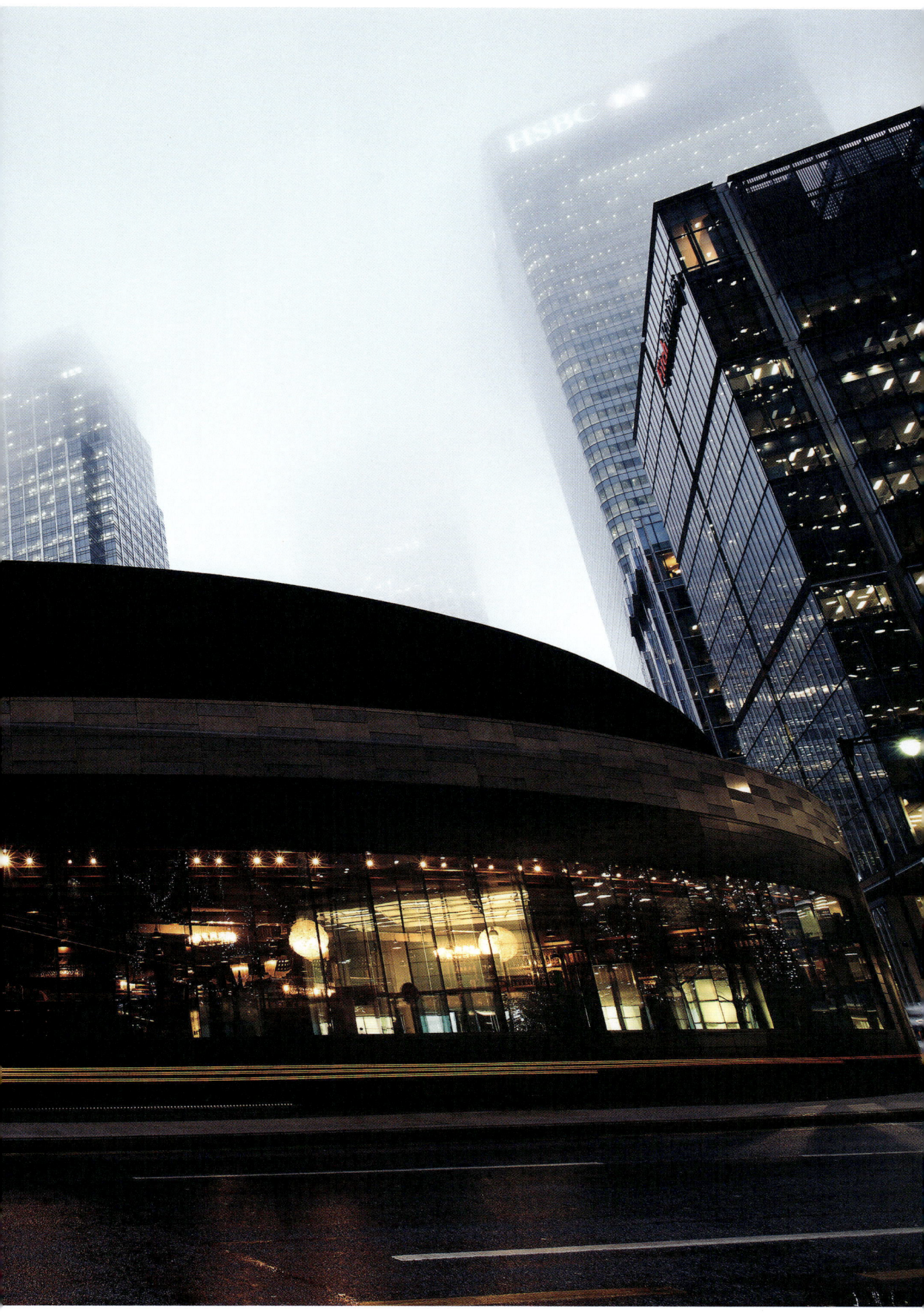

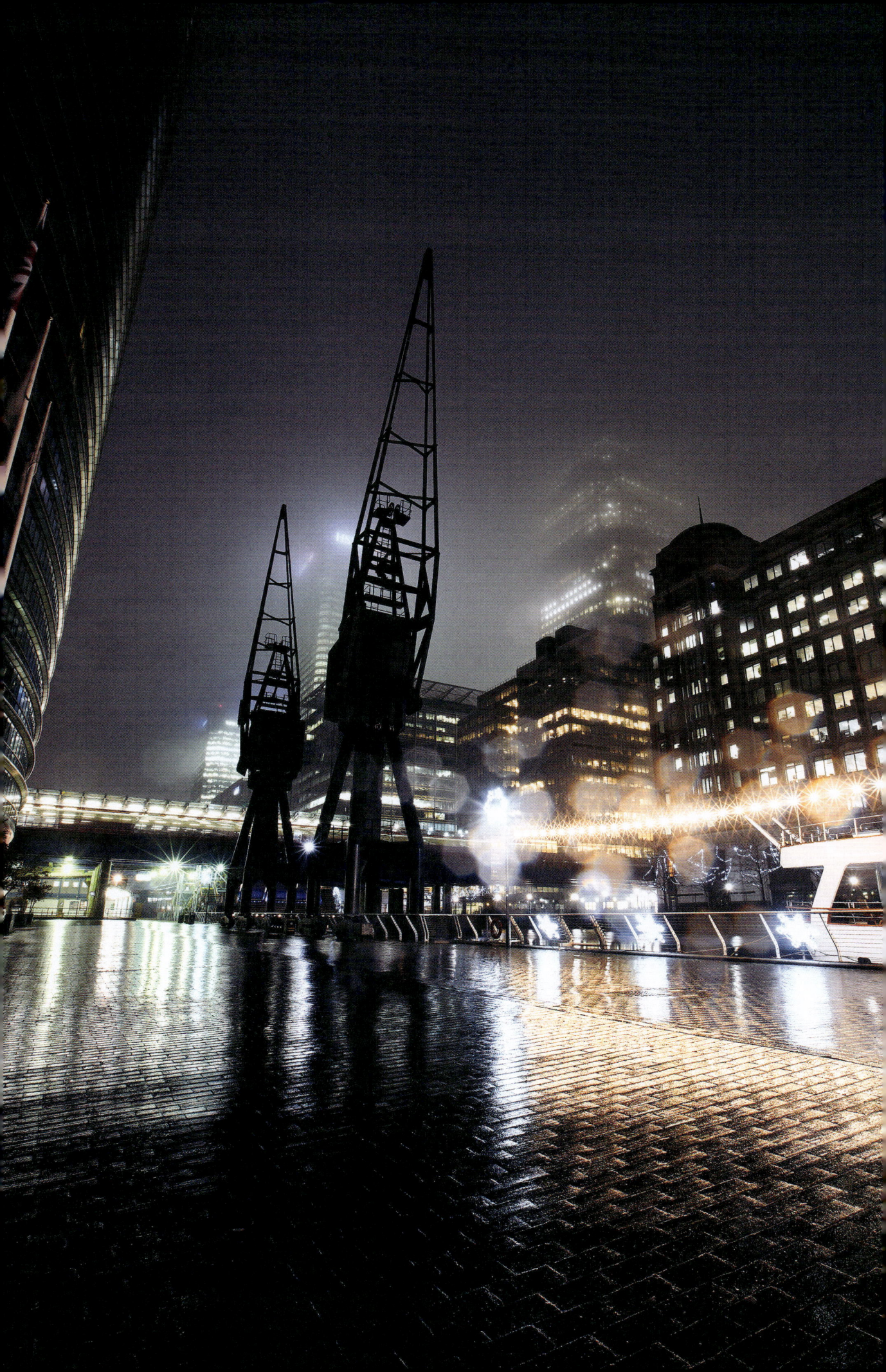

When I started taking pictures I used a camera phone. It's good to learn the fundamentals: composition, light, and focus. I would recommend that anyone looking to get into photography master those first, then master what your camera can do afterwards.

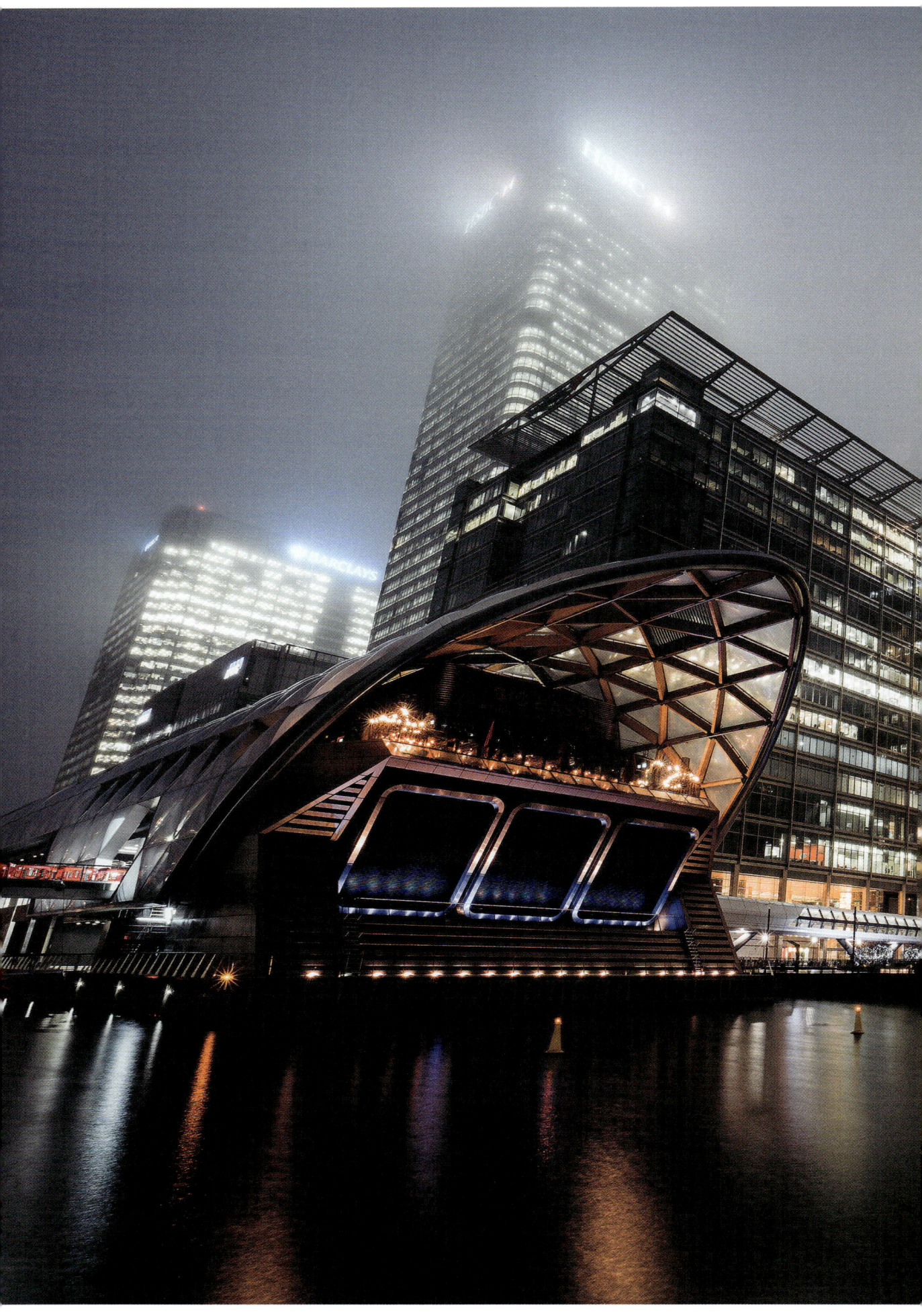

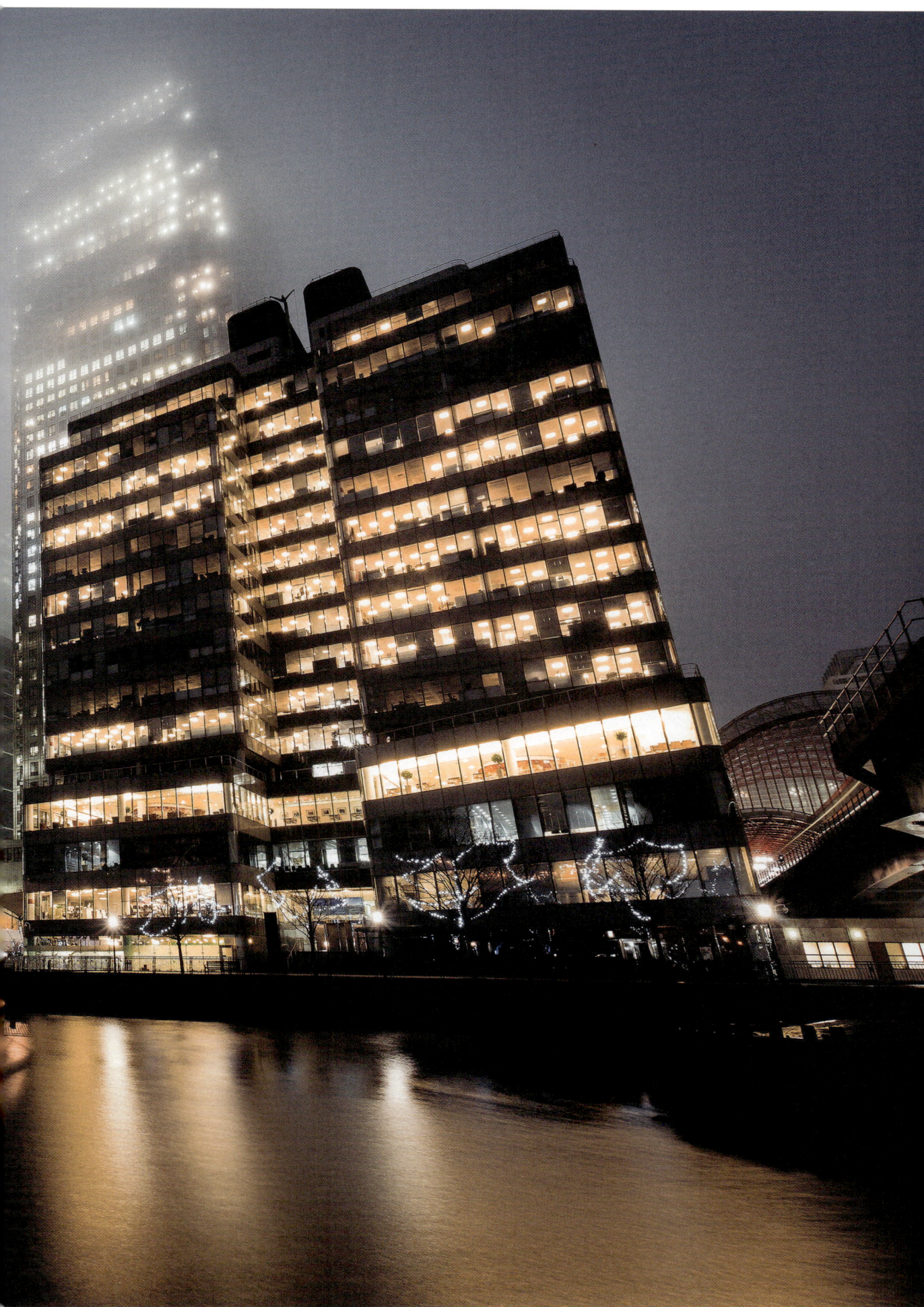

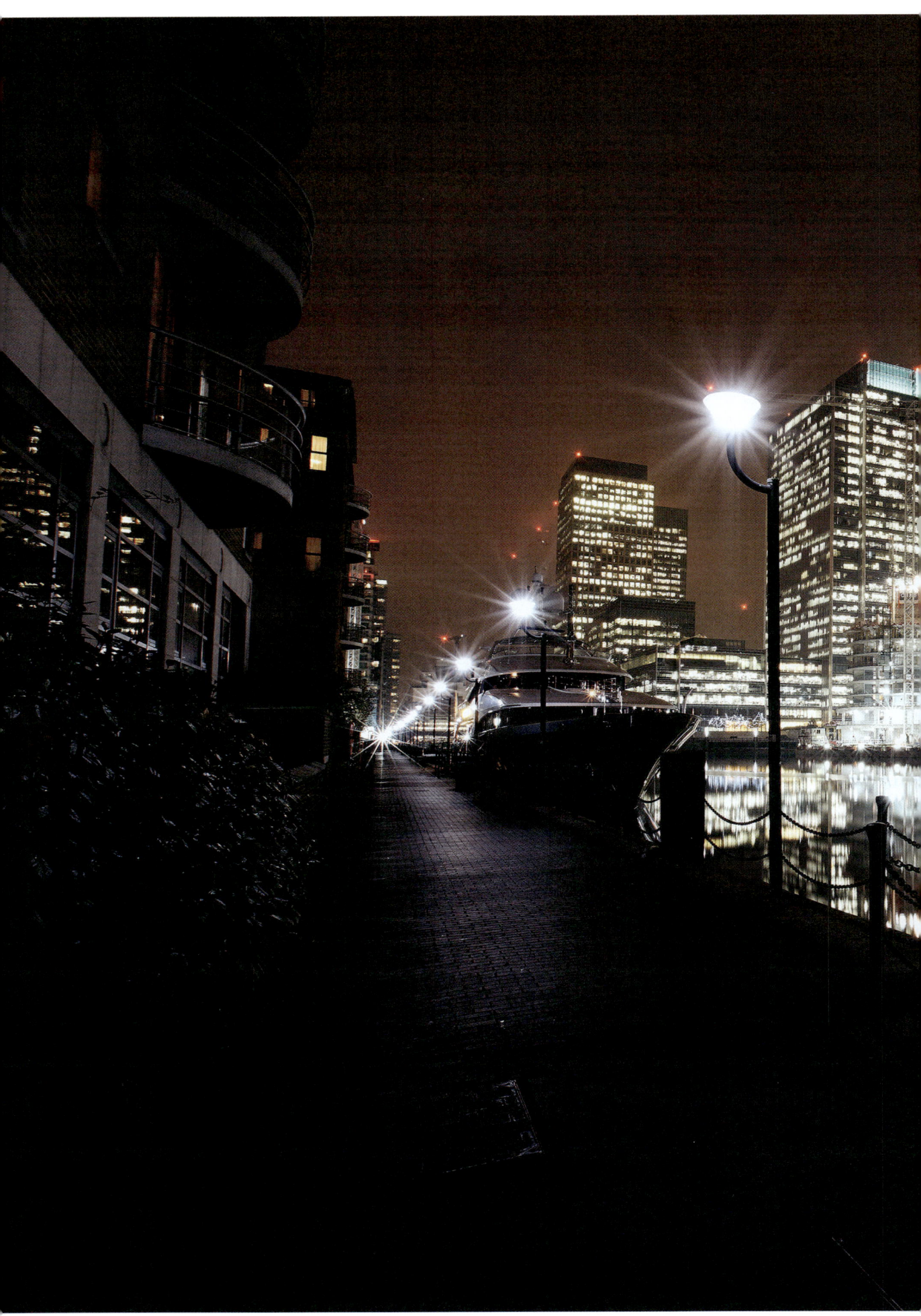

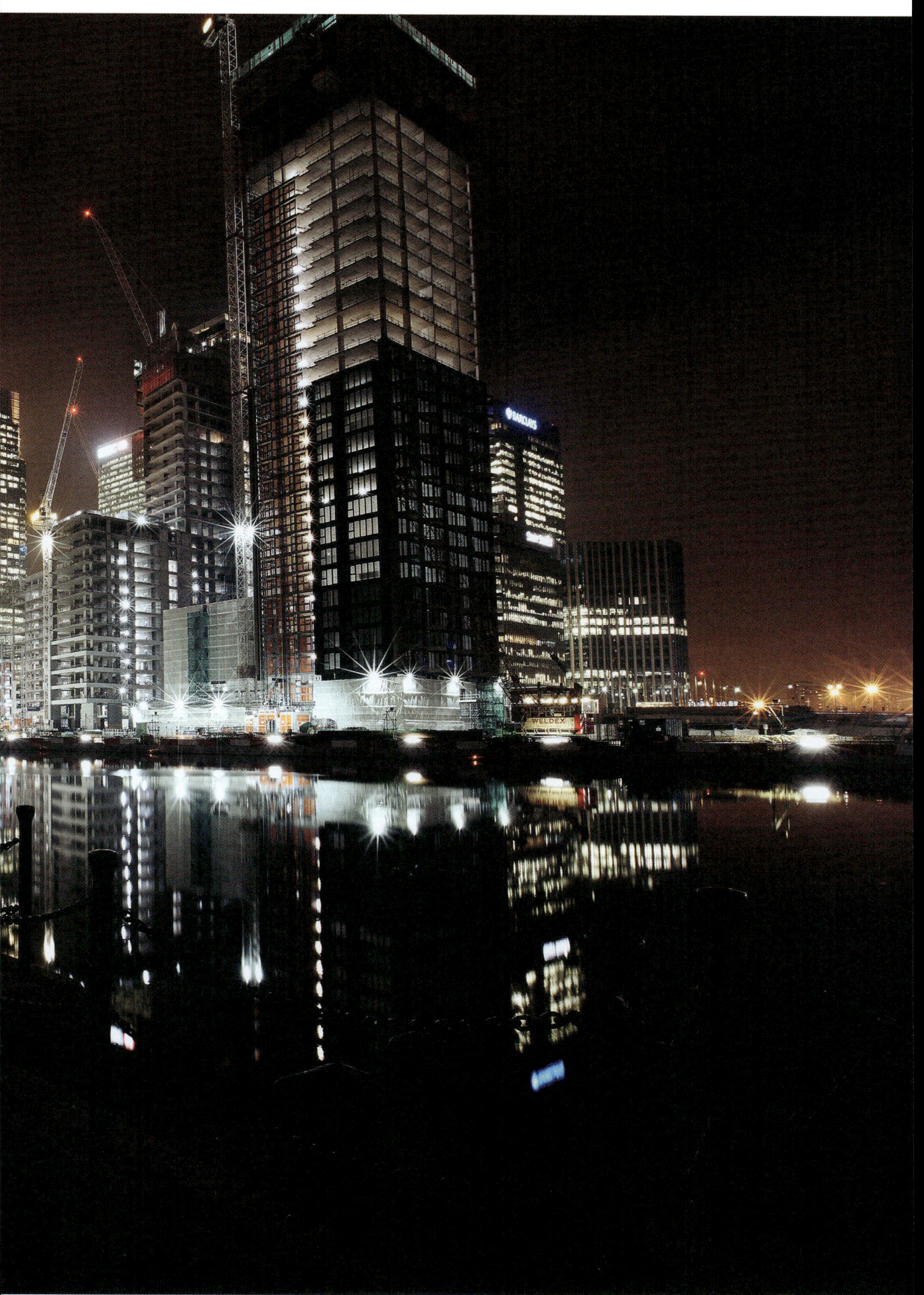

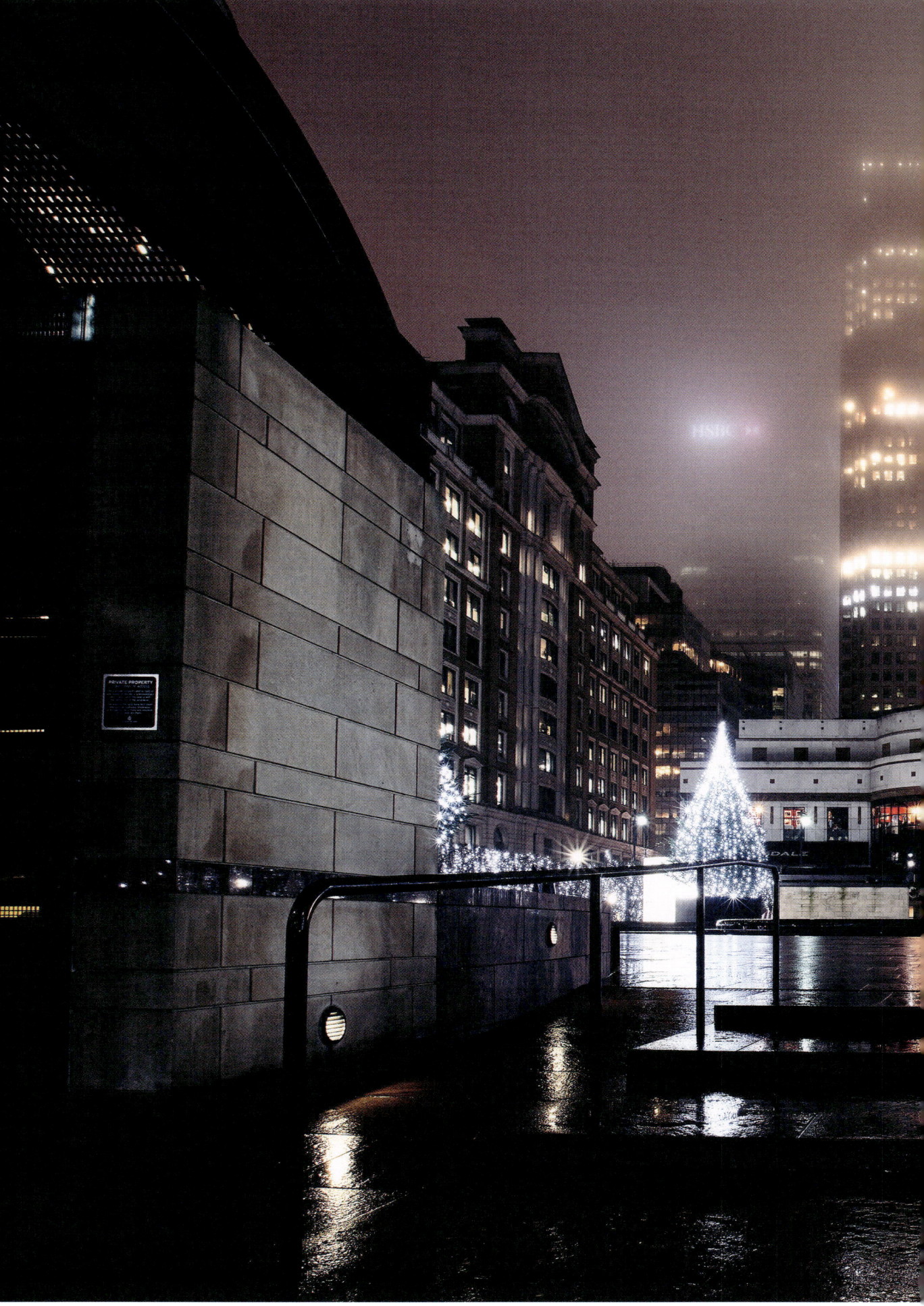

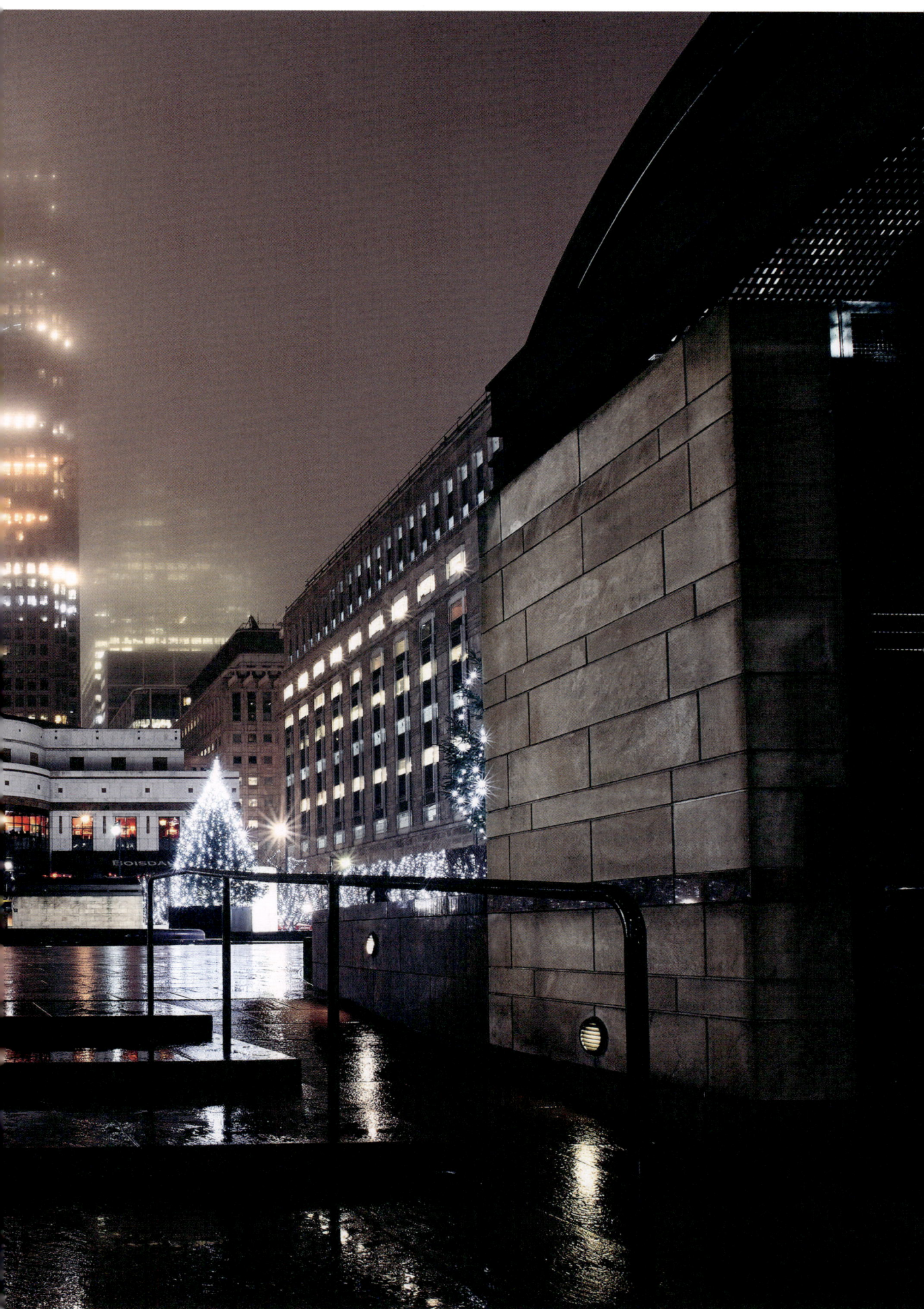

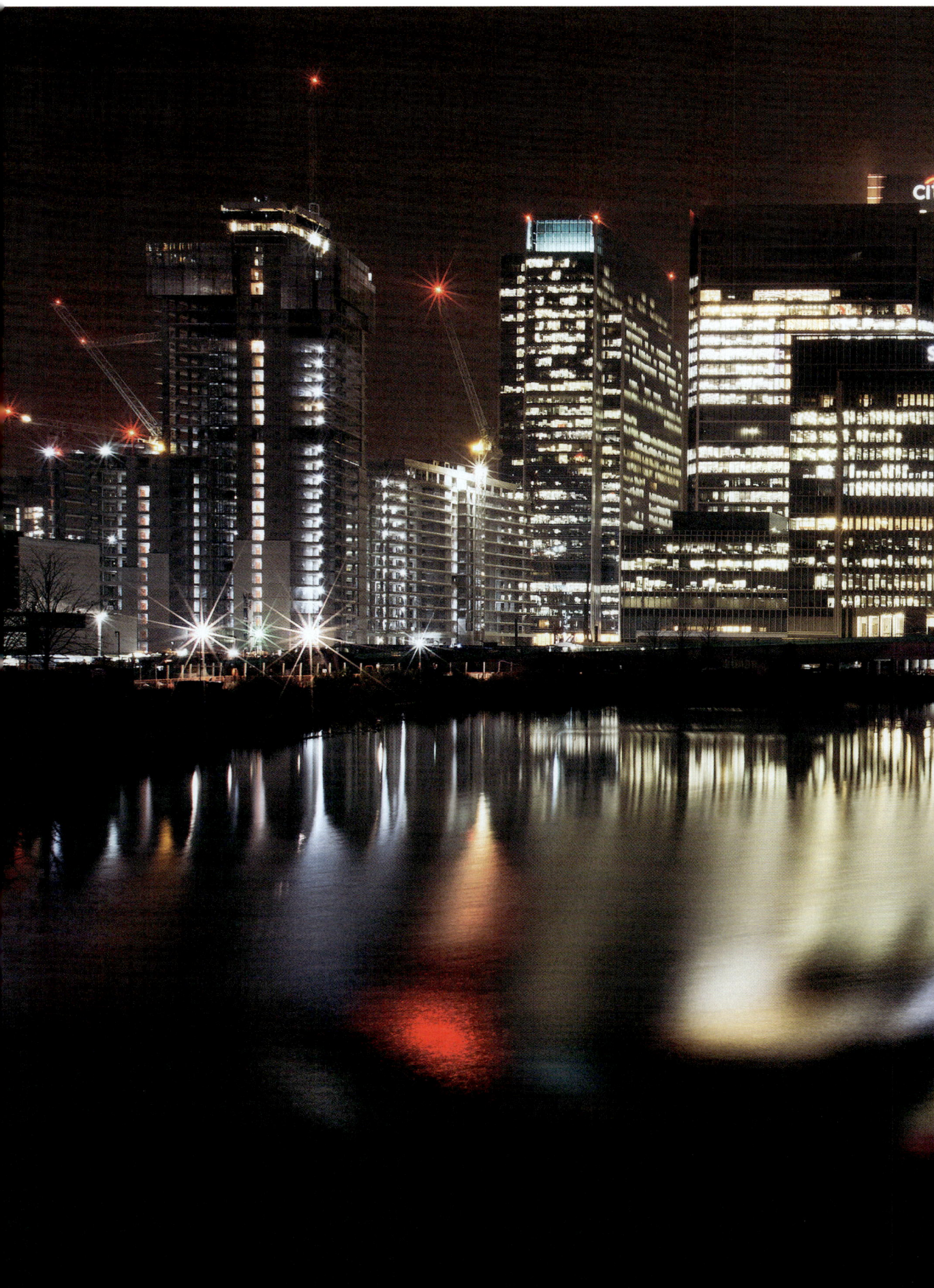

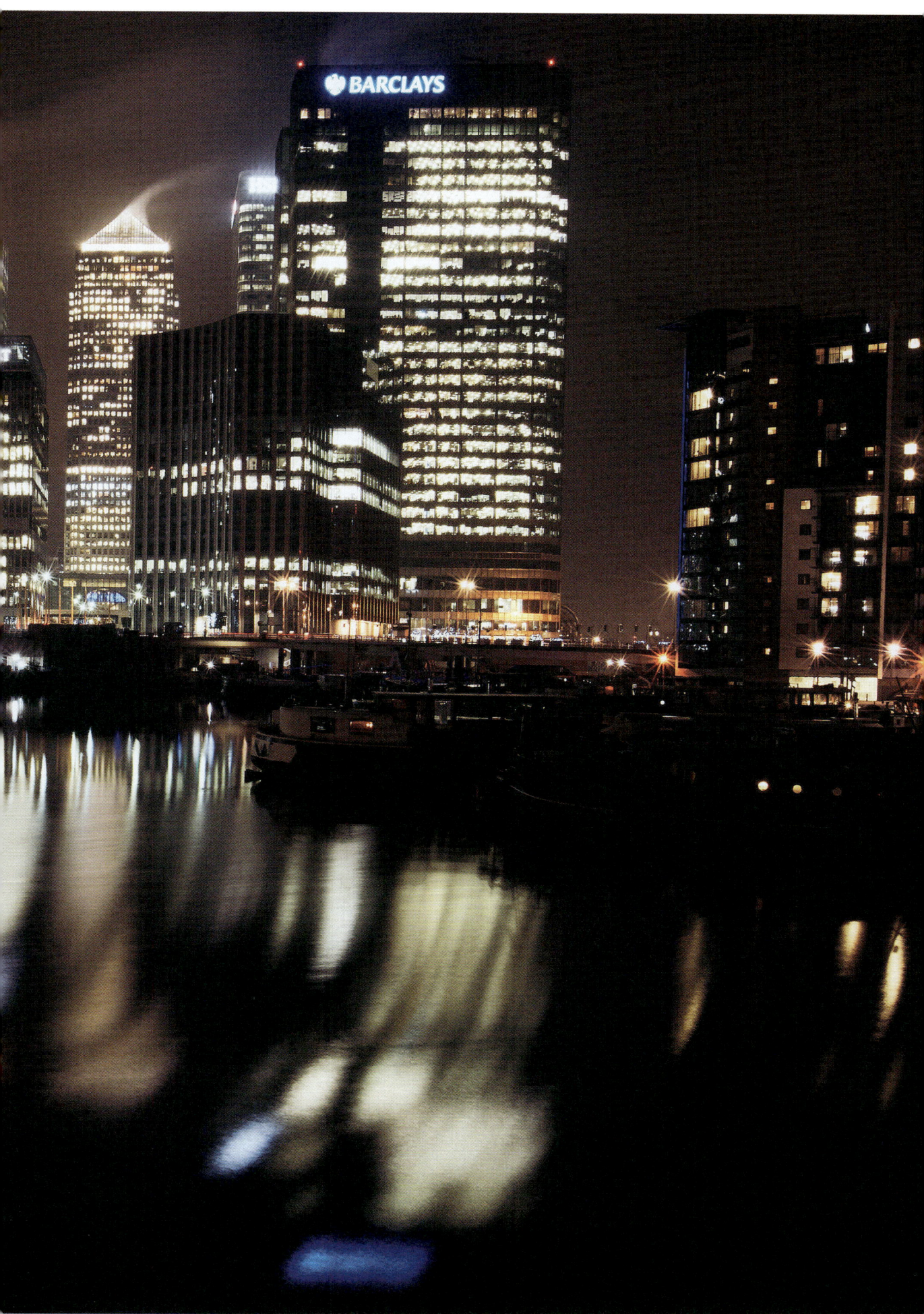

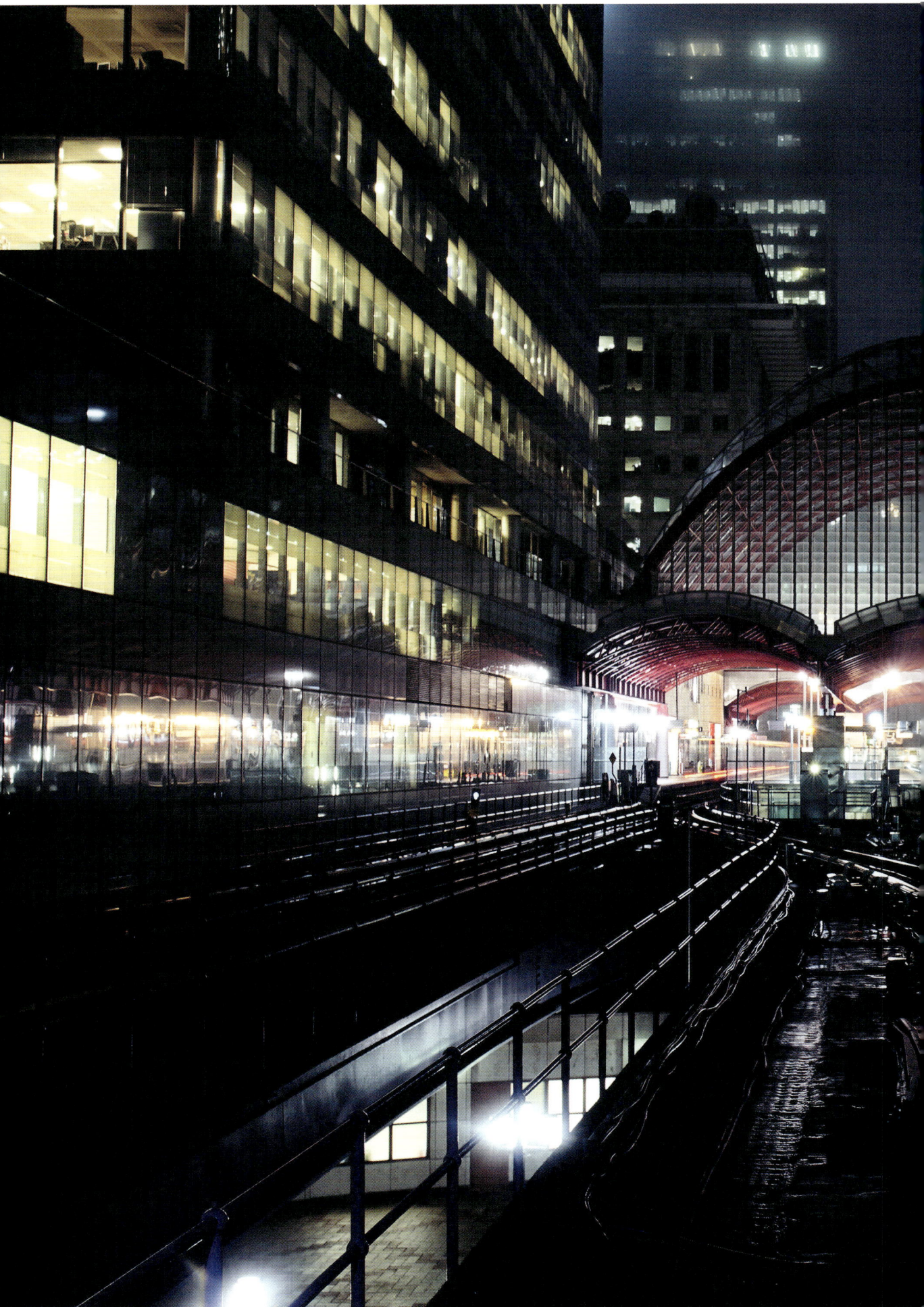

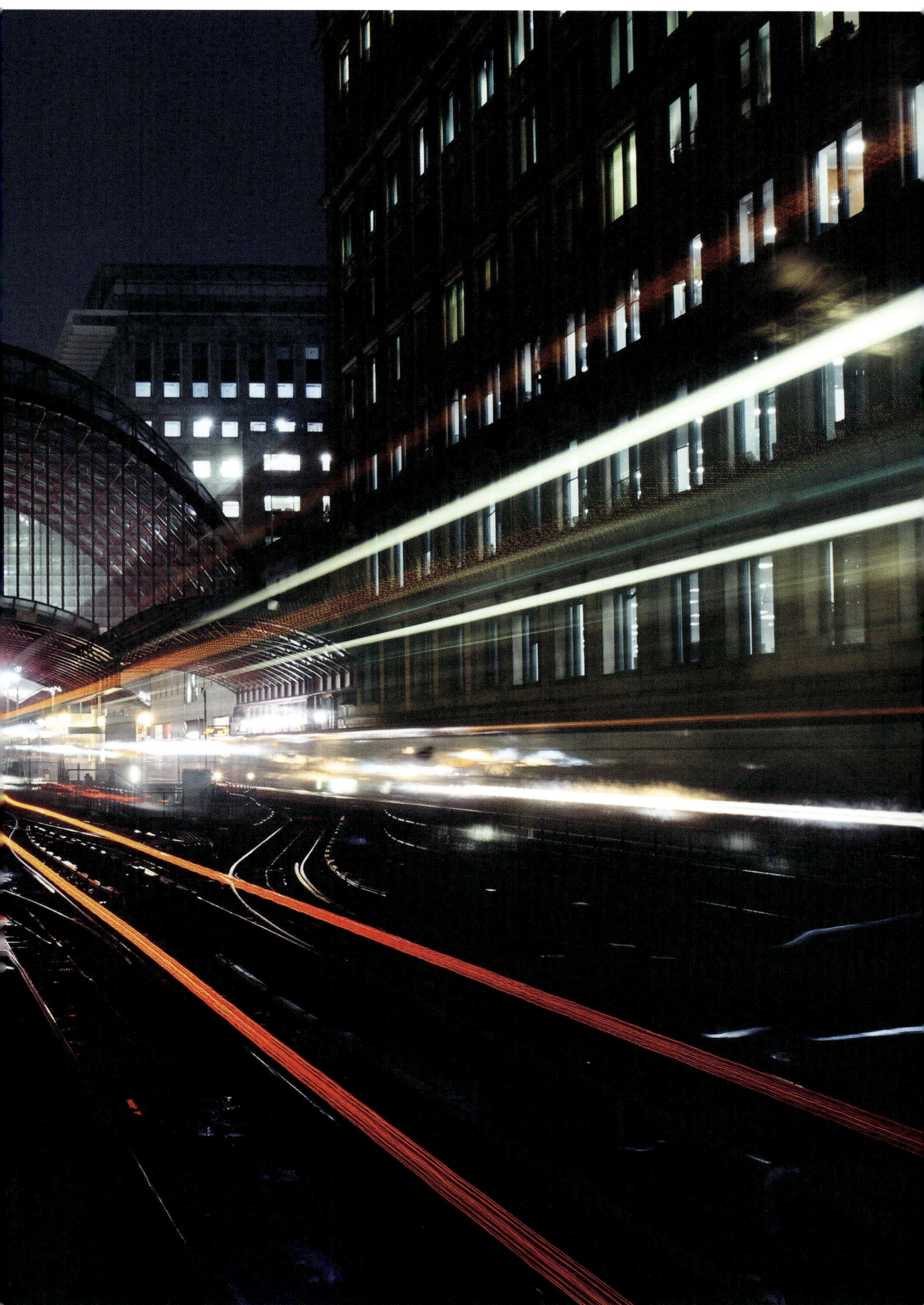

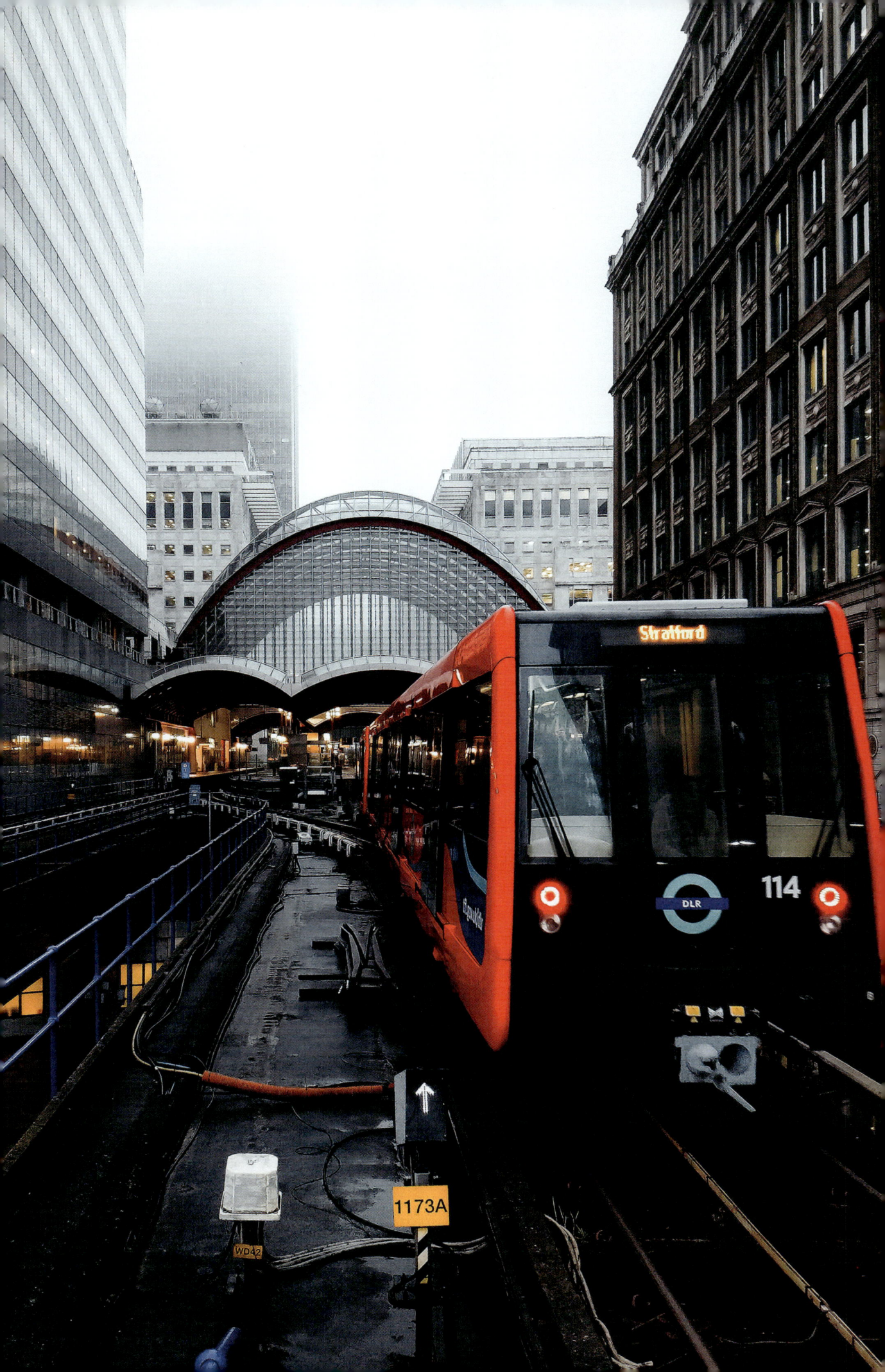

For me, it's all about art, about imagery, rather than being a public figure. I really want to use my influence for good and for change.

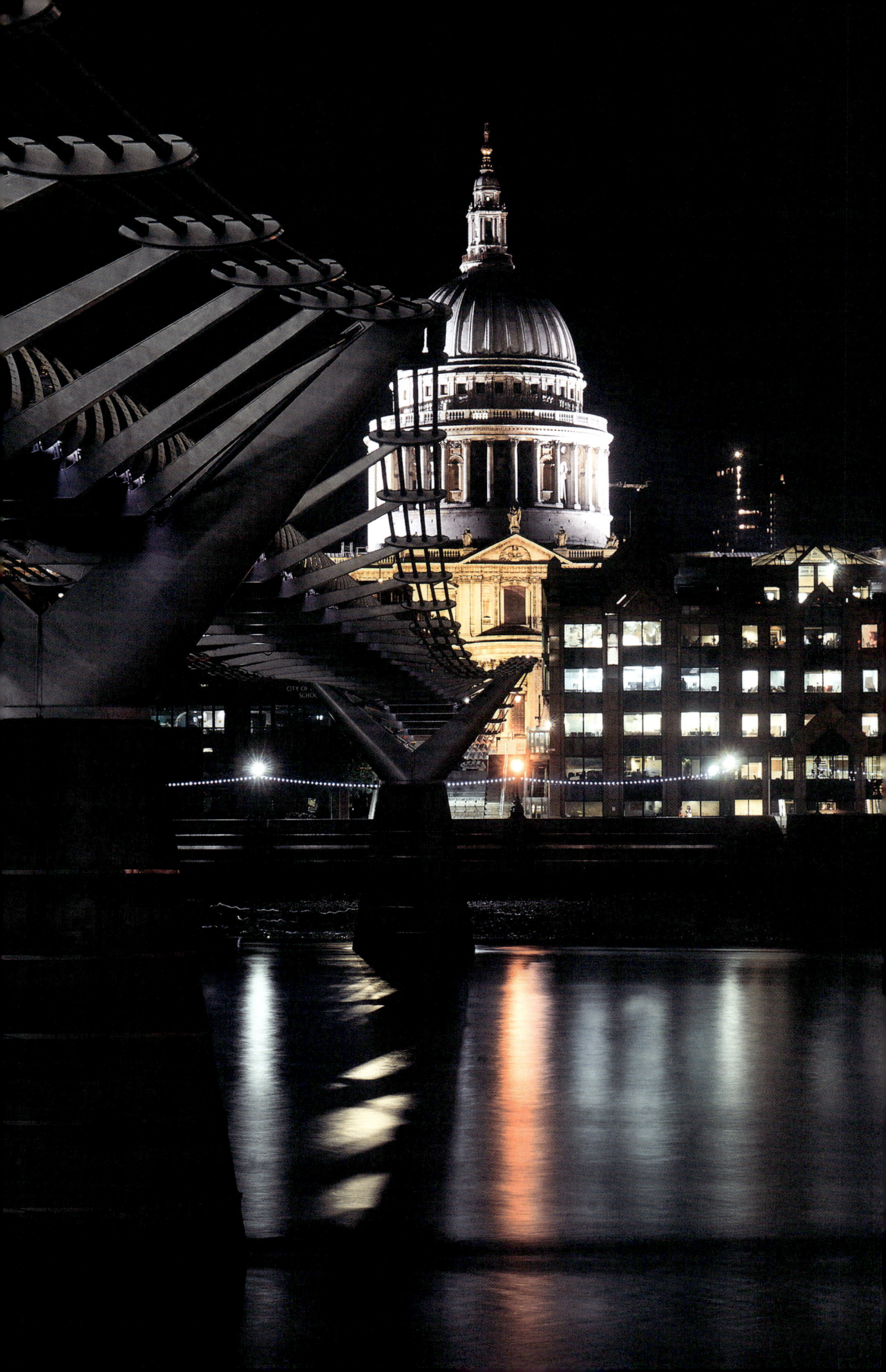

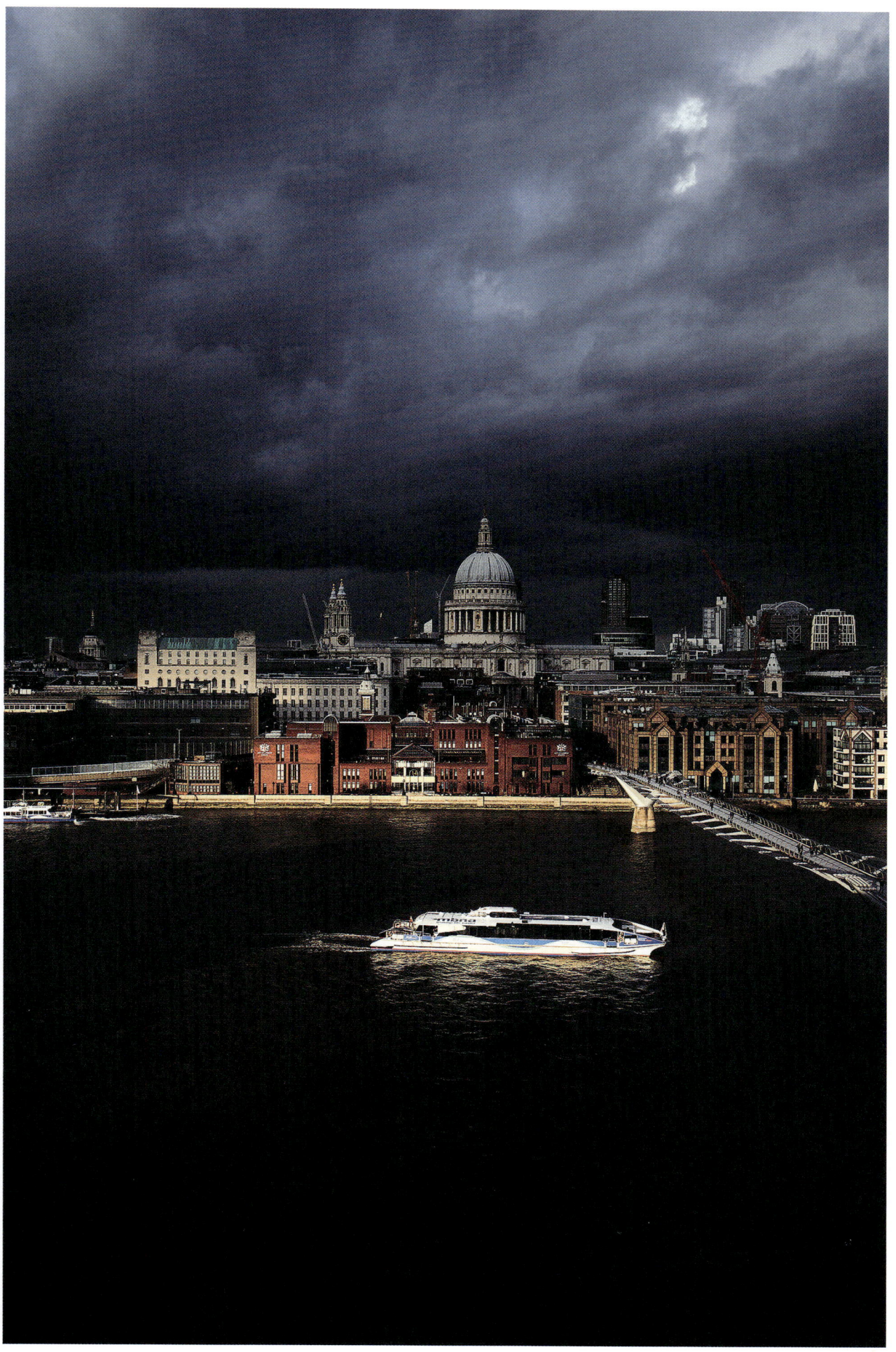

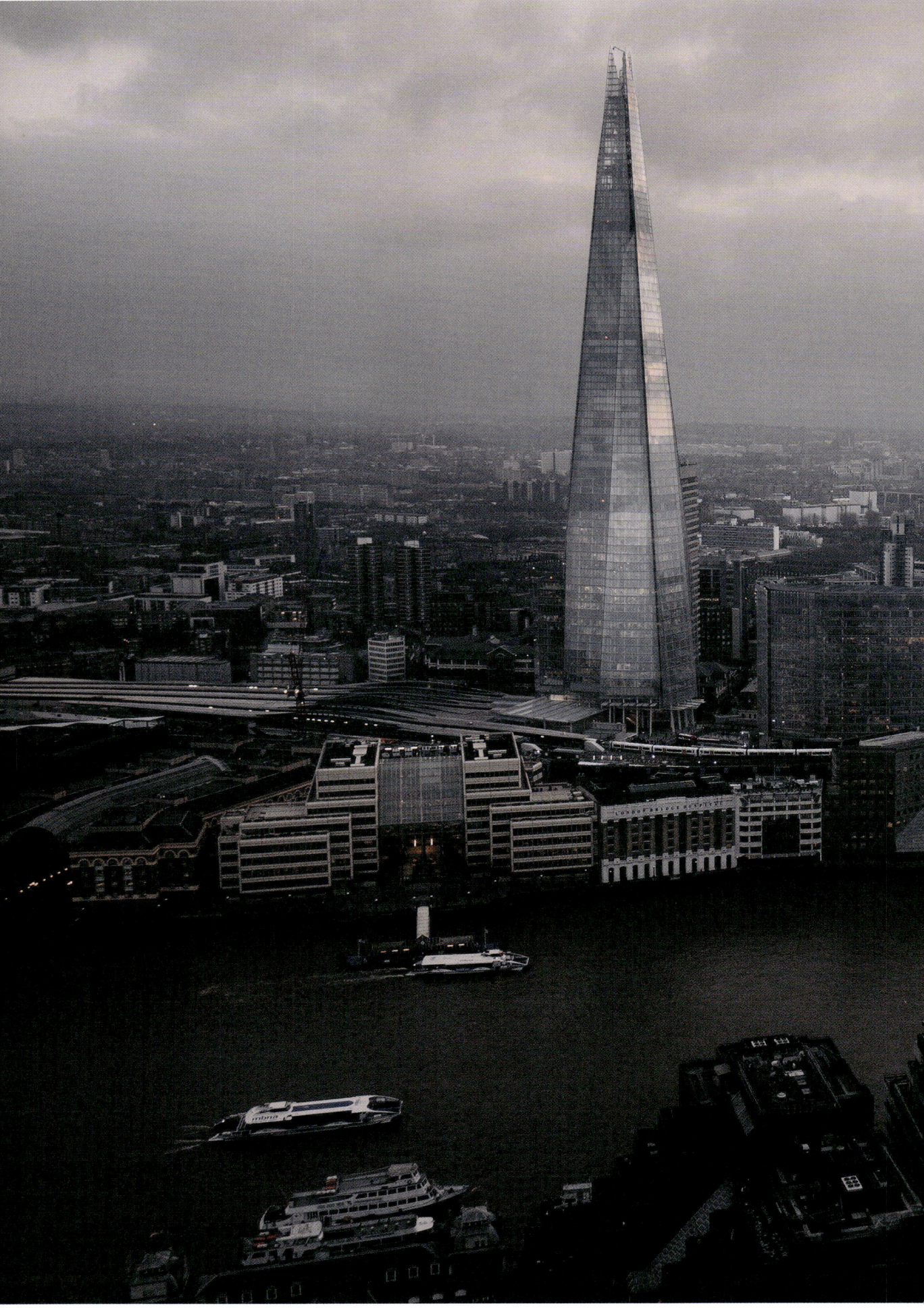

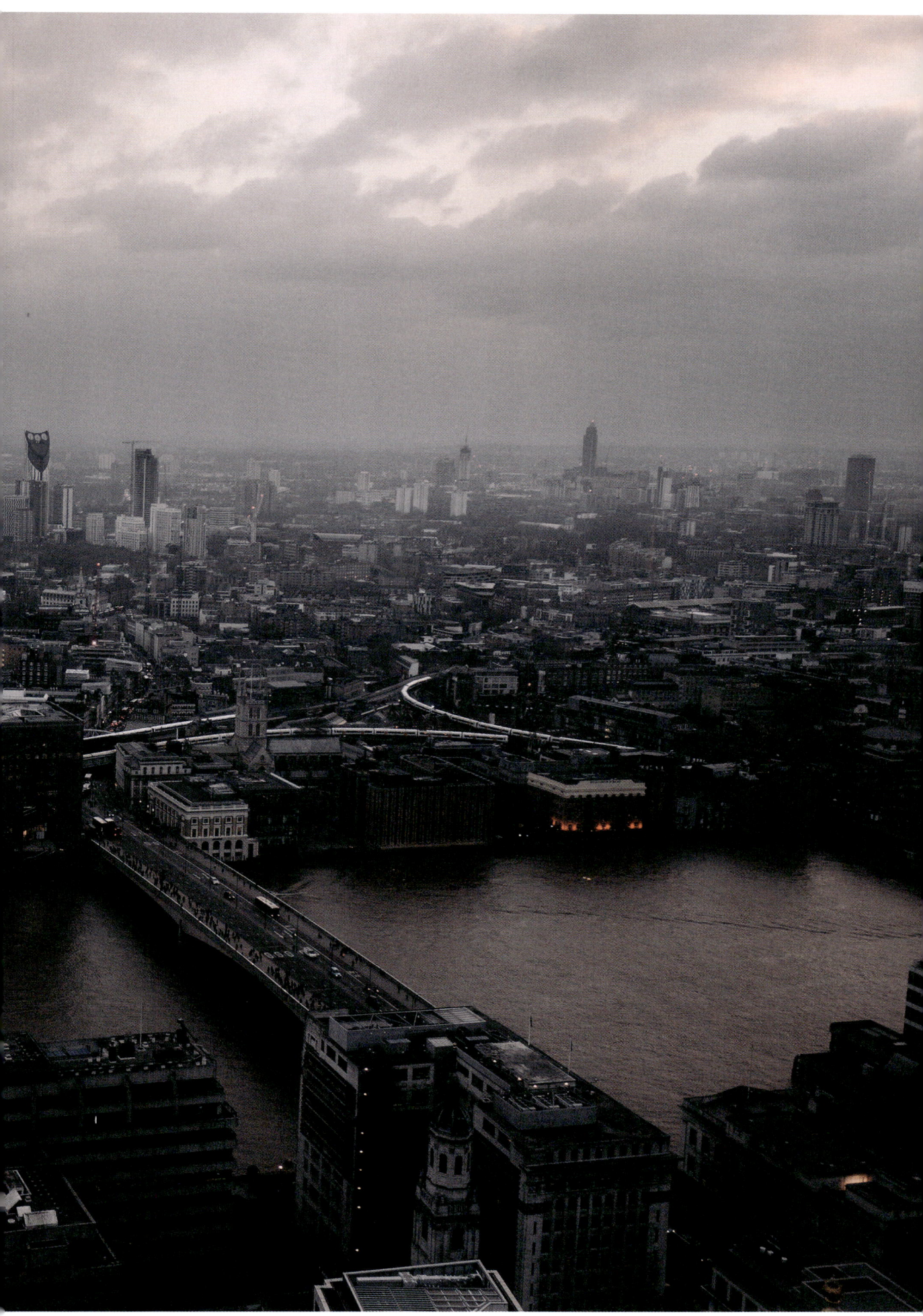

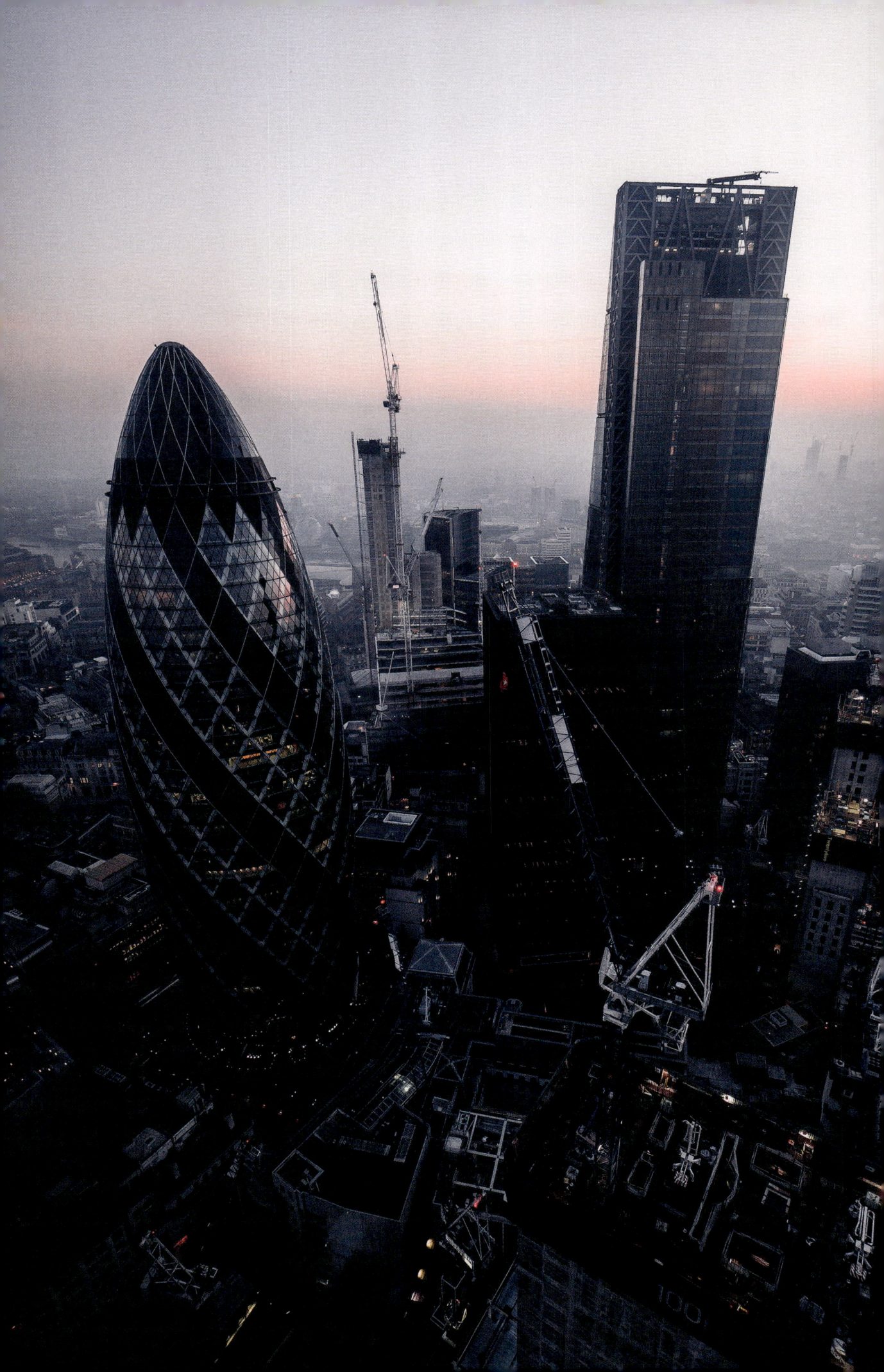

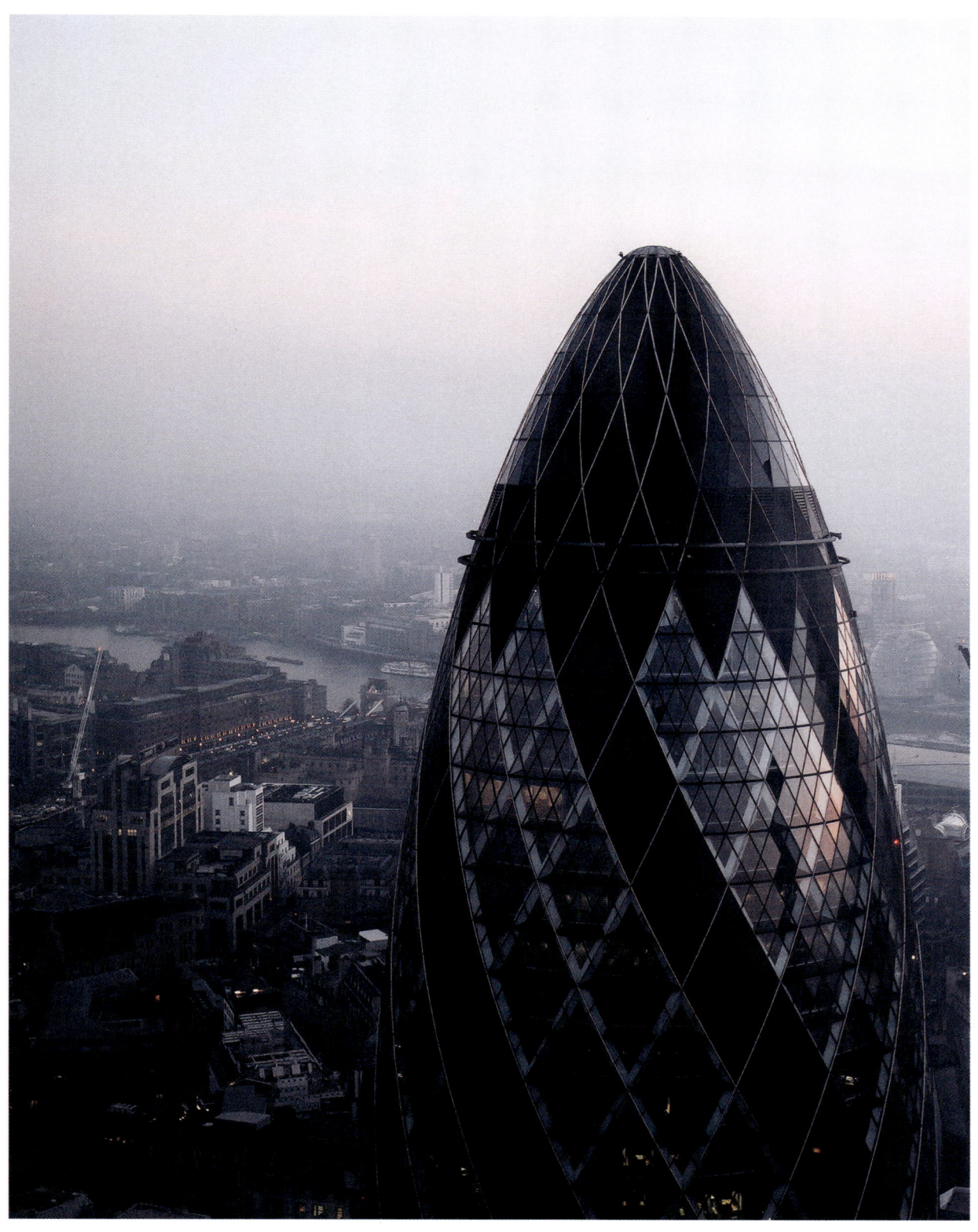

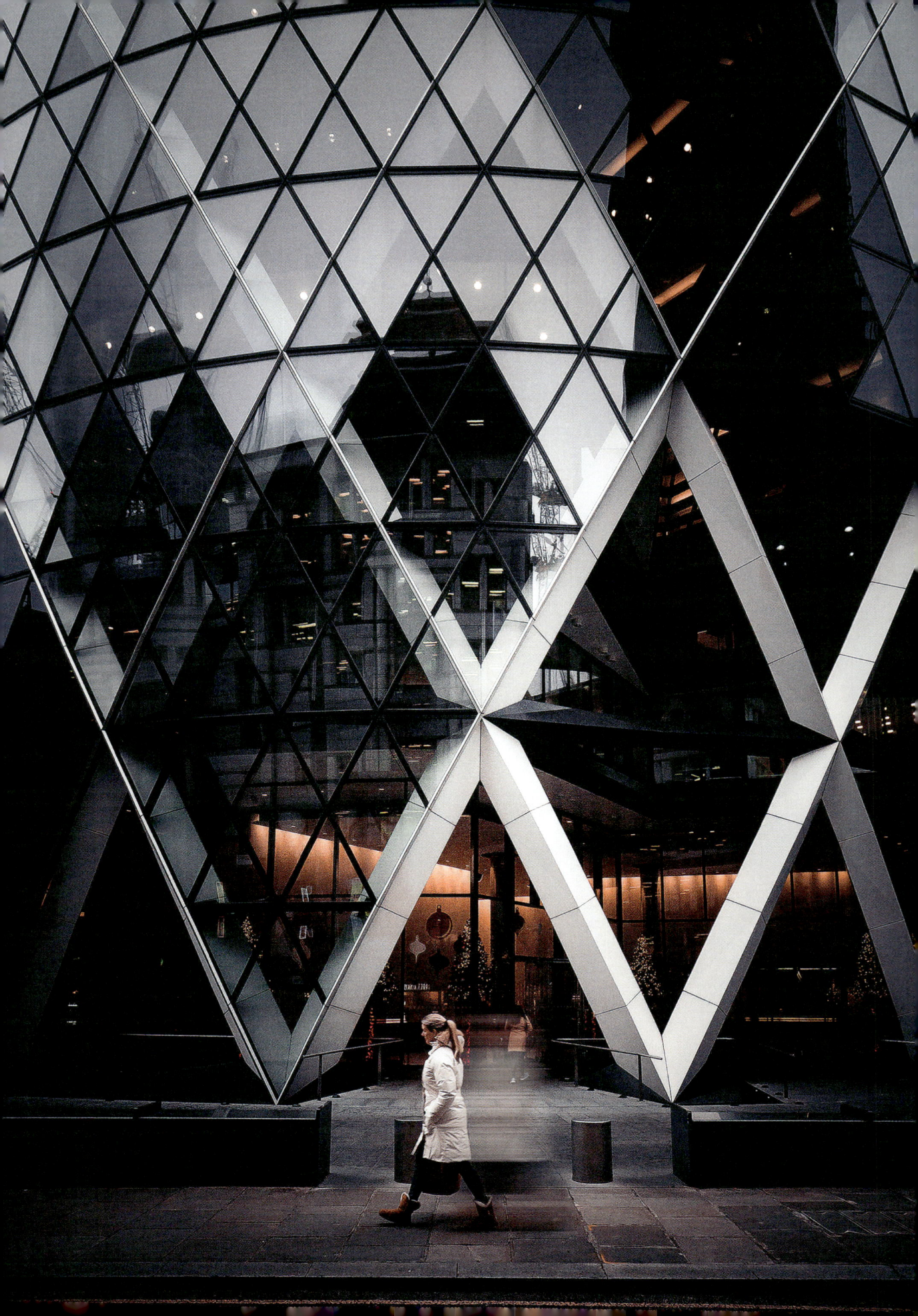

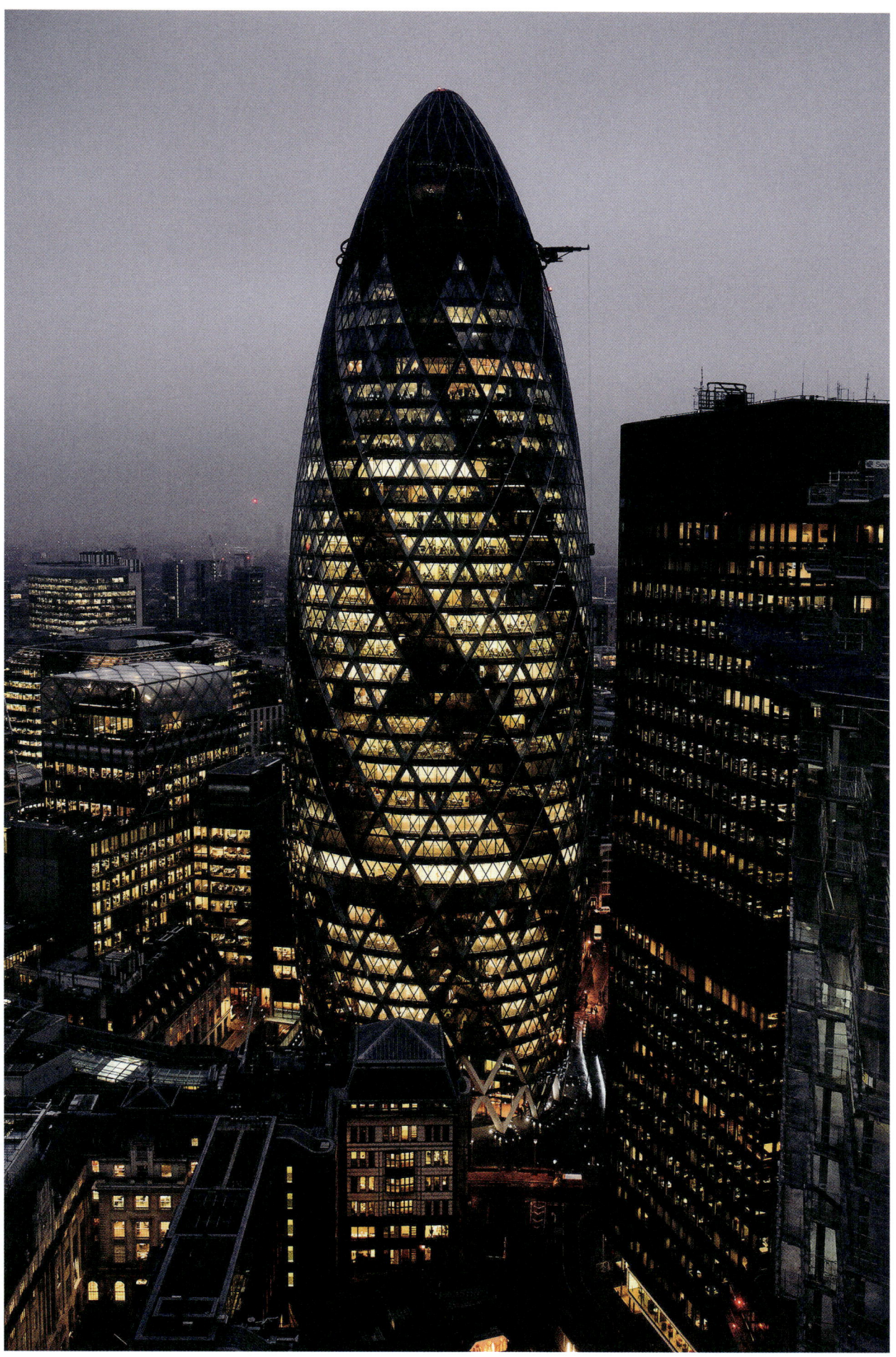

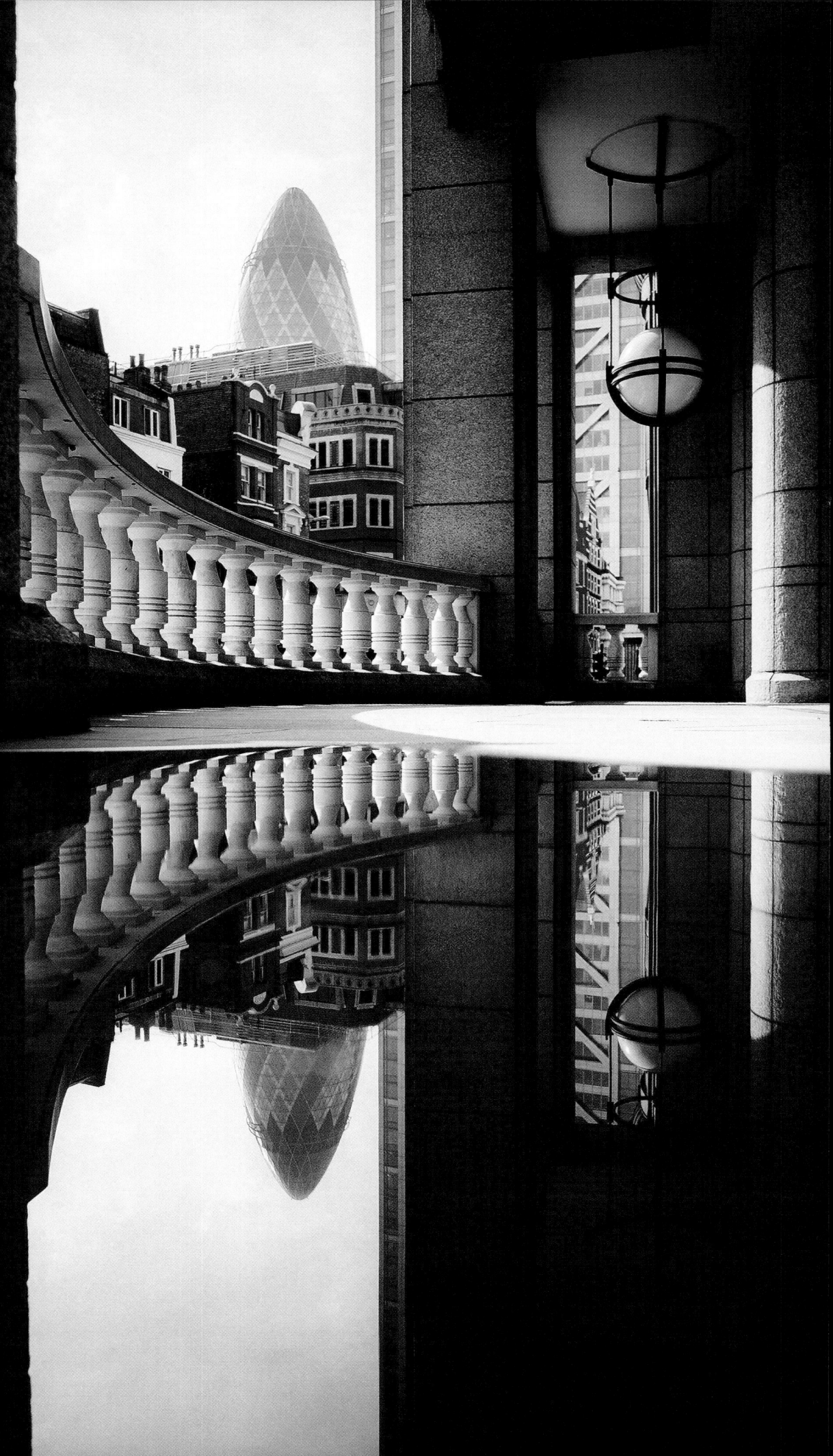

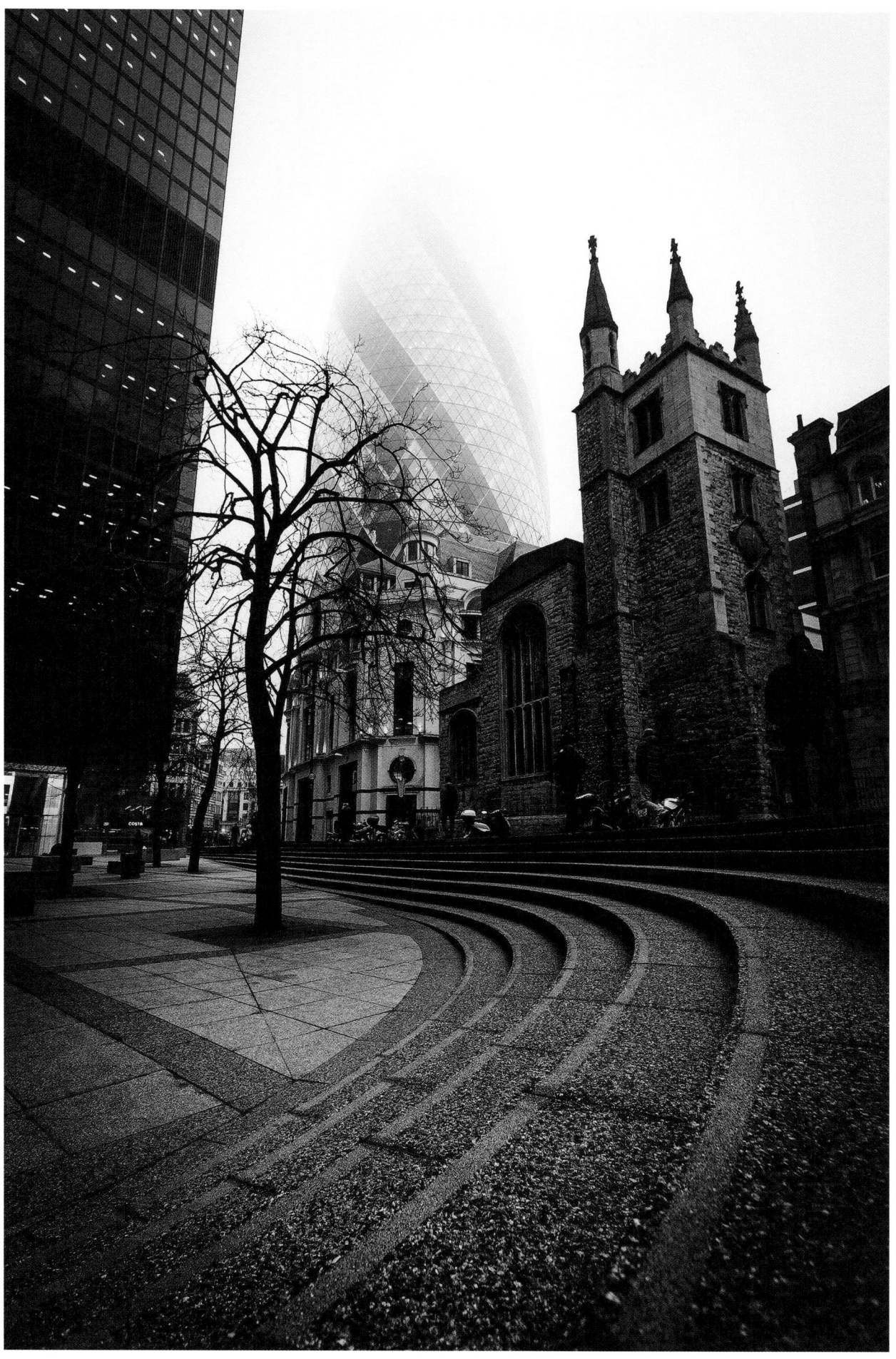

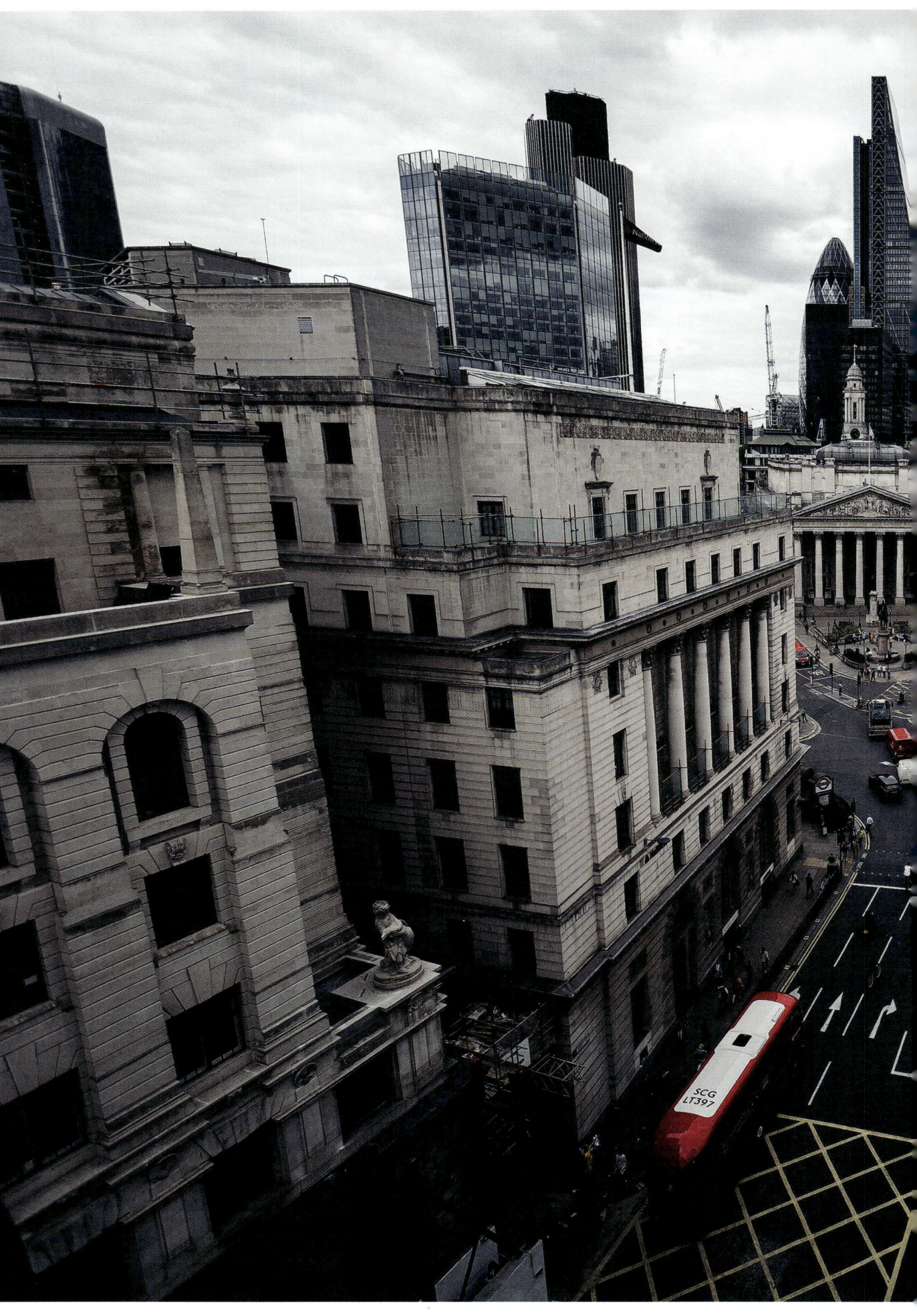

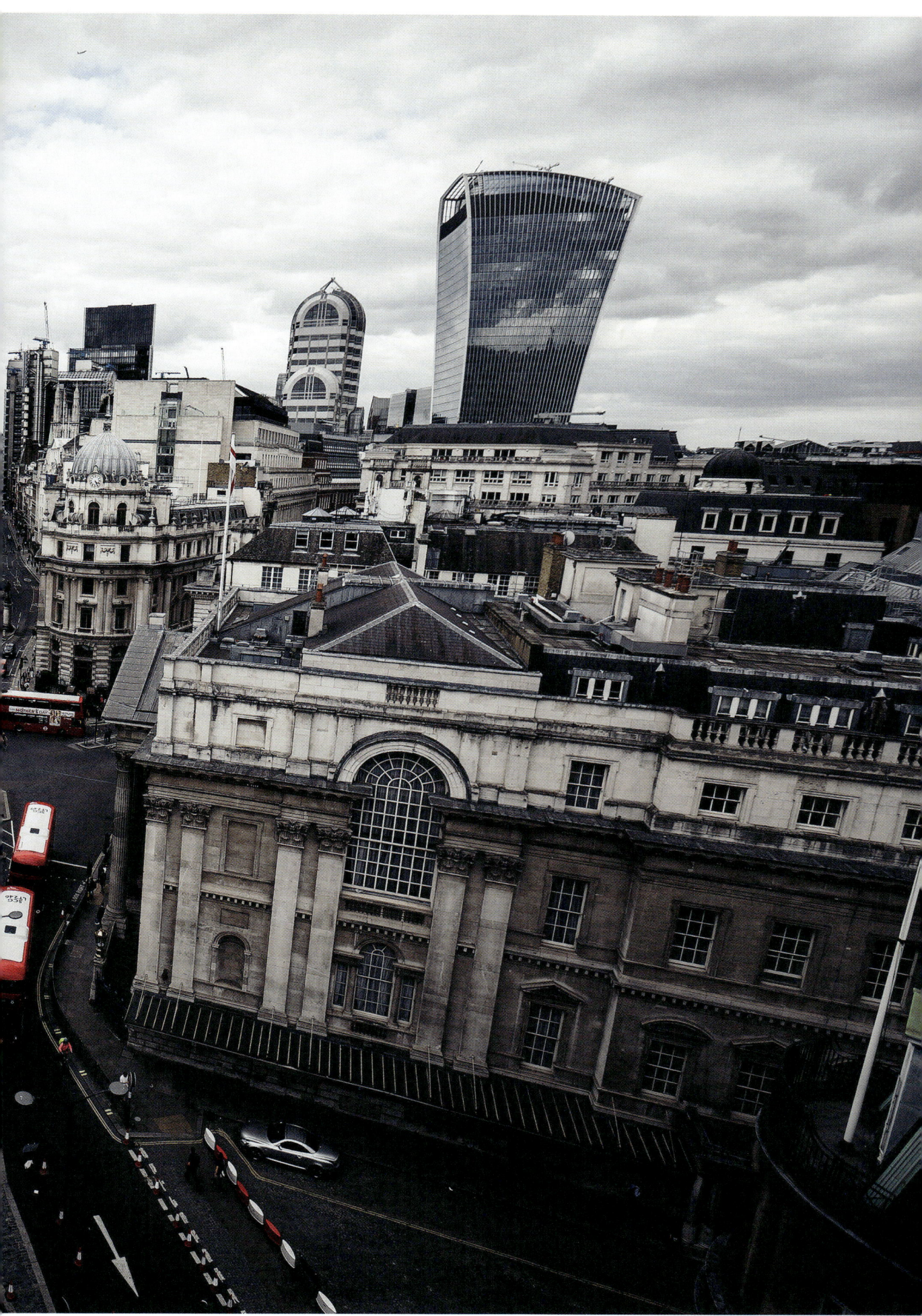

Photography for me is an art form, and I love creating.

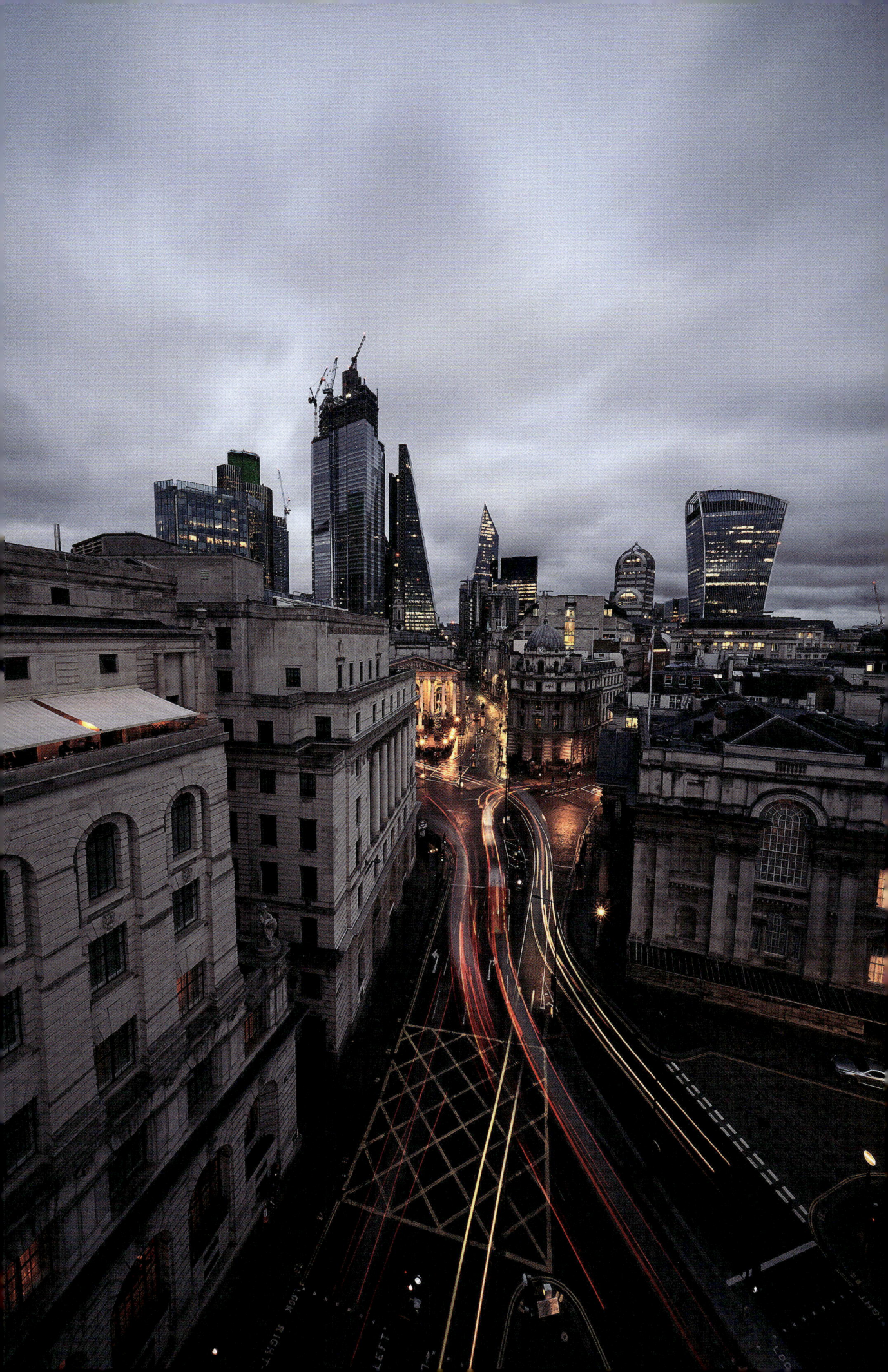

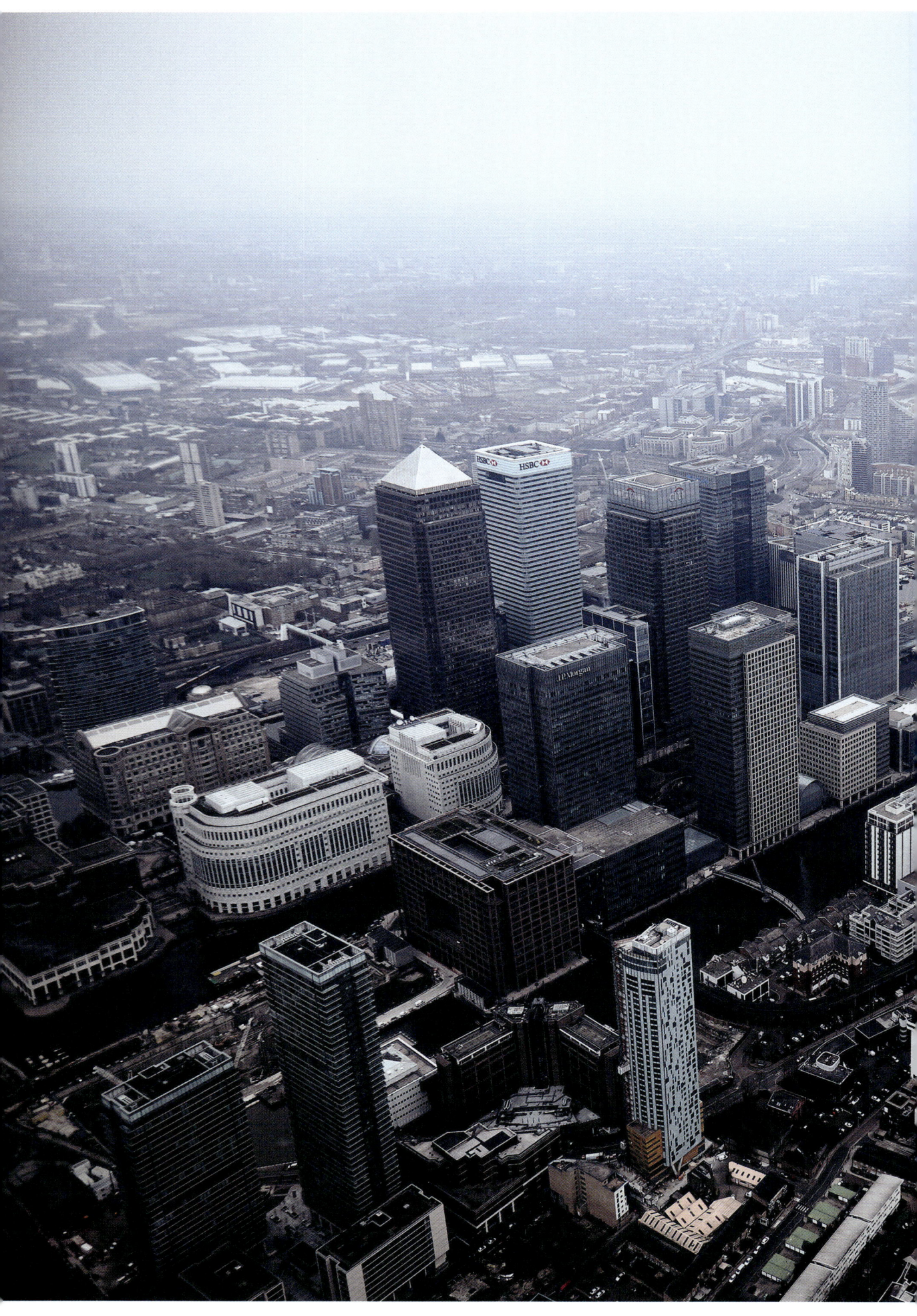

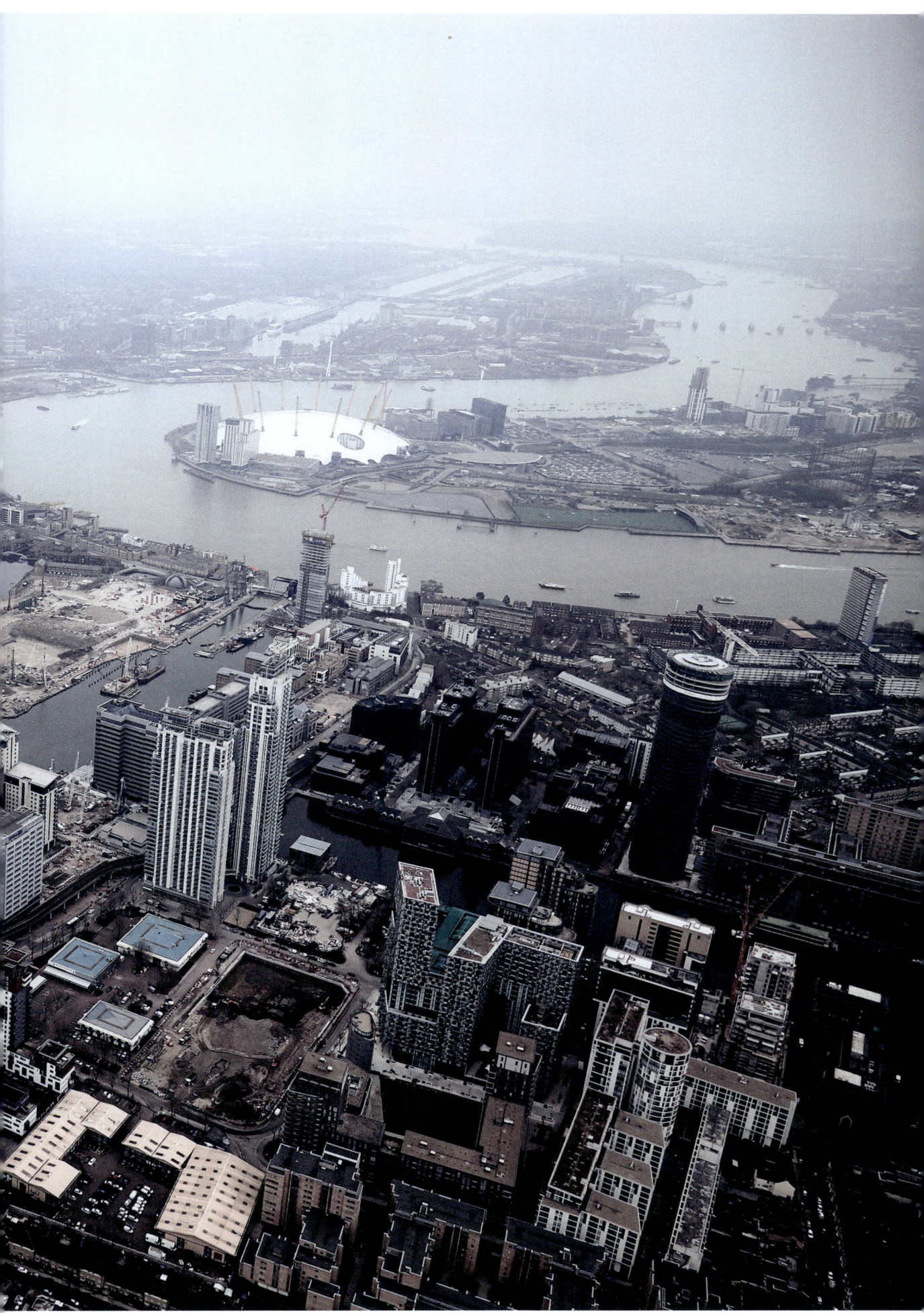

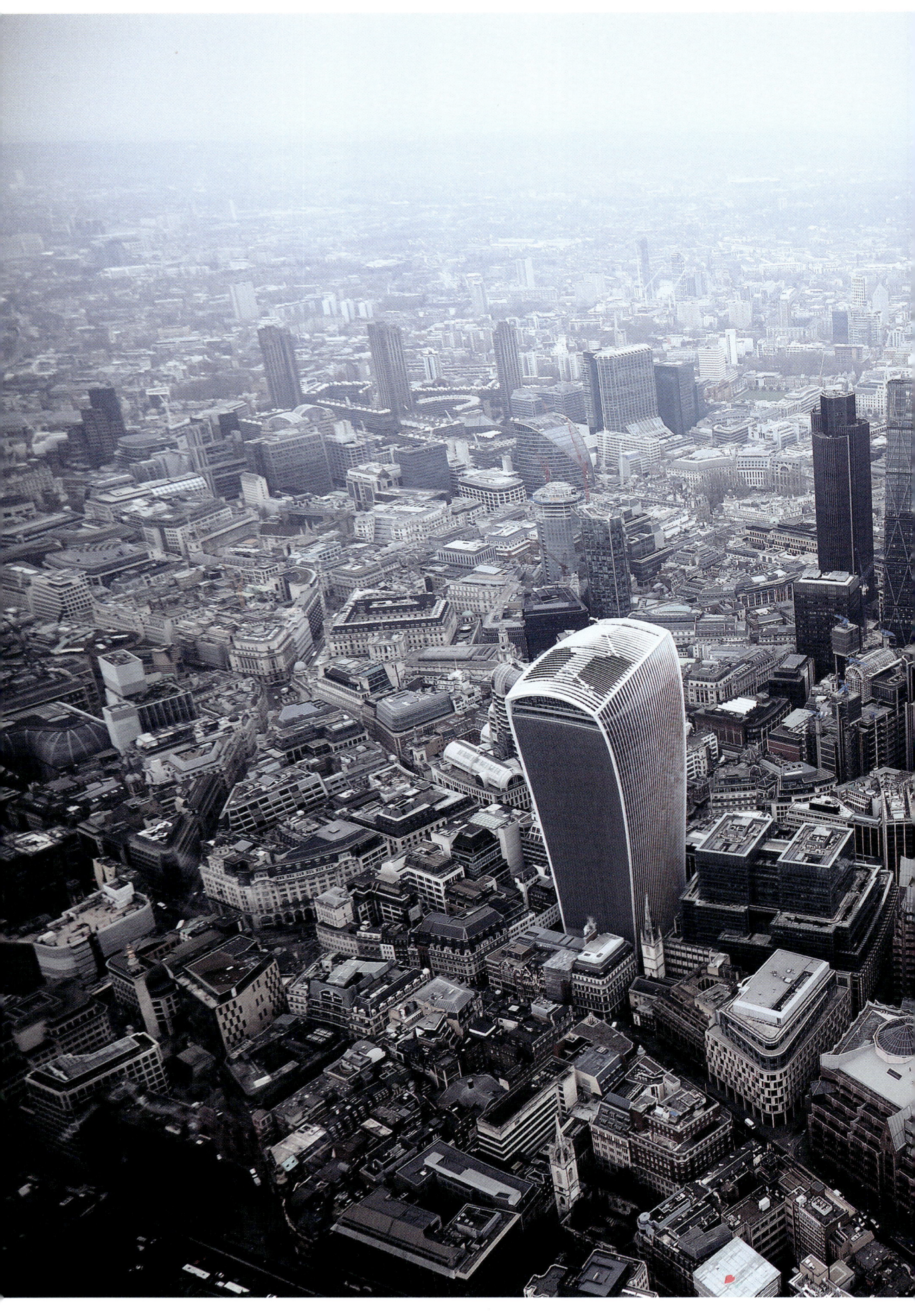

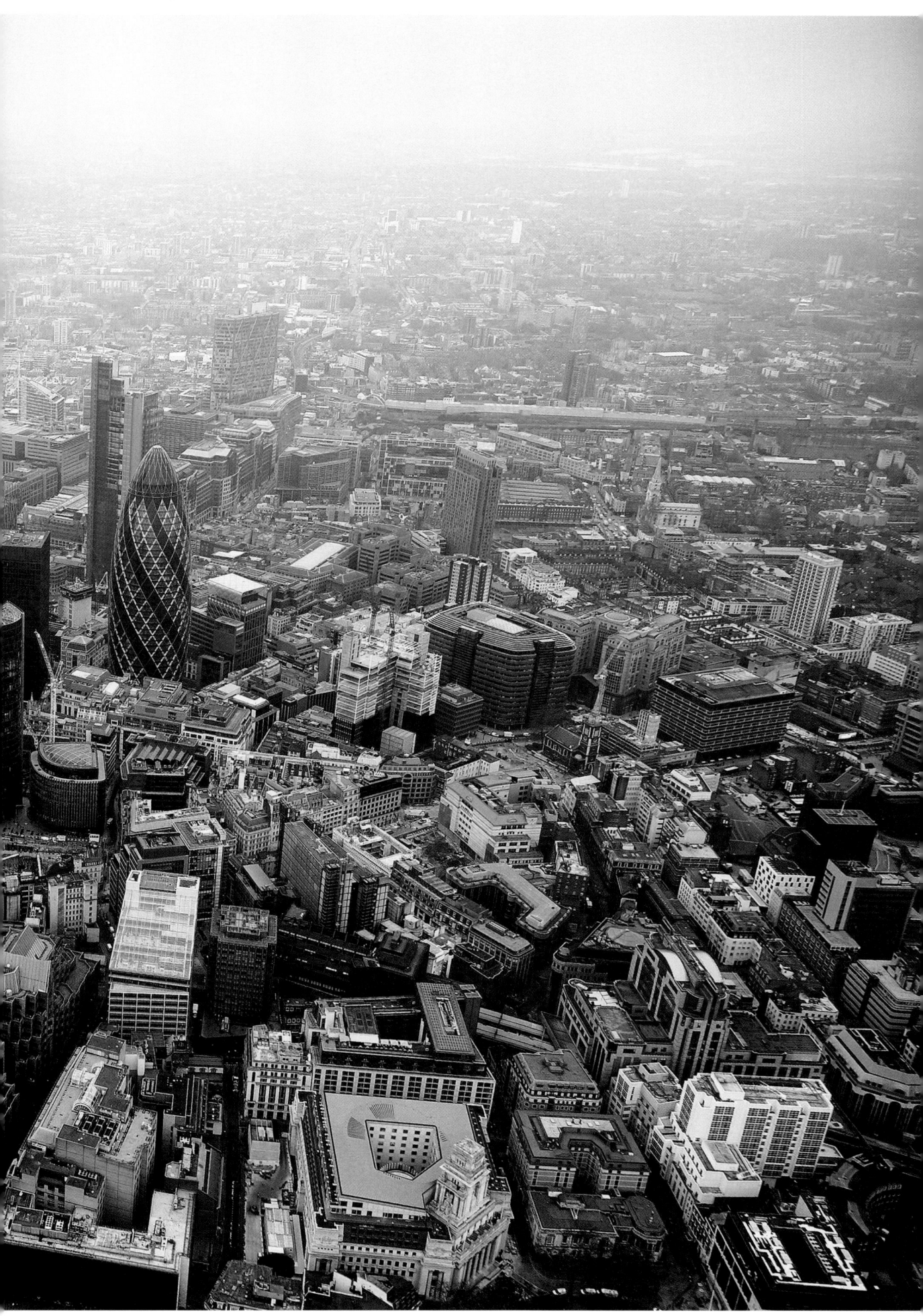

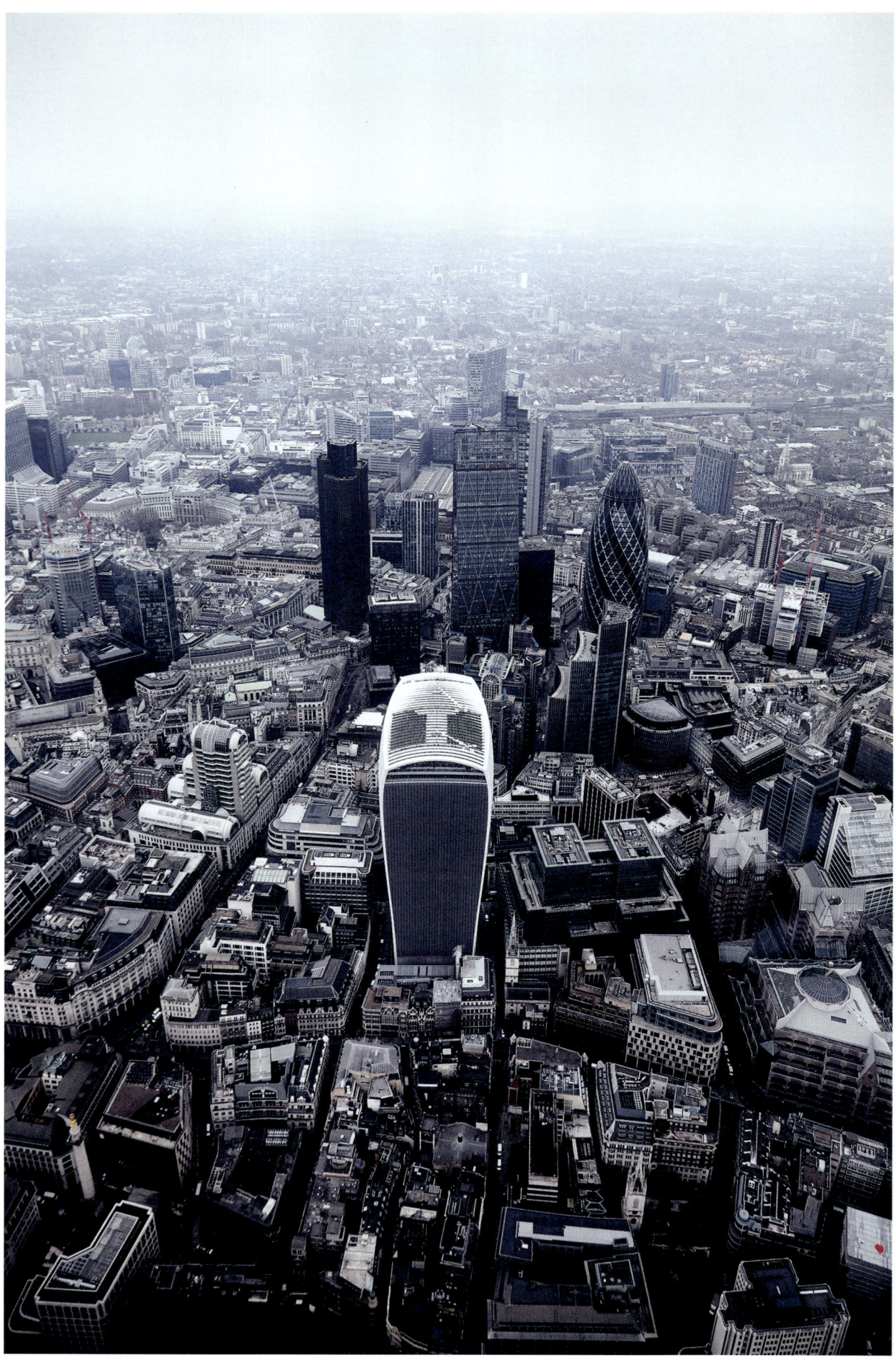

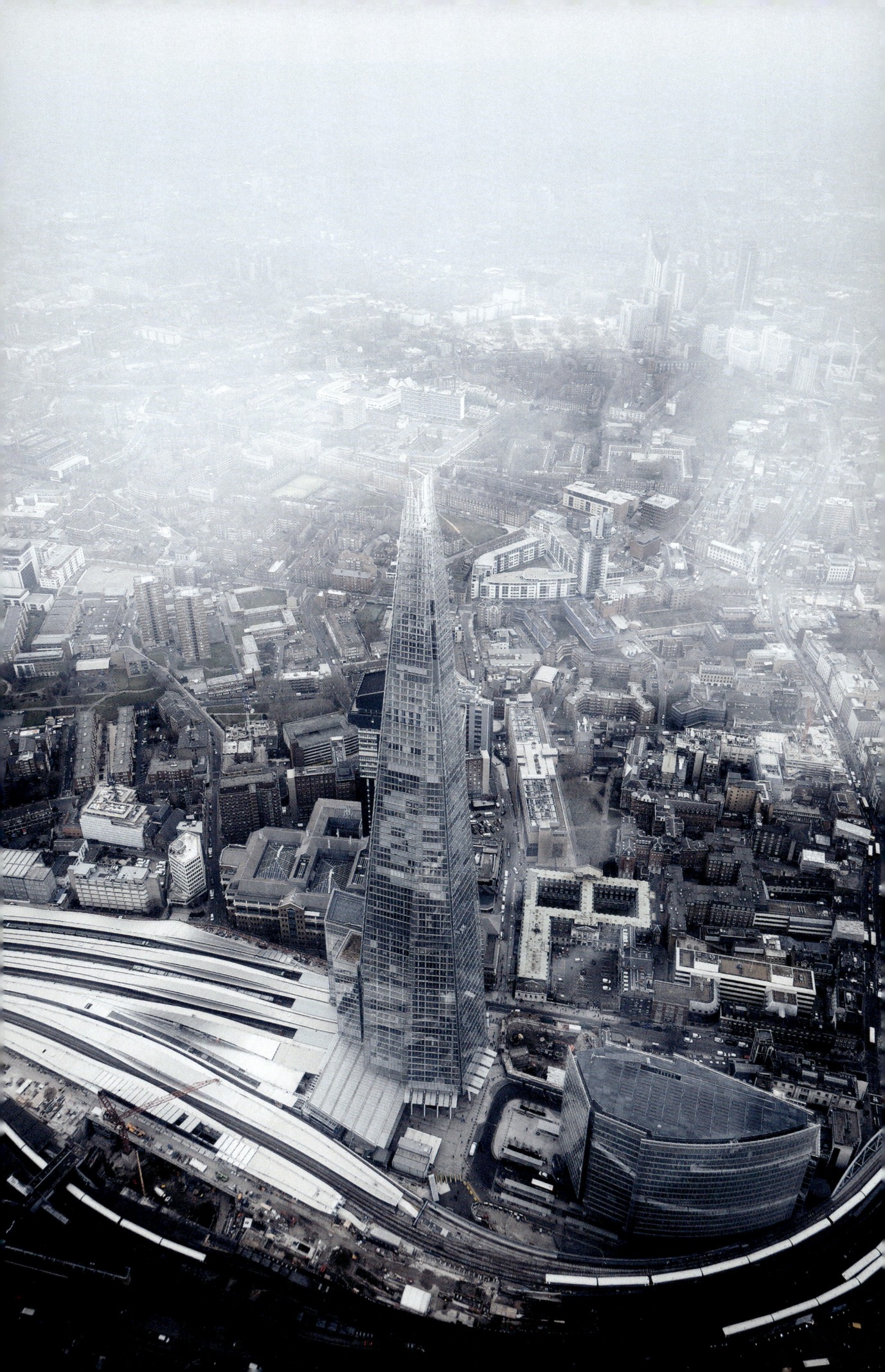

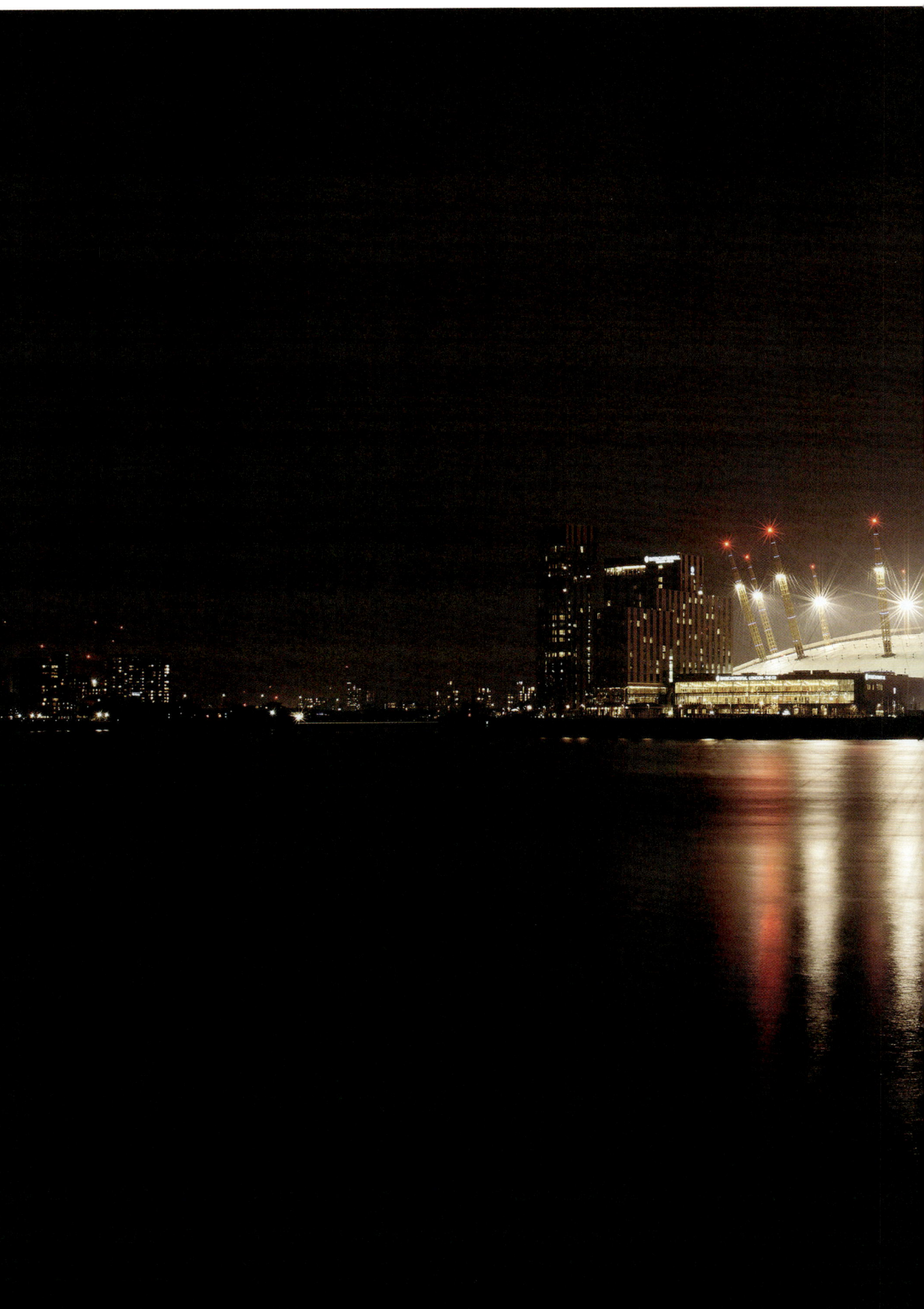

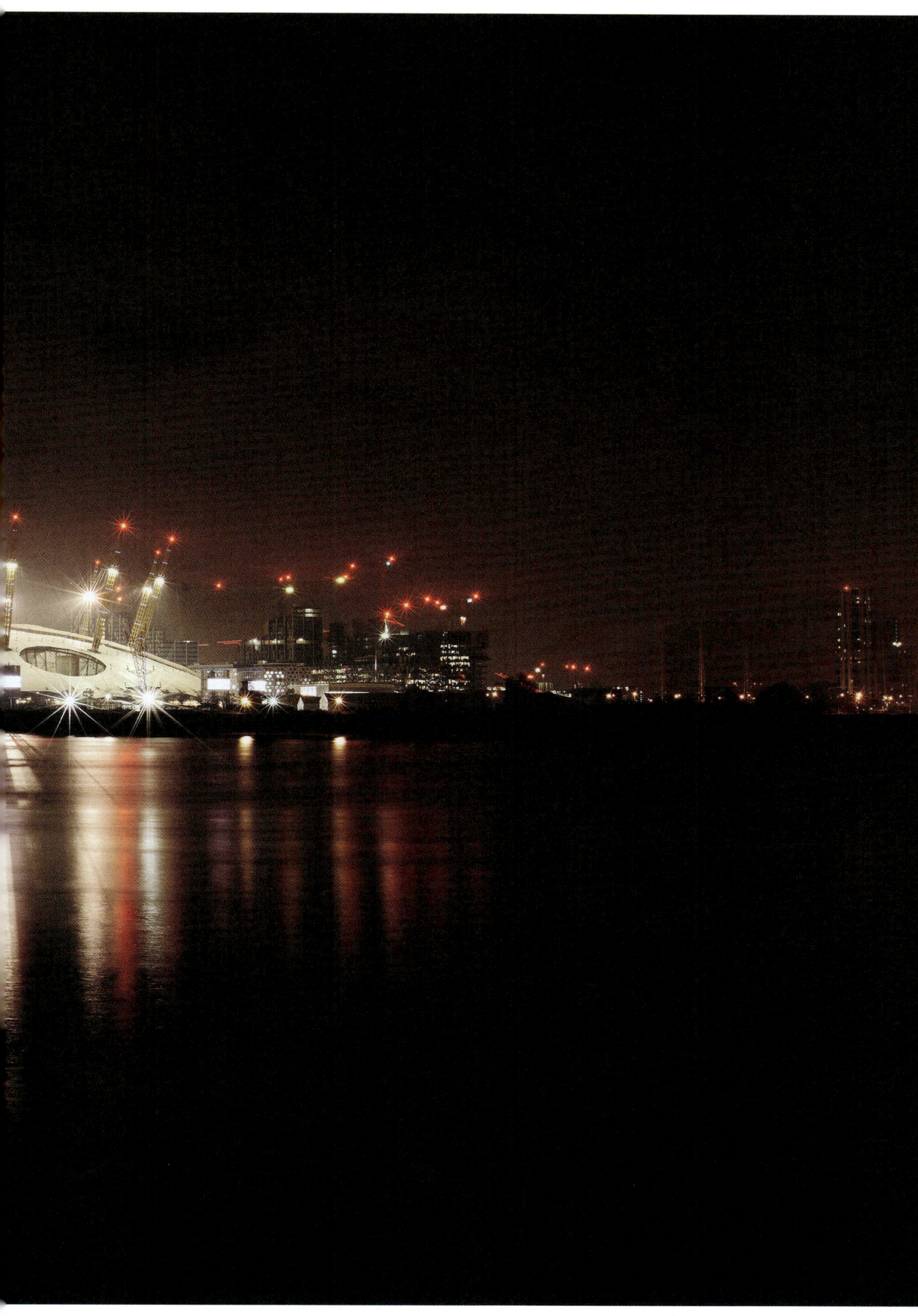

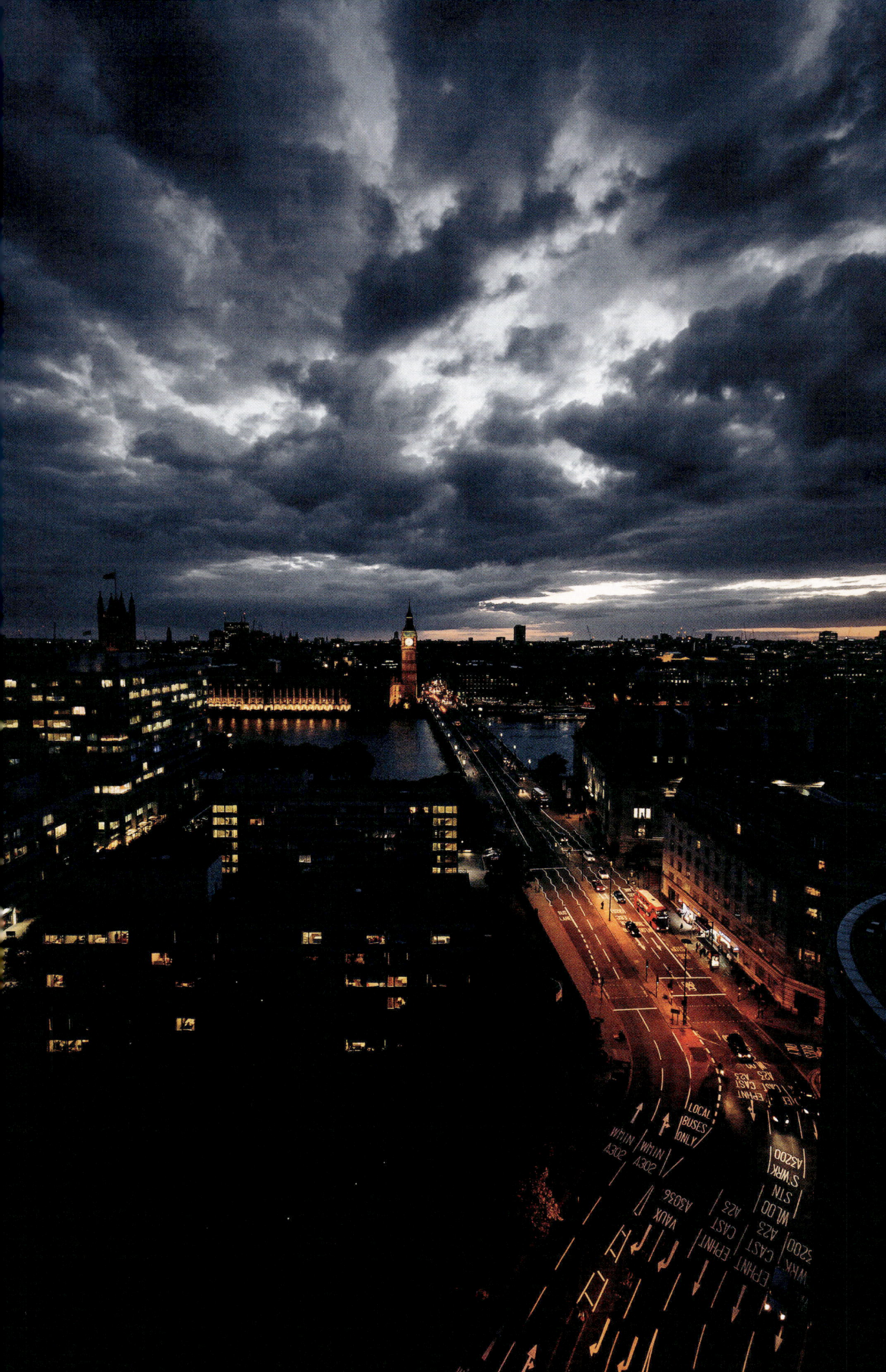

I will go to places in London at times when no one else is around.

London inspires me for a number of reasons, one being the fact that it is so big and there are so many different types of people. It's made me a well-rounded person.

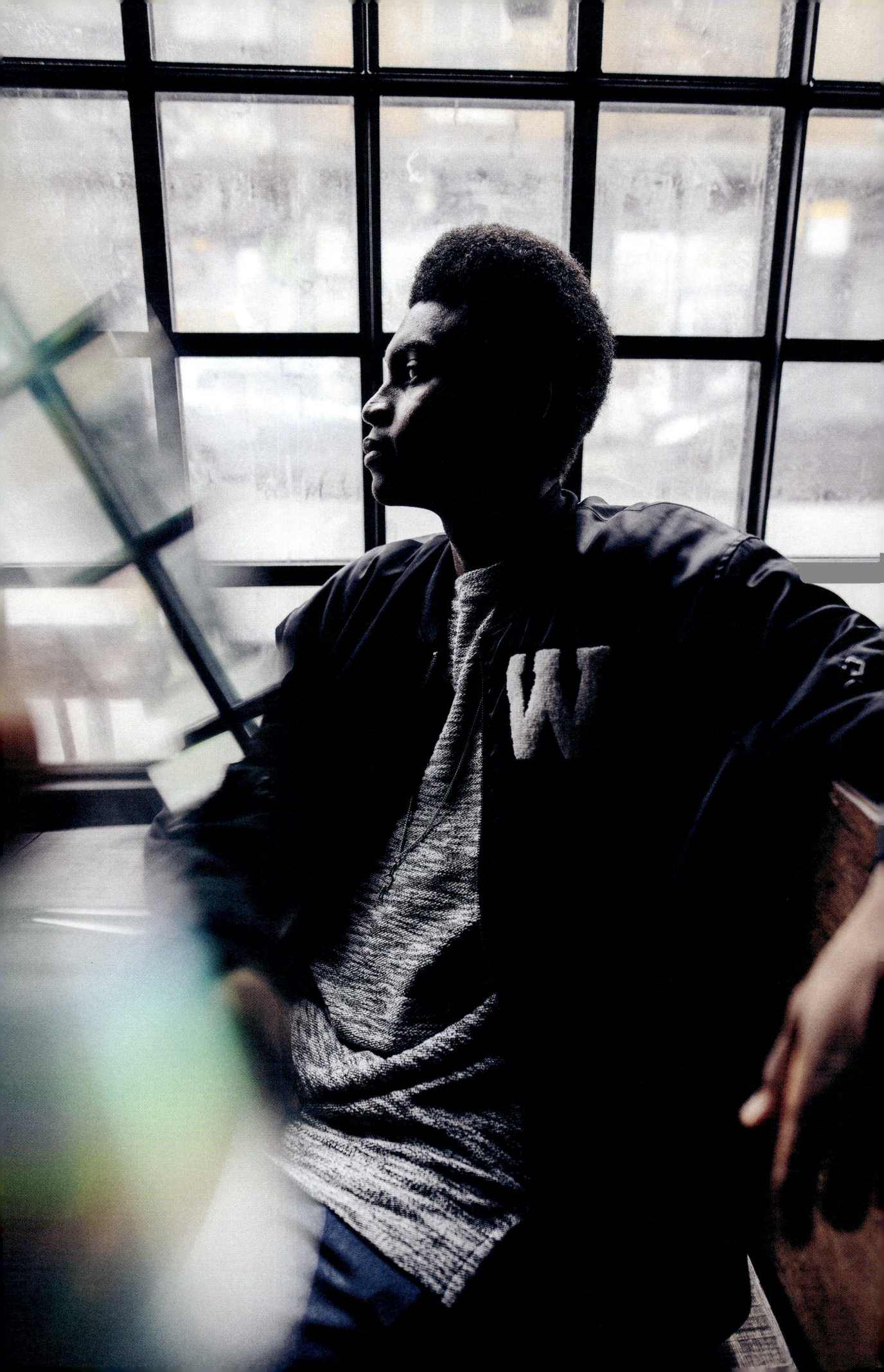

RON TIMEHIN

I graduated from University in 2015 and returned to my home of South London, where I continued to pursue photography as a career, utilising social media to aid me. Over the years to present day, I have worked tirelessly to create compelling content, improve my craft and build my online presence.

The last few years have been incredible, to say the least. I have been able to work with brands such as Google, Nike, Adobe, Canada Goose and Prada, whilst travelling the globe. I have given photography workshops, co-produced documentaries and provided social media consultancy for brands. I've been appointed a Sony Imaging Ambassador, and am honoured to be recognised by one of the world's leading camera brands.

Additionally, my personal work has been included in several publications including GQ, HYPEBEAST, Highsnobiety, The Evening Standard, The Hungry Eye Journal, Disorder Magazine and Resource Photography Magazine.

I hope to continue learning about photography and grow to work in different mediums. @rontimehin

Portrait by Ope Odueyungbo

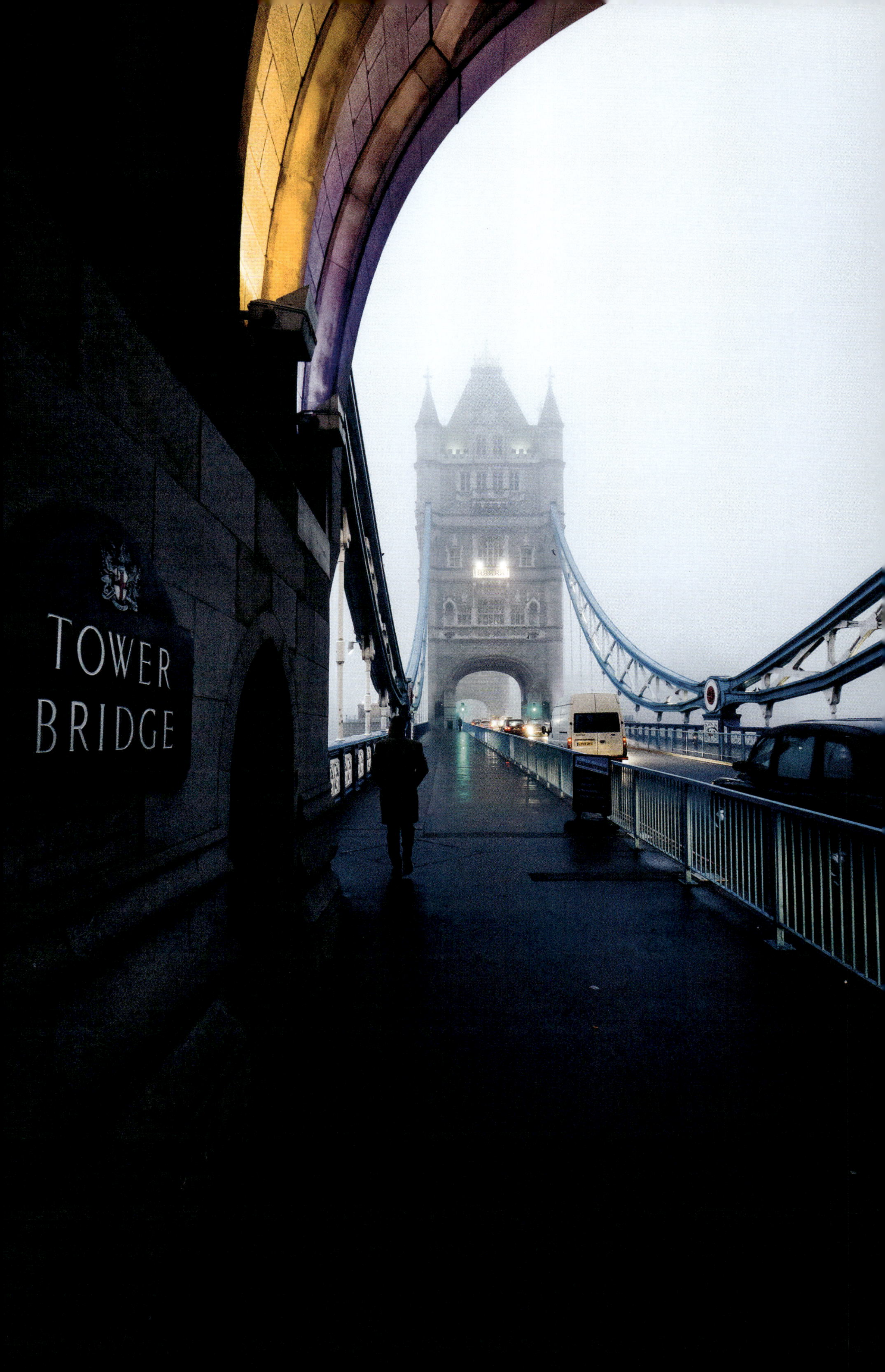

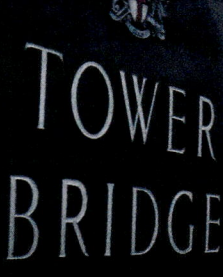

ACKNOWLEDGEMENTS

I would like to thank the following people.

Sam Landers, Tom Maday & Lindy Sinclair for making this book a possibility and supporting both my art and photographic career. Furthermore, for being shining examples of good work ethic and professionalism.

Terry Maday & crew – Terry has a hustle and drive like no other. Thank you to you all for your hard work!

Clive Timehin, Elwina Timehin & Carl Timehin for being a supportive family, no matter what my career choices happened to be. I love you all.

Tobi Shinobi for being like an older brother, a mentor and over all, a good friend from the start.

Ope Odueyungbo – Ope was the first photographer I followed on Instagram from South London who later became a good friend. Thank you for the constant support, inspiration and motivation.

Bromley Youth Music Trust – BYMT is the organisation that accelerated my growth as a young trumpeter and in turn allowed me to perform around the world. BYMT is a real asset to South London and I am eternally grateful for the opportunities you provided.

David Brinkley – My trumpet teacher throughout my educational period. Thank you for so many amazing memories and really instilling in me the ethic of continual and targeted practice.

Paul Showell – Music teacher and mentor through secondary school. Thank you for always pushing me to be the best that I could be, believing in me even when times were low. You are a gem in the schooling system, thank you.

LCCN: 2019937918
ISBN: 978-1-7320618-8-0

Printed and bound in Latvia
First printing, 2019

Trope Publishing Co.

+ INFORMATION:
For additional information on
the Trope Edition Series, visit
ww.trope.com

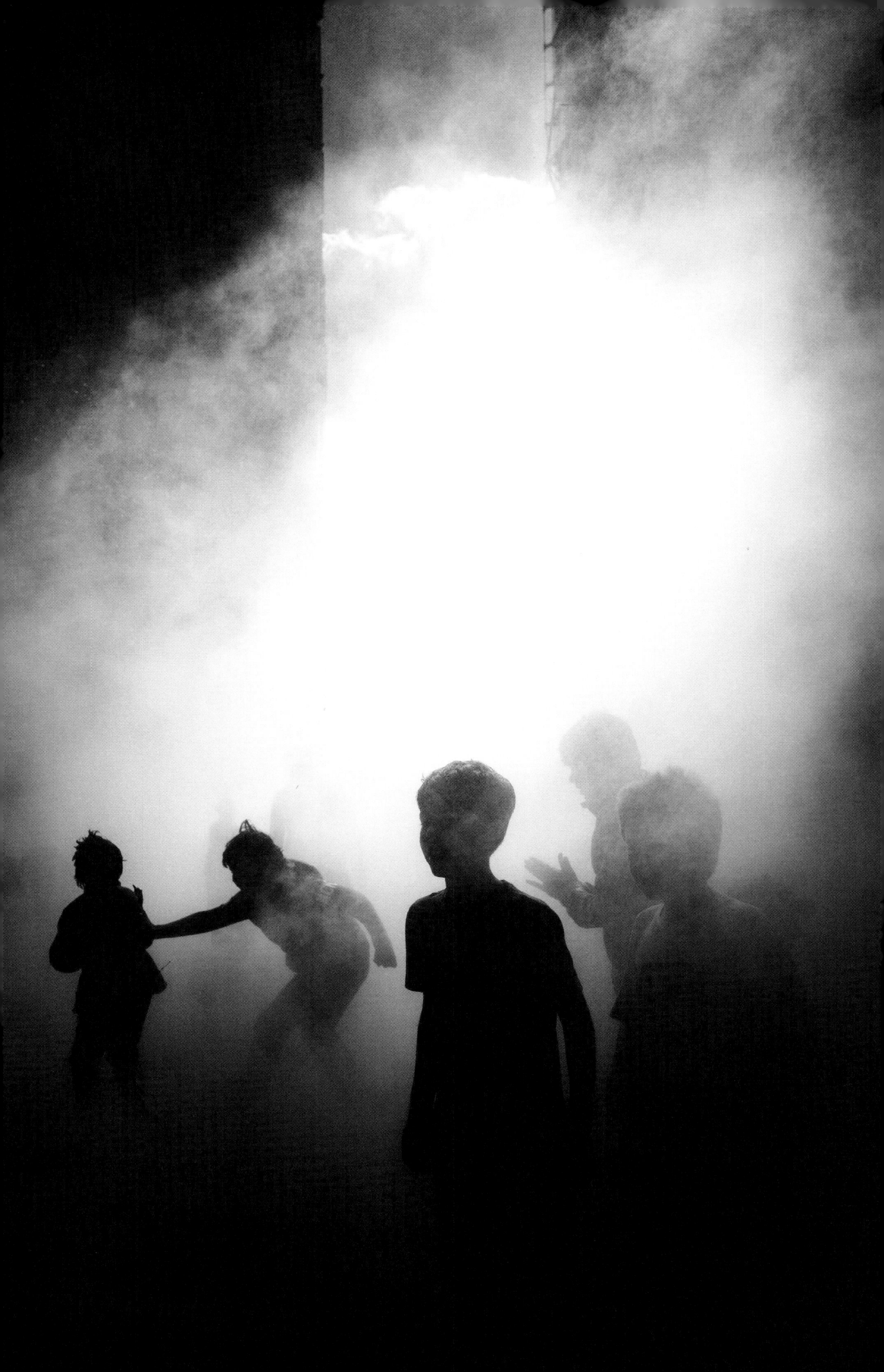

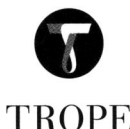

TROPE